On My Terms

On My Terms

From the Grassroots to the Corridors of Power

SHARAD PAWAR

SPEAKING TIGER

SPEAKING TIGER PUBLISHING PVT. LTD
4381/4, Ansari Road, Daryaganj,
New Delhi–110002, India

First published by Speaking Tiger in hardback 2016

ISBN: 978-93-85755-39-2
e-ISBN: 978-93-85755-41-5

10 9 8 7 6 5 4 3 2 1

Typeset in Adobe Jenson Pro Capt by SÜRYA, New Delhi
Printed at Gopsons Papers Ltd, Noida

Dedicated to all the people of India

Contents

Preface

My Father, My Hero

EVERY CHILD THINKS, QUITE rightly, that his or her parents are the best in the world. Ditto with me. As I write these lines, I realise that we, the Pawars of Baramati, have learnt to live happily—taking adversities in our stride, cherishing every moment of affection and togetherness, re-inventing ourselves to keep pace with constant change—in good times and bad. With never a dull moment. For this and much more, I am ever grateful to my Aaiee and Baba.

My mother has played a huge role in my father's long and fruitful innings in the field of politics and public administration. Aaiee has stood behind Baba like the Rock of Gibraltar. He has drawn strength from her steadfast dedication and sense of commitment. Equally our family and our close friends, as well, have stood by him through thick and thin, rain or sunshine. We all hold Baba in the hollow of our palms.

In turn he remains the caring patriarch. For instance, Baba just can't stop thinking of me as a little girl who needs to be told what is what. I often remind him that he need no longer be so protective of me as I am, well, a mother of two now! Needless to add, my mild protest doesn't really help. Once a parent, always a parent, I suppose.

Despite the unrelenting claim on his time as a public figure, he has all the time as a family man, and, even more, as a doting grandparent. Baba's love for his grandchildren and theirs for him is unconditional.

Baba is a man of few words. Very few, indeed. He is never liberal with compliments. I gave a good speech? I did a few good things in my constituency? Fine and thank you. No need to brag or boast. Move on. Start working on a new project.

On the other hand, a wrong turn of phrase in my speech, a small factual error, or faulty diction upsets Baba. He promptly pulls me up. No, this is not merely a fault-finding exercise. This is a worrying father's concern for his daughter. He wants her to constantly evolve, improve herself and keep trying to be the best. Always. After my election to the Lok Sabha, his advice to me was: 'As you walk up the steps of Parliament, remember the people of Baramati who have voted you as their representative. As an MP, work with a sense of commitment and gratitude to those who have elected you. Bond with people. Work to better their lives.'

Being with the people—India's Common Man—is the central tenet of Baba's life. Whether in Pune or Patiala, Baramati or Burhanpur, he likes to meet and engage with people, be one with them. Regardless of the time he goes to bed at night, he is up and about, ready to meet people at 7 a.m. sharp. Every day without fail.

Measured on an electoral yardstick, Baba's standing is impressive. He has an uninterrupted record of being democratically elected 14 times since 1967. Till now 48 years, almost two-thirds of his life, have been invested in public service. Baba has never lost his sheen, his relevance. He continues to be a player. And what a player he is!

The media may love to hate him, but can't do without him either. So be it, he says. He hates to offer explanations to his detractors. Do your job well and go home is his motto. Period.

His job involves people and that delights him. His generous capacity to lend a patient ear to anyone seeking his advice never ceases to amaze us. How does he put up with this day in and day out, my cousin Ajit and I often ask each other. 'Take it easy, Baba,' we tell him. But such is his regard for others that he is certainly not going to take it easy.

People keep him grounded in reality. Despite our cellphones and e-mails, we are far less informed about the heat and tumble of public life than Baba is. His people network gives him an easy lead over us. He prefers travel by car or train to aircraft. Road journeys keep him familiar with the sounds and smells of rural India. His feet firmly rooted in the soil and his head firmly screwed on his shoulders, Baba is like Maharashtra—rough-hewn and solid.

He likes simple food cooked by Aaiee. No frills, no fuss. His energy is infectious, his enthusiasm at 75 can shame a young undergraduate. He is strong as steel, cool as a cucumber. I have never, believe me, never seen him explode in anger. When faced with adversity, he stays calm and focussed. He knows how to forgive and forget; how to move on without ill-will or rancour.

Baba displayed exemplary courage while combating cancer which coincided with the 2004 Lok Sabha elections. As soon as doctors allowed him to leave the hospital, he hit the road, addressing poll meetings, strategising, meeting party candidates.

Baba's mantra is simple. Take life as it comes. Tolerance, according to him, is respecting the good in a person and ignoring the not-so-good. He is unmoved by success and failure. For him, life is like a river. Quiet, deep and forgiving. Always on the move.

Baba loves his family, his kith and kin. He has been chiefly instrumental in keeping the clan together, despite occasional hiccups and heartburn. His involvement in our lives is constant and complete—for instance, he loves to buy saris for the female members of the clan. He insists that women in the family should pursue their vocation, their passion. For him, women's empowerment is not merely a policy document, but an article of faith.

Baba is open to suggestions, even criticism. When we meet for dinner many sizzling topics are on the menu card. Politics, books, plays and films, controversies and personalities and much more. I suppose the more we argue and the more we differ with each other, the greater is the appetite for food. Baba encourages everyone to speak. And he enjoys a good argument.

Both Aaiee and Baba love to have people from all walks of life over for dinner, and Aaiee's wonderful hospitality and her excellent culinary skills are much admired by our friends. For the young ones in the family these dinner conclaves are a source of both entertainment and education.

Baba's biggest USP is his willingness to acquire new knowledge. You tell him about a new innovation and his antennae go up. A small fact, some interesting trivia about science, technology, farming, water and soil management or Indian classical music fascinates him no end. I think that he is young at heart because of his quest for pure knowledge.

He has a sharp eye for detail. Even as simple a task as, say, sending out invites for a cricket match, he executes with precision and great care. And yet, Baba is not a control freak. He believes in delegating responsibility, even as he keeps an eye on the nitty gritty, without grossly interfering.

My heart swells with pride and happiness as I present this book to readers on the occasion of Baba's 75th birthday. It is an autobiography that traces Baba's roots and chronicles his long and rewarding career in public life—as chief minister of Maharashtra (four terms) and as Union minister (three terms) at the Centre.

Baba draws from his personal experience to shed light on the political events that have given shape to post-Nehruvian India and Maharashtra. Readers will also gain insight into various issues of governance and national life through Baba's ringside observations on administration, agriculture, cricket and coalition politics, among others.

This book is in an 'as told to' form and was put together following a series of interactions Baba had with Anand Agashe, veteran journalist and chairman, MediaNext Info-processors Pvt Ltd. I thank Mr Agashe for his effort.

I wish Baba many more years of public service, infused with good health and joy.

SUPRIYA SULE
Mumbai
November 2015

On My Terms

ONE

Bai and Baramati

I HAD MY FIRST brush with administration when I was barely three days old, cradled in the arms of my mother. Sharadabai Govindrao Pawar had a meeting to attend at the Pune Local Board[1], of which she was a member, on 15 December 1940. Although she had delivered a baby boy just three days earlier, she was not one to miss her call of duty. Neither the harsh winter nor the four-hour-long arduous journey, in a crowded bus, from the tehsil town of Baramati to the district headquarters in Pune could deter her from attending the crucial meet.

Board chairman Shankarrao More, a respected Leftist leader, loudly applauded Sharadabai as she entered the meeting hall armed with a bundle of joy! Sharadabai's contribution to the functioning of the Board was already much appreciated and her colleagues were anyway in awe of the feisty woman in their midst. That day her esteem went up several notches in their eyes. I was, of course, oblivious to it all.

Bai, as we addressed our mother, has undoubtedly been the biggest influence on my life. I rarely use superlatives when talking about a person, so I wouldn't call her a 'superwoman', an epithet her peers used to describe her, but she was truly an extraordinary person—intelligent, progressive and bold. Coming from a poor agrarian family near Kolhapur in southern Maharashtra, she stayed in Seva Sadan, a girls' hostel in Pune, to complete her studies up to vernacular final, a Raj term for the seventh standard.

[1]The Local Board was an early form of a self-government body set up in every district under a regulation promulgated by Viceroy Lord Ripon in 1882. Several decades later, in 1934, women were allowed to contest for the board membership. Sharadabai was the first woman to get elected to the Pune Local Board.

My mother was all of eight (she was born on 12 December 1911 and I came into this world on the same date 29 years later!) when she joined the Seva Sadan boarding school in Pune. It was founded by the well-known social reformer Ramabai Ranade in 1915 to impart formal and non-formal education to girls with a view to making them self-sufficient in all respects. Given the male-dominated culture in the early twentieth century, it was a rare feat for a non-Brahmin girl in Maharashtra to enrol herself in a boarding school and do well in academics as well as social activities.

Bai was born in a village called Golwage, at the foothills of the Panhala Fort. Such was her luck that her parents died young. But such was also her luck that her elder sister's husband, Shripatrao Jadhav, took her in and made himself responsible for her education. He was himself an agricultural officer in the court of Chhatrapati Shahu Maharaj, one of the most enlightened rulers of his time. Shahu Maharaj's progressive thinking must have influenced the family, especially his emphasis on 'education for all'. Of course, it is all speculation at this remove, but perhaps that was why Bai was sent to Seva Sadan in Pune and acquired a fine education that was to hone her native intelligence and her keen mind.

My father Govindrao worked as senior officer in Neera canal cooperative society in Baramati. He was known for his integrity and progressive views. Thus it wasn't surprising that after Sharadabai and Govindrao tied the knot in 1926 in accordance with the Satyashodhak[2] custom, both should adhere to the norms of the movement, and make strident efforts to pass on the values of simplicity, integrity and frugal living to their children. I was the ninth child amongst seven sons and four daughters.

My father was a disciplinarian who followed a tough daily

---

[2]Satyashodhak literally means seekers of truth. The Satyashodhak movement was initiated in the late nineteenth century by the celebrated social reformer Jyotirao Phule to mobilise public awareness against Brahminical tyranny.

regime. Up at four in the morning, he would be ready by 6 o'clock to meet the day. After reading the newspaper, he would step out of the house to return at around 6.30 in the evening, and would be in bed by 8 pm. A man of few words, his stern demeanour made us keep our distance from him. This was especially true when one made a mistake or did not do well in studies. I wasn't particularly good in academics at school. Needless to add, asking father to sign my monthly report meant inviting trouble. It was easier to ask Bai to sign it and that was what I would do.

Bai was far ahead of her time in more ways than one. She was not just a terrific home maker, but was also a dynamic, left-leaning social and political activist. In June 1938, the Congress party asked her to contest the election to the Pune Local Board from the sole seat reserved for women. Though the seat was in the reserved category, the expanse of the constituency covered the entire district. On 9 July 1938, Bai was elected unopposed. She was re-elected for the next fourteen years and carried out several responsibilities in the public health, public works, standing, budget and panchayat committees of the Pune Board.

A freak accident in 1952 brought Bai's remarkable political career to an abrupt end. She was attacked by an injured bull she was trying to tend to. The attack left her crippled and she was on crutches for the rest of her life. But even though this put an end to active political work, it did not slow her down much in any other way.

I remember Bai as a caring mother, and a hard taskmaster too. She balanced her political work and her Pune Local Board responsibilities on the one hand, and her domestic chores and farm work on the other, with great aplomb. Such deftness is often missing in among most people in public life. They either tend to become too involved in the lives of their kith and kin at the cost of their public obligations, or get completely engrossed in public life, neglecting their domestic duties. My mother did not compromise on either front. She attended to her political engagements and looked after her children with equal sincerity and dedication. She had an amazing capacity to put in long hours of work in order to attain the goals she had set for herself in various walks of life.

Good habits and formal education topped her list of priorities for her children. Bai did not pamper us but she did acknowledge our individual abilities and lent us her unconditional support in pursuing whatever we were capable of achieving. This was true in the case of both boys as well as girls in the family. There was never any gender bias. She made sure that none of us became bookworms at the cost of carrying out our domestic responsibilities. We were encouraged, even forced, occasionally, to help her in her daily chores, both in the house and outdoors.

True to her progressive outlook, she insisted that her daughters should finish their graduation, if not more, in a stream of their liking so that they could become financially independent. Looking back, I realise how all this has imperceptibly guided me through life.

Since my elder brothers were pursuing their studies in other towns during most of my school years, I had a lot of time to talk to my mother on issues ranging from domestic responsibilities to state and national politics. These interactions with Bai were intellectual, even rigorous. They were my real education, and became more substantive as I grew up, moved to Pune for college education and kept coming home from time to time.

When Bai was young, she was an ardent supporter of the Congress Party. This changed soon after Independence. Men like Shankarrao More, Tulsidas Jadhav and Kakasaheb Wagh began to feel that the Congress was ignoring the interests of the farming community and rural Maharashtra, and they left the party to form The Peasants and Workers Party of India in 1947. Bai saw what they were trying to achieve and shifted her loyalties to them. This didn't surprise those who knew her well. She had long been attracted by leftist thought and was an avid reader, particularly of books from the People's Publishing House which published leftist literature.

I too found communist ideology alluring, but democratic values attracted me more. Bai was of the opinion that in a political system like ours, only a handful of people controlled the opportunities to create and enjoy wealth. I differed strongly as I felt democracy alone could offer equal opportunities to all. I also advocated that creation and equitable distribution of wealth, and not distribution of poverty, was the real solution. We argued often and long. To her credit, she was very tolerant and never imposed her views on me though I was young and inexperienced. 'You think differently. Study ideological issues in greater depth and then form your opinion,' was all that she would say. When I was about to join the Congress Party, she sat me down and we had a long conversation. She tried her best to dissuade me but she never used emotional blackmail. She spoke about ideology, she used logic and reason. I hope I countered with rational argument too, defending my reasons for joining the party. At the end of a long and tiring session, she sighed and said, 'I can see you have the courage of your convictions. You must follow them. But whatever ideology you espouse, you must try and be honest.'

Bai's approach to issues and people, as well as her tolerance of views contrary to her own have left an indelible imprint on my mind. As a result, I have never allowed ideological differences to obstruct the process of dialogue with anybody.

Bai's correspondence with my brothers Madhavrao and Suryakant when they were overseas (Suryakant still is) also had less to do with domestic niceties and more with exchanging information and views. The issues discussed in those letters generally pertained to lifestyles, politics and current affairs at both ends. In short, Bai's interactions with her children were never emotional in nature but cerebral.

When I entered electoral politics, Bai gave me a piece of advice. 'The common man must always feel reassured that your political positions on all issues are in his interest,' she said. After I became minister in the state, she spent a lot of time with me in

Mumbai while continuing her medical treatment. Her love of reading remained unabated even at a ripe age. Consequently, our discussions and arguments acquired added vigour. This continued right till the end when she was hospitalised in Pune and passed away on 12 August 1975.

My most vivid memory of the day India became independent is of a silver coin and one Ravalgaon toffee. My school in our village, Katewadi, where we lived at that time, wore a festive look and there was gaiety all around. The hoisting of the tri-colour was followed by the rendering of patriotic songs and inspiring speeches. As a not-yet-seven-year-old, I could gather that something very important had happened in our country but obviously did not understand the full import of the event.

Each of us was given a silver coin and a Ravalgaon toffee by the school as part of the celebration. While the pleasure of the toffee lasted a few minutes, the memento was my cherished possession for a long time.

The town of Baramati is about 10 kilometres from Katewadi. After completing my education up to the fourth grade in Katewadi, I joined the Baramati municipal school. When I was in the eighth standard, I was enrolled in the Shahu school under the aegis of the Rayat Shikshan Sanstha[3] founded by Karmaveer Bhaurao Patil[4] as part of his mission to educate the masses. My father's close ties with Bhaurao Patil were from the Satyashodhak movement of which both my parents, like Bhaurao, were active

[3]Founded in 1919 in the Satara district of South Maharashtra, the main focus of Rayat Shikshan Sanstha was on an 'earn and learn' scheme for the downtrodden. At present, the institute has 42 colleges, 17 post-graduate institutes, 438 middle schools, 28 primary schools, 17 pre-primary schools, 68 hostels, eight ashram shalas, two ITIs and one engineering college in different parts of Maharashtra. Sharad Pawar is the chairman of the institute.

[4]Bhaurao Patil (1887-1959) was a social activist and educationist. Besides being a freedom fighter, he was also closely linked with the Satyashodhak movement started by Mahatma Phule.

members. Then in the ninth standard I moved to a school run by the Maharashtra Education Society.

As to my older siblings, one was in Baroda and the others were in Pune to pursue higher education. My mother used to get up at 3.30 in the morning every day, cook two meals (lunch and dinner) and send the huge tiffin by public transport to Pune for all of them. I did not ever help to cook as I was entrusted with two other responsibilities at home. One of them was to do all the household purchases and take bananas, grapes and other agriculture produce for sale from our farm to the market.

The other responsibility that I had was to manage all the social gatherings that took place in our house. I was more than happy to carry out all that work. In fact, I feel lucky to have got opportunities so early in my life to host events and interact with a cross section of people in the market and elsewhere.

Baramati, Walchandnagar and Daund were the three places in our vicinity where weekly markets (bazaars) were held on three different days. Farmers and residents from the neighbourhood would flock to these markets to buy and sell various commodities. Walchandnagar is about 25 kilometres from Baramati, while the Baramati-Daund distance is about 50 kilometres. For nearly four years, I went to the Baramati bazaar regularly and also took our farm produce by train to the other two markets. It turned out to be a very valuable experience.

At times, I took our farm produce to the vegetable market in Mumbai which then to us was a distant thunder. Agriculturists in the neighbourhood used to hire a large vehicle and share the transport cost. Balancing myself on gunny bags in the rear of the vehicle was tiresome, but since the seats in the driver's cabin were 'reserved' for affluent seniors, I had no option. Once in a while, I got a chance to sit in the driver's cabin. I would seize the opportunity by keeping the driver in good humour, offering him tea and snacks along the route.

As I belonged to a family of farmers, I got firsthand knowledge about the market dynamics of agriculture products. Like me, there were a large number of sellers, buyers and traders who visited the three markets regularly. One often ran into the same set of people in all the three markets every week. Over the years I developed a close bond with all of them.

Although I did not realise it then, the seeds of my future political work were sown during this time. It was several years later that I started representing Baramati in the state legislature and those people became my voters.

All through my school and college years, I was more drawn towards extra-curricular activities than academics. I was always in the forefront at debates, elocution competitions and plays during the annual school gatherings. The responsibility of organising sports competitions and school picnics also invariably fell upon me.

I distinctly remember a particular incident when I was in the primary school in Katewadi. I was a participant in an elocution competition and each of us was allotted 20 minutes to speak. It so happened that I completely forgot the time limit and continued to hold forth for over half an hour. I paid no heed to the frantic signals from the teachers to wind up. Finally, one of them, quite fed up, pulled my shirt and made me sit down.

It was probably this over-zealousness in 'non-academic' pursuits that prompted my mother to send me away to Pravaranagar (in Ahmednagar district of Maharashtra) for studies when I was in class nine. Vitthalrao Vikhe Patil, who was awarded the Padmashri for his pioneering work in the cooperative movement in Maharashtra, had set up a sugar mill in Pravaranagar in 1950, the first of its kind founded on a cooperative basis in Asia. Well-known economist D.R. Gadgil, who had worked closely with Vikhe Patil to set up the mill, was its first chairman. Annasaheb Shinde, who later became Union minister for agriculture, was a co-founder.

My elder brother Appasaheb was then the agriculture officer

of the sugar mill. Bai probably thought I would focus better on my studies if I joined the Rayat Shikshan Sanstha's Mahatma Gandhi Vidyalaya in Pravaranagar under Appasaheb's eagle eye. She couldn't have been more wrong. It was not long before I was back to my old self. I started volunteering for organising gatherings, picnics and other cultural activities in the school, which was my forte. Naturally, my circle of friends kept expanding with each passing day!

They were truly exciting times!

That was when it all began....

The year was 1955. The movement to liberate Goa from Portuguese rule was at its peak. Batches of satyagrahis led by Senapati Bapat, Mahadeoshastri Joshi and N.G. Goray crossed the Maharashtra-Goa border to stage peaceful protests. They were either arrested or blocked by the Portuguese government.

Despite being more than 500 kilometres away from the scene of action, we at Pravaranagar got to learn about the day-to-day developments of the liberation movement through radio news bulletins and newspapers. Since I had a keen interest in current affairs, particularly political, I kept a close track of what was happening.

On 15 August 1955, about 500 volunteers led by Bhai Vishnupant Chitale tried to cross the Goa border. The Portuguese police resorted to caning and opened fire against the satyagrahis. Tulshidas Balkrishna aka Hirve Guruji, a satyagrahi who originally belonged to Ahmednagar, died in the police firing. This sparked a sharp reaction in several parts of Maharashtra. I too thought it fit to mobilise my school friends. We forced the school to suspend classes for a day.

Emboldened by our success, we then marched to the sugar mill, demanding that it too should stop work. Unperturbed, Chairman Vitthalrao Vikhe Patil came out of his office and asked us why we wanted the one-day close-down.

'As a mark of protest,' I replied. 'Goa must be integrated

with India and therefore we demand that the mill should remain closed for a day.'

Vikhe Patil did not lose his cool. He said, 'Well, if this is the objective, I am prepared to close down the mill permanently. But please tell me how this will facilitate Goa's integration with India.'

I had no answer to this. But the experience of mobilising students for a cause, taking out a protest march and engaging with a stalwart like Vikhe Patil gave me a high I had never experienced before. It was my first significant venture in public life. When the government of India finally liberated Goa on 19 December 1961, I felt happy and proud for having been a part of that operation at some small level.

My mother was, of course, not pleased when she learnt about this. She promptly brought me back to Baramati where I stayed till matriculation. Like my elder siblings, I then shifted base to Pune to enrol in the Brihan Maharashtra College of Commerce (BMCC). As I had done during the years in school, I plunged headlong into the extra-curricular activities of the college from day one. Since I was now staying in a hostel located on the Fergusson college campus, I had ample time to spread my wings. It became a routine to get elected to my college gymkhana as the students' representative every year.

Pune was then (as it still is) a major centre of higher education in Maharashtra. Pandit Nehru had once described it as The Oxford of the East. Students came there from all the other districts, and represented a fine cross-section of rural Maharashtra, from Jalgaon, Dhule, Satara, Sangli and the like. New to the city, they encountered many difficulties, ranging from admissions in the various city colleges to complications with their fees and accommodation. In my capacity as a students' representative, I worked with them to form district-wise associations and conducted elections to make sure that the leadership was elected democratically. This created a much-needed support system for the out-station students. As I developed a close rapport with these associations, I got drawn into students' elections in most colleges. Any student in the city aspiring to contest an election in his or her college would seek my backing! This was how 'Pawar panels' came into being during election time in most colleges. There was never any pre-planning on my part.

Since most of the students supported by me would get elected, I found my sphere of influence spreading across the city's colleges. Many of these students returned to their native places across Maharashtra after completing their education. They continue to hold a soft spot for me even today, thanks to the bond nurtured during my campus days.

During my last year at the BMCC I was selected as a member of the Indian delegation to Cairo, Egypt, to participate in the World Youth Forum conference. As it was to be my first air travel and maiden overseas trip, I was excited. However, my father held a different view.

'You must first complete your B.Com and also get a degree in law. After that you may do whatever you want,' he declared. It was Bai's quick intervention that saved the day. She convinced my father that it was a rare opportunity that had come my way and I must be allowed to seize it.

The conference was held in the vicinity of the gigantic Aswan dam. Youngsters from 90 countries participated in the twelve-day meet, the routine being three or four hours of discussions on contemporary issues and field work thereafter. I was adjudged the 'most popular youth leader' in the conference, of which I was rather proud! I also got an opportunity to talk briefly to President Gamal Abdel Nasser, the legendary president of Egypt, who paid a short visit to the conference.

We were to return by an Air India flight but the take-off was delayed by 24 hours because of a bird hit. The airline staff started serving food and beverages to all those stranded at the airport. We suddenly noticed J.R.D. Tata joining his colleagues to serve the passengers. There were no airs and no fuss which one usually associates with a man of such high stature. When we asked him the reason for his personal involvement, JRD explained in a matter-of-fact manner, 'I am the chairman of Air India. It is my duty, like other staff members, to serve our passengers in an emergency like this. I'm only doing my duty.' He continued with the task at hand, leaving us speechless. JRD's words have remained with me as an everlasting truth of life.

✢ TWO ✢

Entering Politics

LOOKING BACK, I REALISE that entering politics was the natural progression of my sustained inclination for public activities. However, considering the political affiliations of my family, I should have chosen the Peasants and Workers Party of India (PWP), and not the Congress, as my launch-pad. Although elected to the Pune Local Board on a Congress ticket, my mother was ideologically close to the PWP. My elder brother Vasantrao was an active member of that party and had contested the Lok Sabha by-election in 1960 as the Samyukta Maharashtra Samiti candidate.

In the late 1940s and early '50s the PWP, a left-leaning political party, was a force to be reckoned with, though in present-day Maharashtra it has retained its influence only in a few pockets. The PWP was formed by stalwarts Keshavrao Jedhe, Shankarrao More and Datta Deshmukh, who broke away from the Congress Party to set up the new party to aggressively promote Marxist-Leninist ideology. The troika was unhappy with the economic policies of the Congress. The PWP split in 1951, with Jedhe rejoining the Congress. N.D. Patil, my elder sister Meena's husband, leads the party at present.

At home, I was privy to many ideological discussions that took place from time to time between Bai, Vasantrao and Shankarrao More, Keshavrao Jedhe, Raghunathrao Khadilkar and Tulshidas Jadhav. More and Khadilkar were widely respected as intellectuals. Since I was at an age when one was supposed to be seen and not heard, I listened to their discussions in rapt attention. Amongst them, Jedhe was a man who had mass contact and holding conversations with him was much easier. Ditto with Jadhav.

Revolutionary leaders like Nana Patil and Karmaveer Bhaurao Patil were also frequent visitors to our house. Bhaurao was a sage-like figure who was not active in politics, but did pioneering work in the fields of education and social reforms. In short, parallel streams of social activism and political activism were constantly at play in my house. The proponents of both streams were iconic personalities and at that impressionable age I could have gone either way.

I did recognise the importance of social activism. I still do. Yet I opted for active politics when I was in college. This was probably because even at that age I had understood that one had to be in politics since that was the domain where decisions on all critical issues, including social reforms, were finally taken. How could one become truly effective without being part of the decision-making process? In the late nineteenth century and early twentieth century, Maharashtra had witnessed Lokmanya Bal Gangadhar Tilak and Gopal Ganesh Agarkar debating vigorously as to which of the two—political freedom from British rule or social reforms—should take precedence. Though Agarkar was a genuine, passionate advocate of social reforms, Tilak went on to lead the freedom movement, arguing that the reforms could be enforced in a more effective manner once India became independent.

Decades later, Yashwantrao (Y.B.) Chavan, the Congress leader and the first chief minister of Maharashtra who fascinated me the most in my youth, also believed that politics was the most effective medium to bring about social transformation. Besides Y.B. Chavan, Pandit Jawaharlal Nehru too cast a spell over me. Although I appreciated the honesty and sincerity of purpose of the PWP leadership, I became increasingly convinced that the future of India would be safer and brighter in the hands of the Congress. Sometime in 1958, I visited Congress Bhavan in Pune to register myself as an active member of the party.

As general secretary of the college gymkhana during my final year at BMCC, I took an initiative to invite Y.B. Chavansaheb to address the students in our campus. He was a leader of great stature and eminence among the political figures of the time. He was also a very good communicator. Whatever he said was born of his convictions and came from his heart. He delivered an inspiring speech at our college. He was aware that I had taken the initiative to invite him; he called me over after the speech, saying youngsters like me should join the Congress to play an active role in politics. I had already done so and Chavansaheb's words of encouragement further boosted my confidence.

After enrolling as a Congress member, I started frequenting the party office in Pune. Youngsters like me used to spend most of our time around a small compound wall of the Congress Bhavan, and proudly called our group 'Katta Congress' (katta is a colloquial Marathi word for a meeting joint in a public place). Sipping tea and feeding ourselves on pakodas, we discussed political issues and party leaders. We were mostly in touch with senior local leaders like Bhausaheb Shirole and Rambhau Telang. They were hands-on Congressmen involved deeply in the politics of the Pune Municipal Corporation (PMC). In their company, I observed from close quarters how politics often operates at the ground level.

Around this time, elections were scheduled for the post of a committee chairman in the PMC. Since the Congress and the main opposition party, Samyukta Maharashtra Samiti (SMS), had near-equal strength in the committee, the outcome could have gone either way. On the eve of the election, Bhausaheb asked me to hop into his car without disclosing where we were heading. We then picked up an SMS corporator and drove to a dak bungalow about 40 kilometres away from Pune. After some time, the anxious corporator started demanding that he should be taken back to Pune. However, Bhausaheb ignored his pleas and kept him engaged in conversation. I was asked to stand on guard outside the dak bungalow. Next morning when the voting was through in the municipal corporation, we drove back to Pune with the SMS corporator. His party lost the election by one vote! Local newspapers published stories about the 'abduction' of the corporator by a 'senior Congress leader and his companions'. This, the press pointed out, had led to the SMS's defeat. I panicked and rushed to Bhausaheb.

'What should we do now? If my name appears in the newspaper tomorrow, the college will definitely suspend me and I will also be thrown out of home?' I told him.

Bhausaheb was unfazed. 'What are you talking about? I can't understand any of what you are saying.'

That made me panic more. 'All the newspapers have run the abduction story. Now if they report tomorrow how all of us went in your car...'

He cut me short and exclaimed in mock horror, 'Come on! What are you saying? I haven't even stepped out of my house for the last three days.' After I calmed down somewhat, Bhausaheb sent me back home. Fortunately, the issue died down in a day or two.

The 1962 state assembly elections offered me the first opportunity to play some kind of a role in active politics. S.G. Barve, ICS and former municipal commissioner of Pune and a man of impeccable integrity, was the Congress candidate from Shivajinagar assembly segment in Pune. Rambhau Mhalgi of the Jan Sangh was his principal opponent. My task was simple—to go across the city on a bicycle with my friends and put up the campaign posters at prominent locations. I was the tallest in our group. So after locating a suitable spot, my friends would hold the bicycle from either side and I would stand on the seat to plaster the poster high up on the wall. It was all great fun!

Writing out the voters' slips and distributing them was a key task. One afternoon, I knocked on the door of a house in the upscale Prabhat Road neighbourhood in Pune. The nameplate indicated that the house belonged to a Brigadier Rane. An elderly gentleman opened the door, a quizzical look writ large on his face.

'We are Congress workers. We've come to canvass support for our party,' I said.

'Congress? Forget it. I will never vote for your party,' he retorted.

Years later I married Pratibha who was, I learnt, Brigadier Rane's granddaughter.

Meanwhile, Barve won the election and became Maharashtra's finance minister.

The Sino-Indian war broke out in the same year. The country was swept with patriotic fervour. We, the youth of Pune, were also raring to go. Since we had established a network of students in all colleges, we decided to take out a big procession to condemn China.

We went to see Datto Waman Potdar, who then was the vice chancellor of Pune University (now known as the Savitribai Phule University), and requested him to preside over the protest meeting. He turned down our request as he seemed unsure of our ability to organise the event.

Nevertheless, no efforts were spared to ensure that the rally would be impressive. The result was stunning. As the procession snaked its way through the streets, hordes of people joined in at every corner. By the time we reached our destination at the historic Shaniwarwada, the rear end of the procession was some three kilometres behind us. I was one of the speakers at the rally. Veteran freedom fighter and former Union minister N.V. (Kakasaheb) Gadgil was the chief guest. He was all praise for the massive procession and also the speeches we had made.

'I feel reassured today that the future of our nation is secure in the hands of young activists like you.' he said. That was a big pat on the back, indeed.

Around that time, many things happened rapidly. After working for two years as secretary of the Pune Youth Congress, I was elevated to the post of the secretary of the western Maharashtra unit of the party's youth wing. The demise of Congress veteran Keshavrao Jedhe led to a by-election in the Baramati Lok Sabha constituency in 1960. As I said earlier, my elder brother Vasantrao was the PWP candidate and had the support of stalwarts like S.M. Joshi, Acharya Atre and

Uddhavrao Patil. The Congress led by Y.B. Chavan made the electoral contest a matter of prestige because it had to retain the seat in the face of a tough opposition. Gulabrao Jedhe, the late Keshavrao's son, was the Congress nominee. With my brother as the opposition candidate, everyone wondered what stand I would take. It was a piquant situation that called for immense maturity and Vasantrao displayed it with grace. He quickly came to the point and told me in very few, simple words, 'You are committed to the Congress ideology. Don't hesitate when you have to campaign against me in this election.' I did work hard for our candidate. Vasantrao lost the election.

By now my work as secretary of the western Maharashtra Youth Congress was being appreciated in the party. So when I proposed to organise a workers' meet in Baramati in 1962, Maharashtra Pradesh Congress Committee (MPCC) president Vinayakrao Patil and secretary Abasaheb Nimbalkar gave their consent immediately. Needless to add, Y.B. Chavan, who was then the Union defence minister, was the star attraction of the conclave.

When the meet concluded I invited Chavansaheb to my house for a cup of tea. He accepted my request without any fuss. As Chavansaheb sat talking with my mother, he asked her, 'Since all your children are doing very well in their chosen fields, would you please allow Sharad to be under my tutelege?' Bai was as forthright as ever. 'All of us in the house are aligned to the Left ideology, but Sharad has somehow strayed to take your path. I do not have any objection to his going with you if he so desires. My only expectation is that he should always stick to his own convictions and pursue that path sincerely.'

Even though the party saddled me with increasingly heavy responsibilities, I decided to tackle the chronic drought problem that plagued my home turf, Baramati. Because of the Neera left bank canal, which carries water from Bhatghar dam, many portions of present-day Baramati are lush green and a picture of prosperity. In the early 1960s, however, the situation was very distressful. Out of the 67 villages in the tehsil, only 27 had access to water; the remaining 40 perpetually reeled under water scarcity.

Since the average rainfall was barely six to seven inches, I realised that the only solution to the drought was to try and improve the water table by ensuring water conservation in a big way.

Those days the Food and Agriculture Organisation (FAO) of the United Nations used to run a 'Food for Hunger' programme in the region under which wheat and palm oil were distributed free to the poor and the destitute. I approached FAO's office in Mumbai to present my case that the 'Food for Hunger' programme be substituted with a 'Food for Work' programme because we found the former humiliating. The FAO office was manned by a foreigner who found the suggestion worthy of consideration. Since the FAO did not have a 'Food for Work' programme on its list at the time, he asked me to try out a pilot project in the Baramati tehsil.

The members of an Australian NGO called Church's Auxiliary for Social Action (CASA) were engaged in drought relief work in our neighbourhood at the time. The team was led by Hesel Skuces and Edna Wazar, and these two Australian women worked with complete dedication. We were initially apprehensive that there was a proselytising angle to their social work. However, once we ascertained their credentials and found everything above board, I decided to seek their assistance.

We identified a village named Tandulwadi to run the pilot project. Among the college students whom I had mobilised under district-wise committees when I was studying at BMCC in Pune there were some from the engineering college. I got them to prepare a plan and estimates for constructing a percolation tank. The estimated cost was around ₹80,000. I called a meeting of the villagers to seek their active participation in constructing the tank. Everyone who worked on the project would be given three kgs of wheat and one litre of palm oil every week. They readily agreed. I visited the project site almost every week to supervise the work. Though the project was to be completed in one year, we finished it in six months. The final cost also came down to ₹60,000 as against the estimated ₹80,000. The percolation tank filled to the brim during the following monsoon, recharging all the wells in the vicinity.

The FAO was pleased with the result and asked me to scale up the programme to cover other parts of the region. Over the next four years, I literally trekked through the hinterland and used the same methodology to construct nearly 300 percolation tanks by involving local villagers. The work continued for at least five years thereafter. During that period I was on the move from 7 a.m. to 2 a.m., putting in 19 hours of work on most days. I spent considerable time in practically every village and built a strong network among the youth. This served as a backbone for the mammoth task. When the availability of water improved, it changed the face of Baramati.

The success of the model prompted the FAO to substitute its 'Food for Hunger' programme with 'Food for Work' elsewhere too. Years later, in November 2004, the Central government under Dr Manmohan Singh (wherein I was the agriculture minister) formally launched a 'Food for Work' scheme in the 150 most backward districts in the country. Under the scheme, one person from a family was guaranteed work for 100 days a year, with 25% of his or her daily wages being paid in the form of food grains. I found the scheme resonating with the spirit of the pioneering programme that we had implemented in the 1960s in Baramati.

As I was also involved in party work at the state level in the mid 1960s, I could convince chief minister Vasantrao Naik to visit Baramati and take a look at our work there. After spending a day at various sites with me, he went on air to cite the Baramati example as a model for water conservation. The state government subsequently extended financial aid that helped us construct drains for excess water in the percolation tanks.

THREE

Minister at 32

IN 1962, BARRISTER A.R. ANTULAY vacated his position as chief of the Maharashtra Youth Congress after he won the state assembly election. I succeeded him by defeating barrister Raja Bhosale by four votes in a keenly fought contest.

I began to tour Maharashtra extensively, staying in Mumbai for barely two days in a week. Regular visits to Baramati were, of course, part of my tour schedule. Even as I met scores of people from all walks of life, I studied the social trends and cultures in different parts of the state. It was this vigorous ground work that strengthened the organisational structure of the party. Senior Congress leaders such as Y.B. Chavan, Vinayakrao Patil, Vasantrao Naik and Vasantdada Patil were supportive and were pleased with the outcome.

Till 1967, I camped in the party's state head office at Tilak Bhavan in central Mumbai. This helped me bond with party workers from all over Maharashtra. Also, I made it a practice to get introduced to thinkers and stalwarts from different fields because I knew that it would shape and strengthen my intellectual and ideological foundation. The noted scholar Tarkatirtha Laxmanshastri Joshi[1], educationist Govardhandas Parikh, editors Govind Talwalkar and H.R. Mahajani, industrialists S.L. Kirloskar and Neelkanth Kalyani, vocalist Bhimsen Joshi,

---

[1]Laxmanshastri Balaji Joshi (1901-1994) was a Vedic scholar, thinker and Marathi writer who was widely respected for his critical inquiries into Hindu religious traditions. Granted the title Tarkatirtha, which literally means 'Master of Logic', he was a recipient of a Sahitya Akademi fellowship and the Padmabhushan award. In 1960, he was appointed as the first president of the Maharashtra State Board of Literature and Culture. A twenty-volume Marathi encyclopaedia brought out by the Board was one of his most significant works.

cricketers Vijay Merchant, Madhav Apte and Chandu Borde were some of the luminaries I met at the time.

While I was working as president of the youth wing, I started a magazine called *Nav-yuvak* which soon became quite popular. Aiming to expose party members to a wide range of subjects, it published informative articles, interviews and profiles of well-known personalities from different fields. Also at this time MPCC chief Vinayakrao Patil deputed me as member of the All India Congress Committee (AICC) from Maharashtra. Soon, I was elected as an executive committee member of the party's apex body. Arjun Singh (Madhya Pradesh), Jaipal Reddy (Andhra Pradesh), Jaffer Sharief (Karnataka) and Vayalar Ravi (Kerala), who were also part of the Indian Youth Congress, were my collegues.

The Maharashtra Congress during that era functioned like a well-knit organisation which not only responded quickly to people's issues but also groomed young party workers like me. Brainstorming sessions, initiated by Chavansaheb, were a regular feature. Senior leaders met in the camps to discuss threadbare many of the party's socio-economic policies. The outcome would be sent to the chief minister who, in consultation with his cabinet colleagues, would prepare the government policy.

In one such camp at Mahabaleshwar, Chavansaheb spelt out his vision for Maharashtra. The state, he felt, could no longer afford to rely solely on agriculture and therefore industrial development, including agro-based enterprises, was essential. Once this concept of agro-industrial Maharashtra found acceptance, a foundation was laid by the government for setting up sugar factories, spinning mills and milk societies in the cooperative sector. After V.S. Page (who went on to become the state assembly speaker) floated the concept of employment guarantee in a party camp at Nashik, the government formulated a scheme to translate it into reality. Baburao Tanpure and Annasaheb Shinde (who later became a central minister) organised a session at Rahuri (Ahmednagar district) to assess government policies and schemes. The exercise led to a refinement of these measures.

As a party functionary, it was my responsibility to take notes, prepare minutes and write out the draft resolutions in these sessions. It helped me gain insights into the decision making mechanism and also matured me as a political leader.

On 17 May 1964, Prime Minister Jawaharlal Nehru called a meeting of the national executive members of the Youth Congress at his Teen Murti residence in Delhi. Also present there was Indira Gandhi in her capacity as head of the advisory committee of the youth wing. Such was Panditji's charisma that when we, members of the national executive, entered the meeting hall, we could not take our eyes off him. It was our first—and, sadly, the last—meeting with the legendary leader. Ten days later he died. A glorious era drew to a close.

What I have said about the state Congress of the time also held true at the national level. Free expression of thoughts on Congress policies was encouraged and even criticism of the party's and government's programmes was not frowned upon. I remember the first time I participated in a national convention of the party, held at Bhubaneshwar at the behest of Biju Patnaik. Among the speeches that I still recall for their scholarly content and forthrightness were those of N.V. Gadgil and S.K. Patil. Delegates hanging outside the pandal would troop in as soon as a good speaker took the mike. Listening to those speeches was a huge learning experience.

In 1966, I was delegated by the Congress party to attend a United Nations programme called 'Promising Youth Leadership'. If memory serves me right, N.D. Tiwari was also selected as a delegate. The programme required each of us to spend fifteen days in the office of a prominent political leader of the country assigned to us. During the brief internship, we were expected to pick up things about office administration, party functioning, interacting with the media, and so forth.

My first stint was in the office of the Japanese prime minister, Eisaku Sato. It was followed by working in the offices of the Canadian premier, Lester Pearson, and the California senator, Robert Kennedy. In October that year, I reached Denmark to intern in the office of Prime Minister Jens Otto Krag. As soon as I landed there, I received a telegram from the party asking me to return home for 'something urgent'.

On reaching Bombay (as the city was then known), I learnt that elections to the Maharashtra assembly were to be held soon and state party chief Vinayakrao Patil wanted me to apply for a Congress ticket from the Baramati constituency. I had no reason to decline but I knew it was going to be tough to break through the entrenched local leadership. The prevailing party practice entailed applying for a ticket at the tehsil level from where the recommended name would go to the district committee and then to the state committee for a decision. It was very rare that the Congress high command in New Delhi overruled the state unit's list.

The Baramati assembly constituency received twelve applications in all, including mine. I was barely twenty-seven years old then. Some of my seniors in the party were considerably tense, knowing well that I stood a fair chance to win the state assembly election because of the hard work I had put in. If elected to the assembly, I would be on a firm footing and it would be hard to dislodge me for at least a decade or more, they thought. Those arrayed against me included the tehsil party president, the local zilla parishad member and sugar factory directors. All eleven applicants said they wouldn't mind any one among them being selected as the party candidate. However, they were unanimously opposed to my nomination. The issue went to the Pune district Congress committee which too ruled against me because, they said, my chances of getting elected were 'nil'. It was finally left to the state parliamentary board to take a call.

The meeting was held at Riviera, Chavansaheb's Marine

Drive residence in south Mumbai. Though I was an ex-officio member of the parliamentary board in my capacity as the state Youth Congress chief, I stayed out of the meeting. The MPCC president endorsed my candidature but the party's district unit persisted with its stiff opposition on the ground that my 'elective merit was low'.

Finally, Chavansaheb intervened. 'How many assembly seats do you expect the Congress to win out of the total 288 seats in the state?' he asked my detractors.

'About two hundred,' came the reply.

'Alright,' Chavansaheb said, 'That means we shall lose 88 seats. Let Sharad contest from Baramati even if that means losing 89 seats.'

As soon as my candidature was okayed, the entire tehsil-level team of Congress functionaries resigned in protest. Babalal Kakade, chairman of the Someshwar cooperative sugar mill, was set up by them as an Independent candidate against me. However, at the ground level the picture was entirely in my favour. I had a very strong following among the youth. Students of the local college steered my poll campaign with great enthusiasm.

About 600 students from Baramati who were studying in Pune colleges came home to join the campaign. The networking I had done in the course of my work for the construction of percolation tanks as well as my visits to the weekly bazaars some years earlier also helped. Chavansaheb drove down from Mumbai to address a big gathering which gave a fillip to the campaign. As the voting day approached, I noticed that many traders, doctors, lawyers and teachers who generally kept away from the heat and dust of electioneering, extended support to me.

My elder brothers Dinkarrao and Anantrao played a major role in monitoring the campaign. My mother, a hardcore PWP person, had never voted for the Congress in Independent India. While returning from the polling booth, she told me with a grimace, 'This is the first time I stamped on the pair of bulls (Congress symbol) and not the bullock cart (PWP symbol).'

My maiden electoral victory was impressive. While I polled about 35,000 votes, my opponent could muster just 17,000. Those who had contested my elective merit had been proved terribly wrong. But they were right in one respect—once elected, I never lost an election from Baramati.

After winning the Baramati election, I was required to work on three fronts simultaneously. I had no complaints about that. In fact, I welcomed every additional responsibility that I was entrusted with. I was determined to absorb as much as I could in every role I was assigned to play. In the very first term, I got unanimously elected as secretary of the Congress Legislature Party. I made it a point to sit through the entire day's proceedings in the House. It helped me understand the nitty-gritty of the legislative business. Observing how the treasury and the opposition benches engaged each other during the question hour was equally educative. This self-learning equipped me to participate confidently in the House debates.

The second area of my responsibilities pertained to party work. When Vasantdada Patil became president of the state Congress, I was elected as the general secretary. V.N. Gadgil and Tushar Pawar were the other two general secretaries. It was around this time that I found myself at the centre of a minor storm in the party. It had to do with sugar cooperatives.

The cooperative sector had struck firm roots in Maharashtra. This was especially true of the cooperative sugar factories. A gentleman called Lalubhai Samaldas had first started an agricultural cooperative in the early twentieth century. This was a unit in Baramati, but it failed. Some three decades later, in 1945, the eminent economist Professor D.R. Gadgil, who later became the vice-chairman of the Planning Commission, first mooted the idea of a sugar cooperative. It was another three years before the first such cooperative could be set up, at Pravaranagar, but it was such a success that by 1954, the government was granting sugar factory licenses only to cooperatives. In the 1950s, fourteen new sugar factories had been set up by the cooperatives. Annasaheb Shinde and Vitthalrao Patil were among those who went to the farmers and convinced them to join the cooperatives.

However, there was a growing feeling that power was becoming concentrated in the hands of a few in that sector. I tabled a resolution at the party forum that sought to bar any office bearer in the cooperative sector from holding office for more than ten years. Vasantdada opposed it vehemently. He was supported by several party MLAs who, like him, had a firm grip on the cooperative sector. If MLAs and member of Parliaments could get re-elected any number of times, why should the cooperative sector be made an exception was Vasantdada's argument, while Dnyaneshwar Khaire, Vasant More and I argued that a new class of powerful leaders in the cooperative sector had started leveraging their financial muscle to influence politics and this called for remedial measures. Chavansaheb agreed with us.

This sparked a heated debate within the party. Following a division of votes in the Congress Legislature Party, our resolution was passed. Later, the Maharashtra Cooperative Societies Act was suitably amended on the floor of the House.

The Congress party's truly democratic culture at that time permitted such frank discussions. Though Vasantdada and I took opposing stands on the issue, and it created some distance between his followers and me, the conflict also resulted in the elevation of my stature as a future leader within the party. Youth workers in the Congress, including approximately 50 MLAs, gradually rallied around me. I realised from this episode that workers appreciate a leader who takes a stand. However, what was most remarkable in all of this was that while, as a senior leader in the party, Vasantdada could have asked me to withdraw the resolution, he allowed a free debate and risked getting defeated. Such open-mindedness is rare in today's politics.

The responsibilities of the legislature and the state party unit could not keep me away from the exciting development projects

I had initiated back home in Baramati. An excellent local team of my friends and colleagues had dedicated itself to the work. I somehow squeezed time from my busy schedule to visit Baramati and spend time with the team. There were problems, but they were resolved in a spirit of camaraderie. My elder brother Appasaheb Pawar, who was stationed in Baramati, was a big support in this journey. In time, the work we did evolved into what is widely known at present as the 'Baramati model of development'.

Any hard work always pays off, and that in itself becomes a reward. For me, it also brought about rapid political progress. Unlike in 1967, there was hardly any opposition within the party to my candidature from Baramati in the 1972 assembly elections. I had garnered about 35,000 votes in 1967. My tally in 1972 touched 50,000. Soon after, Chief Minister Vasantrao Naik inducted me as minister of state, thanks to the timely intervention of Yashwantrao Chavan.

It so happened that Vasantrao Naik had prepared a list of ministers and got it approved by Prime Minister Indira Gandhi. He then called on Chavansaheb with the list. Saheb was upset that my name did not figure in the list. 'Do we not need to groom young leadership? I don't see that angle reflected in this list,' he said to the chief minister.

As instructed by Y.B. Chavan, Naik then included my name in the list and got it re-approved by Indiraji before returning to Mumbai for the swearing-in function. Chavansaheb's private secretary Shripad Dongre told me later that he had never seen saheb get so upset earlier. Apparently saheb and Naik had a long meeting, with saheb doing most of the talking, which had finally resulted in my inclusion as minister.

Frankly, I had not expected to be made a minister so soon. I was only thirty-two and had completed just one term as legislator. Therefore, just as I was not disappointed when my name did not figure in the first list, I was not over the moon when the list was revised to induct me. That was probably because at that time I only dreamed of becoming a very good parliamentarian. Secondly, I was already a state Congress general secretary, a position that commanded a lot of respect within the party.

However, I fully appreciated Chavansaheb's insistence on grooming young leadership and tried to pursue the policy myself whenever I could. Soon after I became minister, I convinced a young Sushilkumar Shinde to quit his job in the police force and contest the state assembly election on a Congress ticket. Shinde resigned from service but unfortunately could not get a ticket because Congressman Tayappa Hari Sonawane, another party worker, got the nomination at the behest of Babu Jagjivan Ram. Sonawane died six months later, which led to Shinde getting the ticket and winning the election in 1974. I managed to convince Naiksaheb to induct him as minister of state in the very first term. Shinde was put in charge of the animal husbandry department.

Coming back to my ministership, after the Vasantrao Naik government took over the reins of office, the chief minister asked me in the first meeting to select portfolios of my choice. 'It is your prerogative, Sir,' I replied. He entrusted me with the prestigious home, general administration (GAD) and legislative affairs portfolios. This allowed me to work directly under the chief minister. There couldn't have been a better opportunity to learn from within how a government functions. The minister in charge of GAD, in particular, gets access to the entire government machinery, and since the portfolios of home and legislative affairs were also with me, I could pick up the nitty-gritty of administration in a relatively short time.

Vasantrao Naik reposed full faith in me and did not stifle my enthusiasm in any way. Though I was a debutant minister, he gave me full freedom to take appropriate action regarding police officers, including their transfers, excepting those from the IPS (Indian Police Service) cadre. This was quite significant because it had never been done earlier. He was as supportive in the legislature as in the administration. He would sit through the entire session in the House but he made it a point to ask me to respond to any issues and questions pertaining to 'our' portfolios. Only when he thought I needed support did he intervene.

I remember a particular incident when teachers of a Mumbai municipal school had refused to let their students recite 'Vande Mataram', citing religious reasons. As I started making a statement in the state assembly on the issue, arguing that the teachers' logic was wrong, the opposition unleashed a barrage of criticism against me. The chief minister promptly intervened to put up a spirited defence of my position. Such support by senior ministers means a lot in the beginning of one's legislative career. While it keeps one on one's toes, it also boosts one's confidence to do better.

A natural calamity that struck Maharashtra in 1972 put me straight into action. Many states in the country reeled under severe drought that year. The situation in Maharashtra was particularly grave. Of the 35,800 villages in the state, 30,000 were hit badly. The 1971 Bangladesh war and the attendant burden of nearly one crore refugees from the erstwhile East Pakistan had already strained the Indian economy. Shortage of industrial raw material and electricity had affected industrial production, worsening the shortage of several essential commodities. In this scenario, the failure of the rains dealt a severe blow.

As the water supply got hit and foodgrains became dearer, the anger of the common man boiled over. There were reports of scarcity and distress pouring in from all parts of Maharashtra. In Mumbai, women took to the streets, protesting against the government. Led by Mrunal Gore, Ahilya Ranganekar, Kamal Desai, Sushila Patel and Malatibai Bedekar, they targeted their ire at Chief Minister Vasantrao Naik and civil supplies minister Haribhau Vartak. When thousands of women marched to the state secretariat with rolling pins in their hands, it created national headlines.

Vasantrao Naik put me on the job of drawing up emergency

measures to tackle the shortage of foodgrains in the state. I suggested that we could tap other states which had surplus production of foodgrains. The state of Maharashtra and its leaders Chavansaheb and Naiksaheb enjoyed a lot of goodwill in many states, which made my task somewhat easier. Though a junior minister, I was received very well by Giani Zail Singh in Punjab and Bansi Lal in Haryana. The states of Tamil Nadu and Karnataka also agreed readily to supply rice over and above the quota allotted to them by the central government.

Uttar Pradesh (UP), however, did not respond favourably to drought-hit Maharashtra's needs. This should be attributed to the meeting I had with Chief Minister Kamlapati Tripathi. He was relaxing on a charpai with his legs stretched out. I greeted him with folded hands and started to converse. I found that he was ignoring me completely. One of the IAS (Indian Administrative Service) officers from the Maharashtra cadre who accompanied me to UP was a native of that state. He signalled that, in keeping with the region's prevailing practice, I should touch Tripathi's feet. Now it was my turn to get even with Tripathi. I chose to ignore the officer's advice. If the aim of feet-touching was to show respect, I had already done so by doing a 'namaste' to him. That seemed to have decided it for Tripathi. My attempt to revive the discussion about getting foodgrains from Uttar Pradesh proved futile. That year Maharashtra did not get any supplies from Tripathi's state.

Another big problem during the drought pertained to transport of fodder. The moving of fodder from one district to another was banned at that time. It created a ridiculous situation because while some badly hit districts in Maharashtra were struggling to keep cattle alive in the absence of green fodder, other districts had ample stocks because they had received relatively good rains. After I pointed this out to the chief minister, he immediately issued orders to facilitate cross-district transport of fodder. That came as a huge relief to the farming community in the state.

The battle was over, but the war for making Maharashtra self-reliant in foodgrain production was yet to be won. Soon, Shankarrao Chavan replaced Vasantrao Naik as chief minister and allocated the agriculture portfolio to me. Prime Minister Indira Gandhi took personal interest in the issue. She held a meeting in Pune and made it clear that she wanted Maharashtra to attain 100% self-sufficiency in agriculture.

Following a meeting of the state cabinet, I was asked to take the lead to achieve this objective. Maharashtra's foodgrain deficit at the time was to the tune of ₹120 crore a year. After apprising myself of the research work done in agriculture universities across the state, I realised that it was imperative to strongly encourage farmers to opt for high-yielding crops. There was initial resistance on two counts. One, a hybrid plant was significantly shorter than a traditional plant. Since that meant less fresh fodder, farmers were reluctant to switch to the hybrid variety. Two, it was generally felt that food items prepared from hybrid crop tasted 'different', that is, inferior.

I decided to take the bull by the horns. We opened demonstration farms in all districts of the state. The following year, the bumper hybrid crop in those farms created a buzz, prompting the farmers to overcome their doubts and adopt hybrid seeds in a big way. The controversy over hybrid crops died down in less than two years.

An interesting and totally unexpected fallout of government efforts on food supply in the early 1970s was the emergence of the term 'Congress grass'. The seeds of this weed accidentally entered India through bulk imports of wheat from the United States and some other countries. The weed grew very fast in any climate all over the country—something similar to the Congress party's pan-India growth—and the farmers started calling it 'Congress grass'. The term has come to stay in the state's political lexicon.

FOUR

The PDF Saga

FOR CONGRESS ACTIVISTS WHO believed in democratic values, the Emergency years (1975-77) proved to be harrowing.

As a middle-level party leader at the time I was witness to the rapidly deteriorating situation in the country, and I was unhappy with the way the party high command was handling it. It all started with the 'Navnirman movement' in Gujarat. The movement was steered by students, and it intensified as various sections of society joined in, culminating in the resignation of Chimanbhai Patel, who was then the chief minister of Gujarat. In April 1974, Gandhian leader Jayaprakash Narayan launched a movement for 'total revolution'. The railway employees union, the largest union in the country, went on a nationwide strike in May-June that year. The government came down heavily on the strikers, putting thousands of them behind bars.

Even as things kept sliding, the Allahabad high court, in its historic judgement, held Indira Gandhi guilty of electoral malpractices on 12 June 1975. She challenged the decision in the Supreme Court, but the latter too upheld the high court's ruling. That proved to be the last straw. On 25 June 1975, Indira Gandhi acted on the advice of her senior party colleague Siddhartha Shankar Ray, who was then the chief minister of West Bengal, and clamped Emergency on a palpably nervous nation.

For the Congress party, democracy was an article of faith. We just couldn't reconcile with Indiraji's decision to curtail people's democratic rights. We did feel that Jayaprakash Narayan's call to the armed forces to disobey government orders was fraught with high risk, however, we thought the issue could have been tackled without resorting to the extreme step of imposing Emergency.

While seniors like Chandrashekhar and Mohan Dharia quit the Congress in protest, Vasantdada Patil felt stifled and resigned as minister from the state cabinet. Even Vitthalrao Gadgil, a known Indira Gandhi loyalist, was not happy with the imposition of Emergency. Yashwantrao Chavan was abroad when Emergency was declared. Cutting short his foreign trip he rushed back home to convey his anguish to Indiraji. The latter defended her decision by showing him some Intelligence Bureau reports. That did not diminish his discomfort, but he was ignored. Devkant Baruah, the Assamese politician who had earlier given the slogan 'India is Indira; Indira is India', was now the Congress president. Dissent was discussed in hushed tones.

The party was told that Emergency was a bitter pill which had to be administered to a troubled nation, a short-term measure in view of unprecedented circumstances. Among other party colleagues who were my contemporaries, I remember Ambika Soni was a little restless in the beginning, but once the party appointed her the Youth Congress president, she spared no effort in implementing the Emergency programmes. In Maharashtra, support came from an unexpected quarter: the Shiv Sena. Following a meeting between Indira Gandhi and Balasaheb Thackeray, held at the behest of Mumbai Pradesh Congress Committee president Rajni Patel, the Sena backed Emergency.

As far as I was concerned, I withdrew myself to some extent from party work and focused all my attention on the state ministries which I held, especially agriculture. During my statewide tours I noticed that common people were happy with Emergency, at least in the initial period, because it brought down the crime rate, curtailed price rises and induced a sense of discipline in public life. The Gandhian leader Vinoba Bhave went to the extent of hailing Emergency as 'Anushasan Parv' (Era of Discipline). But the tide soon turned. Reports of administrative excesses began to pour in. The government machinery went all out to achieve the targets set for vasectomy operations. This triggered a sharp reaction, especially among the minority communities. Emergency became a hated word. I used to share the feedback with Chavansaheb whenever we met. A similar exercise with Chief Minister Shankarrao Chavan was, however, not possible as he was a staunch supporter of Emergency.

As Maharashtra chief minister (CM), Shankarrao Chavan implemented the government programmes ruthlessly. In cabinet meetings he regularly reviewed the progress of the vasectomy campaign, wanting to know how many operations were scheduled over what time frame, and so forth. He also ordered the arrests of all those who spoke against Indira Gandhi. As a result, most jails in the state were packed with political prisoners. Sanjay Gandhi visited various states to inspect the implementation of government programmes. He and his coterie never treated chief ministers with respect. Yet, Shankarrao Chavan always accompanied him when he was in Maharashtra. I did not participate in any of those visits, barring, I think, a solitary case.

Some of us also skipped many cabinet meetings on some pretext or the other. Many of my friends and acquaintances like Bapu Kaldate were sent to jail. We used to meet them clandestinely and also help their families. Generally speaking, the party atmosphere was hostile to anyone who did not agree with the Gandhi couterie, and therefore those opposed to Emergency reached out to like-minded friends in whichever ways they could.

Emergency was lifted on 18 January 1977 but the political turbulence persisted. We in the Congress were mentally prepared for poll reverses, but certainly not to the extent of the shocking defeat of Indiraji and her son Sanjay who had become extremely unpopular during Emergency. Both lost their traditional seats and, worse, the party was thrown out of power. V.N. Gadgil lost on a Congress ticket from my hometown Baramati.

However, the Janata Party government, under Prime Minister Morarji Desai, that replaced the old regime, was unstable right from the beginning. As the creaky government began to crumble, the Congress too split once again. On 18 December 1977, Indiraji resigned her primary membership of the party. In the first week of January 1978, she formed Congress (Indira) to take on the parent party (the Congress [S]) led by Brahmanand Reddy and Yashwantrao Chavan in elections to the state assemblies of Maharashtra, Karnataka and Andhra Pradesh. Vasantrao Naik, Vasantdada Patil and I were among those who stayed with the Chavan-led Congress in Maharashtra.

Shankarrao Chavan, who belonged to Nanded in the Marathwada region of the state, left the Congress to set up his own party called the Maharashtra Samajwadi Congress. Nashikrao Tirpude, the leader from the Vidarbha region, aligned with Indiraji. In the February elections that year, we won sixty-nine seats as against sixty-five of the Congress (I).

Indiraji got in touch with Sardar Swaran Singh, who then headed the Congress (S), to assess the possibility of a coalition government in Maharashtra. The composition of the new House was such that notwithstanding the split, Congress (S) and Congress (I) had no other choice but to come together to form a government with Vasantdada Patil as chief minister and Tirpude as deputy chief minister. I was sworn in as minister for the industries department.

The coalition government, however, was not destined to last long. The Congress (I) ministers used to meet separately before cabinet meetings to strategise on how to corner the chief minister. Things came to such a pass that after Vasantdada briefed the media on the decisions taken by the state cabinet, Tirpude would hold a separate press conference, and would use offensive language while talking about the chief minister and other leaders from the Congress (S).

In private conversations, too, Tirpude would make derogatory remarks about our leaders. Chavansaheb too was not spared.

'We care little whether we stay in power or not,' Tirpude once told journalists. 'In that case, why do you continue to be in the government?' mediapersons asked. To which his reply was, 'I joined the government only because Indiraji asked me to do so. Leaders of the Chavan-Reddy Congress cannot survive without power. It was because they literally begged Indiraji that the coalition was formed.'

This caused a sense of deep hurt and anger among Congress (S) workers across the state. Vasantdada was livid. In a meeting of Congress (S) MLAs, he gave vent to his feelings using very harsh language. He called me over one day to say, 'I am fed up with Tirpude's antics. Do you think we should simply walk out of the government? Please talk to Chavansaheb about this.' Vasantdada said he would also consult Janata Party president Chandrashekhar, with whom he had very cordial relations. Chavansaheb himself was unhappy with the coalition experiment and was fast veering to the point of asking us to disband the government. In popular perception too the government was not expected to survive long.

Senior Congress (S) leaders Abasaheb Kulkarni and Kisan Veer took the lead in working out the nitty gritty of a split with the Congress (I). Govind Talwalkar, editor of Mumbai's leading Marathi newspaper *Maharashtra Times* was very close to Chavansaheb. In fact, it was popularly perceived at the time that Y.B. Chavan's political views were often reflected in Talwalkar's writings. After a meeting between the two, Talwalkar wrote an article in his newspaper with the title 'He sarkar jaave hi Shreenchi ichcha' ('It is God's will that this government should go'). This was a clear signal for us.

We rushed to Delhi to meet Chavansaheb. He was not as unambiguous as the heading of Talwalkar's article, but he did not conceal his displeasure with the coalition, and hinted that we did not have to drag along a partner with whom we could no longer get along. We got down to work after the meeting. Vasantdada was with us all along. However, at a later stage, for reasons best known to him, he changed his mind and chose to keep his distance.

Indira Gandhi got wind of the political developments in Maharashtra. She made a phone call to Vasantdada, the very chief minister her party people were insulting, and asked him to be on guard. After Vasantdada informed Rajni Patel about Indiraji's call, the latter took me along to meet Vasantdada. We talked for a long time about a number of issues. But the topic of disbanding the government did not come up.

Subsequently, Congress seniors, including Abasaheb Kulkarni, Kisan Veer, Dadasaheb Deotale, Prataptao Bhosale and a few others met at Ramtek, my official bungalow. Abasaheb called up Chandrashekhar from Ramtek and briefed him about the latest developments. The two shared a good equation.

I too had a close rapport with Chandrashekhar, and given the important role he would play in my career at this time, I must digress to describe our association. Our friendship went back to my early days in politics in the 1960s. I won my first state assembly election in 1967, a year after Indira Gandhi became prime minister. Before she started to assert herself, a band of Congressmen forged a 'ginger group' within the party to mount pressure on the prime minister to lend a Socialist slant to government policies. The Socialist Forum, as the group was called, was led by Mohan Kumaramangalam, Siddhartha Shankar Ray and Chandrashekhar. The group steadily gained in strength. I was aligned with its activities in Maharashtra.

Five years later, as Indira Gandhi strengthened her hold on the Congress, another bunch of young party members started voicing their views, a tad freely, on the party's programmes and policies. The group came to be known as Young Turks. Chandrashekhar was its leader. He was accompanied by Mohan Dharia, Krishna Kant and Ramdhan. The Young Turks were growing restive because of Indira Gandhi's autocratic style of functioning and also in no small measure due to Sanjay Gandhi's frequent interference in party and government affairs.

Around this time, elections to the Congress Parliamentary Board were scheduled during the party's national meet at Shimla. However, Chandrashekhar's name did not figure in the list of the 'official' panel. We urged him to contest and I worked as his campaign manager. He was elected to the Parliamentary board, and with his victory the Young Turks moved further away from Indira Gandhi. In the process, I grew closer to Chandrashekhar, and we remained friends even after he left the Congress and, later, became president of the Janata Party. It was against this backdrop that Chandrashekhar backed me in 1978.

Developments unfolded very fast in Mumbai and Delhi that summer. After Abasaheb Kulkarni spoke to Chandrashekhar, the latter spoke with me. He said, 'You will have to play a key role in this.' Janata Party leaders in Maharashtra were keen on forming a government in the state. Chandrashekhar held talks with S.M. Joshi and Uttamrao Patil, after which we moved on to the next stage.

Sushilkumar Shinde, Datta Meghe, Sundarrao Solanke and I wrote out our resignations and sent them to the chief minister. While this was underway, Indira Gandhi spoke to Yashwantrao Chavan in New Delhi, asking him to intervene. When Chavansaheb called me at Ramtek, I was with more than thirty-four MLAs present there. Chavansaheb asked me to put a halt to the move to withdraw support to the coalition government. This put me in a fix. I told him, 'Our resignations have already reached the chief minister. We will have to pay a heavy political price if we go by what you say at this stage. However, we will still abide by your wish. We won't proceed further.'

Kisan Veer was standing next to me when I said this to Chavansaheb. Kisan Veer was a veteran. His equations with Chavansaheb were such that he could talk to him on equal terms. Snatching the phone from me, he told Chavansaheb, 'Things have gone too far. There can be no turning back now. Don't ask us to do something that will ruin the future of these youngsters.' Then he disconnected the line.

I told Kisan Veer that I would not go against the wishes of Chavansaheb if he was insistent on maintaining the status quo. But Abasaheb Kulkarni brushed aside my viewpoint. 'You have already sent in your resignation. Now don't play around with your political future and that of your associates,' he warned. 'I don't care about my future. I will go by what Chavansaheb says,' I insisted. But all the senior leaders were more than firm on their stand. I was completely overruled.

As hectic parleys were on at Ramtek, in walked Govindrao Talwalkar who had 'expressed' Chavansaheb's views in his article in the *Maharashtra Times* earlier. He had brought a message from Chavansaheb that we should put our plans on hold. However, Talwalkar followed it up by voicing his own opinion in favour of withdrawing from the coalition government.

Congress (S) was not unanimous on the issue. Shalinitai Patil (chief minister Vasantdada's wife), Yashwantrao Mohite (party stalwart from southern Maharashtra) and former chief minister Vasantrao Naik were dead against the move. Yet, thirty-eight MLAs of Congress (S) walked out with me to form a new party called Samantar Congress (Parallel Congress) under the leadership of Dadasaheb Rupawate.

The Maharashtra Assembly session was on at the time. Even while the House was discussing supplementary demands, the government was reduced to a minority, following which chief minister Vasantdada Patil submitted his resignation to the Governor.

CM AT 38

In a joint meeting of the legislature wings of the Janata Party, the Samantar Congress and the Peasants and Workers Party (PWP), Janata Party stalwarts Chandrashekhar and S.M. Joshi announced my name to head the new coalition. My formal, unanimous election as leader of the Progressive Democratic

Front (PDF) happened immediately thereafter. On 18 July 1978, only three ministers, Uttamrao Patil, Nihal Ahmed and Sundarrao Solanke, were sworn in along with me.

The change of guard created a storm, raising the political temperature in Maharashtra. As head of the new government, I faced a major challenge as I was supposed to lead the fledgeling PDF government through the on-going monsoon session of the legislature with a three-member team of inexperienced ministers. I had worked in the government earlier but the other three were debutant ministers.

On the other hand, the opposition benches were packed with veterans such as Pratibhatai Patil, Vasantrao Naik, Vasantdada Patil, Prabha Rao and Yashwantrao Mohite. Two of my ministers, Uttamrao Patil and Nihal Ahmed, confessed that they couldn't muster adequate confidence to speak in the state assembly on behalf of the government. As a result, I had to bear more than 90% of the burden for the remaining eleven days of the session.

Whether it was the question hour or calling attention notices or discussions relating to any of the government departments, the responsibility of presenting the government's viewpoint lay entirely with me. The wide exposure I had got when working as a junior minister in Vasantrao Naik's government proved useful. Abasaheb Kulkarni and Kisan Veer used to watch the proceedings from the visitors' gallery. In the evening, they would pat me on the back on my performance in the House. They would call up Chavansaheb and tell him how well I was doing.

The very first assembly session kept me on my toes and also boosted my confidence to run the government efficiently. Like Abasaheb Kulkarni and Kisan Veer, Narubhau Limaye, a senior Congress leader, had a soft spot for me. Limaye had very strong views on most issues. A journalist and a MLC (Member of the Legislative Council) from Pune, he praised me profusely when he thought I was doing good work. But he was equally harsh in his criticism if he felt I had erred.

For instance, during one of my stints as chief minister, the government decided to give a green signal to casinos. Narubhau did not like the decision one bit and, in an acerbic remark, said my government was hell-bent on promoting the 'Rum (liquor), Ramaa (women), Rummy (betting)' culture. The phrase caught the people's imagination instantly. But I never took umbrage as I knew that Limaye was a man of integrity.

One of the first issues the PDF government tackled was the unresolved problem of the dearness allowance for state government employees. Every time the central government announced a revision in allowance for its own employees, the Maharashtra government employees used to go on strike demanding parity. My predecessor Vasantdada Patil had said a firm 'no' to the demand. However, my government took a policy decision that any revision in the dearness allowance at the Centre would become automatically applicable to the state government employees too. My government struck a chord with the state employees with the announcement of this permanent solution to their problem. The state government's employees' union was led by R.G. Karnik and G.D. Kulthe, both of whom enjoyed a clean image and vast following. The goodwill generated by the announcement about the dearness allowance prompted them to mobilise government employees in a big way whenever the state faced grave challenges in later years.

To quote just two examples, the government employees put in extraordinary efforts, almost like voluntary workers, when serial bomb blasts shattered Mumbai in 1993 and the earthquake devastated Marathwada the same year.

My colleagues in the cabinet lacked experience. They were simple at heart, unaccustomed to the dazzle of power. This would often lead to hilarious situations. To give you an instance, the Australian prime minister and the speaker of the Australian Parliament were on a visit to Mumbai. In keeping with protocol, I and Shivraj Patil, who was then the speaker of the Maharashtra legislative assembly, received the guests at the Santa Cruz airport.

It so happened that both Patil and I were dressed in gulla-bundh. We escorted the Australian prime minister and the speaker to Raj Bhavan where they were supposed to stay. I was to go to Varsha, the Maharashtra chief minister's official Malabar Hill residence, where a state cabinet meeting was to be held. I asked Patil to join me for a cup of tea at Varsha. My cabinet colleagues were surprised to see both of us in gulla-bundh.

I decided to pull a fast one on them, a harmless prank. I told them with a deadpan expression that every minister was entitled to have a gulla-bundh as a gift from Raj Bhavan and that they should give their measurements to a tailor. Soon, the ministers queued up before a master darzi whose worn-out tape did a quick job. Weeks later, they began to make frantic calls to Raj Bhavan to ask whether the gulla-bundhs were ready!

A few days after the PDF government got down to business, some of my cabinet colleagues came to me with a complaint that very few recognised them as ministers when they stepped into the state secretariat. They had a point, as many were beginners or not so well known to the Mantralay staff. So, each of the ministers was given an escort whose job was to walk ahead of the minister as the latter entered Mantralay. The escort was to sport a big brass buckle on his chest, identifying the minister.

However, mutual trust and shared values helped us set Maharashtra on a path of progress as mapped out by Chavansaheb. Thus, the employment guarantee scheme was given legal sanctity during PDF rule. We also took a decision to rename the Marathwada University after Dr Babasaheb Ambedkar. However, the Marathwada region in the state witnessed anti-Dalit riots when the decision was first announced, as a result of which my government suspended its implementation.

In a bid to promote progressive thought in Maharashra, we initiated projects that entailed compilation and publication of the thoughts and works of Dr Ambedkar, Mahatma Jyotiba Phule and Chhatrapati Shahu Maharaj. Our government also took measures for the utilisation of Maharashtra's share of water from the Krishna-Godavari river basins.

I expanded the cabinet after the assembly session. S.M. Joshi pressed for the inclusion of S.B. Chavan because he felt a man of Chavan's experience and scholarship would be an asset to the government. I wanted to induct Rajarambapu Patil as well, though he had been defeated in the elections. When Morarji Desai learnt of this he expressed his displeasure, saying, 'Hey barobar naahi' ('This is not right'). Though a Gujarati, Morarjibhai spoke good Marathi and 'Hey barobar naahi' was his pet phrase to indicate his disapproval. I pointed out to him that he too was made a minister despite losing an election in 1952. On hearing this, he relented and Rajarambapu Patil became a minister.

Our decision to break away from the Congress (S)-Congress (I) coalition was severely criticised in many circles. Vicious attacks of a personal nature were routinely launched against me. I was accused of 'back-stabbing' Vasantdada Patil. Now that I have narrated the exact events and behind-the-scenes happenings during that most talked-about part of my political career, let us leave that aside.

What I am really satisfied about is that the PDF government under me could provide an efficient, forward-looking regime that positioned Maharashtra firmly on the path of development. There was another interesting fallout. As chief minister of Maharashtra, I was required to attend several official meetings in Delhi. It helped me to interact with key political figures from different parts of the country. The network developed during the period became an asset in my subsequent years in politics.

FALL OF THE PDF GOVERNMENT

Following the collapse of the Janata Party government at the Centre in 1979, Indira Gandhi led Congress (I) to a thumping victory in the general elections held in January 1980. I was in Nagpur for the winter session of the state legislature. Two days before the end of the session, I got a telephone call from Union home minister Giani Zail Singh asking me to come to Delhi. I told him that I would do so once the session was over.

On reaching Delhi on 15th February, I got a message at the airport to proceed straight to the home minister's office in North Block. Zail Singh said he had called me on the instructions of the prime minister. 'I was planning to come over in any case because I wanted to congratulate the prime minister on her electoral victory. But, I haven't sought a formal appointment as yet,' I said. 'There is no need for that. Let's go to her right away,' he replied.

The two of us drove down to the prime minister's residence at 24 Willingdon Crescent. As soon as we entered her office, Zail Singh said he would leave because the prime minister wanted to speak to me alone. Minutes after he left, Indiraji walked in. There was an air of awkwardness. After a few minutes of polite conversation, she accepted my compliments on her electoral grand slam. 'Despite odds, you are managing very well,' she said. The remark perplexed me. But it set off an interesting conversation.

Before I could say anything, she put me a straight question, 'What is your future plan?'

'I will continue with what I am doing at present,' I said.

'There is one problem with you. You are not willing to disassociate yourself from your seniors,' she said. Her tone was sharp.

The remark was obviously directed at Yashwantrao Chavan. I maintained silence.

She turned more aggressive.

'Now the younger generation should work together.'

'Are you referring to Sanjay Gandhi?' I asked.

'Why not?' she said, coming straight to the point. 'It is time for young people like you to join hands in the task of nation building. How long can we shoulder this responsibility?'

Refusing to give in, I said, 'How can I take any responsibility as you suggest? The Congress (I) has a clear majority in the Lok Sabha. Our party has bagged just one seat—Yashwantrao Chavan's seat, and his success is due more to his own stature than our party's clout.'

'Don't go by election results,' she persisted. 'Both Sanjay and I had lost in the previous election, but we have bounced back. It is in your hands to back younger leadership to run the nation.'

'I am grateful to you for showing faith in me,' I said.

'I have complete faith in your ability,' she shot back.

'In that case, why don't you support *me*?' I asked.

She laughed out in response. On that note the meeting ended.

I came back to Mumbai. It was Saturday, 17 February 1980. After spending some time with my friends Nusli Wadia, Ajit Gulabchand, Arun Dahanukar and Madhav Apte at the Aarey Colony guest house in Goregaon, I returned to my official residence in south Mumbai. Around midnight, the chief secretary of the state L.S. Lulla came to my house. He read out a central government notification that the PDF government led by me had been dismissed. The development had come about within less than forty-eight hours of my meeting with Indiraji.

A couple of party functionaries and colleagues told me that the Centre's notification dismissing my government had come on 'amavasya', the inauspicious no-moon night! The crux of the matter was that Indiraji was keen on letting me continue as chief minister if I crossed over to her side. However, I was not interested in the offer.

That night, I vacated my official residence and shifted to my Maheshwari Mansion apartment in south Mumbai. My friends who were with me at the Aarey guest house the previous evening helped me pack my baggage. The next day, newspapers splashed reports of the PDF government's dismissal. There was a test match at Wankhede stadium. Pratibha and I drove down to the stadium in my old Fiat. A commentator, who was supposed to closely follow the game, announced my arrival and countless spectators rose from their seats and greeted me and my wife with a thunderous applause—a moment which I chrished for a long, long time.

Looking back, I consider my first stint as Maharashtra chief minister as the most satisfying of my four terms. Running a key state such as Maharashtra at the age of thirty-eight was a huge responsibility. However, I must say that eleven years of legislative experience, of them six years as minister, helped me handle the high-pressure job.

The PDF government I headed was a rainbow coalition. It had leftist, rightist and centrist leaders, none of whom had prior experience in government. However, there were advantages too. Since I was the one with the most experience I could shape government policies and implement them without external interference. For me, S.M. Joshi, the socialist doyen, was the high command. A man of impeccable character, he kept a close watch on the goings-on in the government. It was thanks to his patronage that I could function freely. Even when some leaders from the socialist stream went to him to voice grievances against me, he would pacify them quickly to ensure that the government was not harmed in any way. I feel blessed that I had SM on my side during that eventful phase.

RENAMING MARATHWADA UNIVERSITY

One of the most noteworthy decisions that the PDF government took was to rename the Marathwada University in Aurangabad after Dr Babasaheb Ambedkar. The historic decision displayed the government's courage and commitment. According to some people, it also perhaps, displayed the government's relative inexperience.

The decision sparked violence in parts of Maharashtra which pained me a lot. On looking back, I can say that the decision was fair and socially justified, but we lacked proper preparation before announcing it.

There was a reason why Dalit organisations in the state had been pressing for the renaming of the Marathwada university since the mid-1970s. Marathwada happened to be one of Maharashtra's most backward regions on many fronts, one of which was education. In comparison to other parts of the state, the region had very few schools and colleges of repute. Most boys and girls used to migrate to either Amravati in the Vidarbha region of the state, or Hyderabad in the neighbouring state of Andhra Pradesh, or Pune in western Maharashtra to pursue higher education.

To make up for this major lacuna, Dr Ambedkar had founded Milind College in Aurangabad in 1950. He had also called for the setting up of a university to give a fillip to higher education in the region. After Y.B. Chavan became chief minister, he took a decision to set up the Marathwada university in Aurangabad in 1957. Many Dalit organisations and progressive organisations in the state therefore demanded that the university be named after Dr Ambedkar.

In July 1977, chief minister Vasantdada Patil assured a delegation that the government would consider the demand if the university passed a resolution recommending the renaming. The university senate did so in a short time and there was a general consensus in the state cabinet as well. However, the government did not act on it for a year due to lack of political will. It feared a backlash because of the emergence of an equally strong force in the region that was vehemently opposed to the renaming. I shall come to that later.

Even as the issue was hotting up, the Vasantdada Patil government collapsed. The Progressive Democratic Front government led by me took over the reins of the state on 18 July 1978.

The renaming of the university was listed on the agenda of the new government. The written agenda was finalised at a joint meeting of all coalition partners. After assuming charge as chief minister, I called a meeting of the leaders of all political parties to seek support. The resolution for renaming was passed unanimously in the meeting. After the meeting, Sundarrao Solankhe took me aside. 'There will be a sharp reaction to the decision. Don't be in a hurry to implement it,' he cautioned. His was the only voice of apprehension that reached me at the time.

However, since all political parties had already given their consent without any reservations, I moved ahead. My personal conviction also prompted me to do so. The state already had universities elsewhere named after Chhatrapati Shivaji and Mahatma Phule. If the long-pending demand for naming a university after Dr Ambedkar was not met, I felt it would put an indelible blot on Maharashtra.

On 27 July 1978, I tabled the historic resolution in the state legislature. Discussions in both the Houses went off very well with members of all parties reiterating their support in one voice. The resolution was passed unanimously. And then the trouble started.

I got a message the same night that the Dalit community was being attacked in parts of Marathwada region by forces opposed to the renaming. The latter called for 'Marathwada Bandh', sparking a number of violent incidents across the region. Public property was destroyed, Dalit hamlets were targeted in villages and towns, and members of the community were assaulted at several places.

A youth named Pochiram Kamble, belonging to the Matang community, was killed near Nanded. Govindrao Bhurewar, a police sub-inspector, was burned alive by rioters. While Nanded district witnessed a spate of killings of the most gruesome kind, the violence also started to spread to the neighbouring region of Vidarbha. A committee chaired by Ramdhan, instituted later to probe the violence, concluded that thirteen Dalits and seven police personnel lost their lives. About 137 people were injured in various incidents.

The law and order machinery had failed to stem the arson. I was shocked by the scale and nature of the violence, which indicated that we needed to suspend the decision of renaming the university in order to bring the situation under control and to restore sanity.

'The government shall not implement the renaming resolution unless all concerned sections are taken into confidence,' I announced. That lowered the temperature at last.

S.M. Joshi and I visited the strife-torn region on the fifth day of the riots. We got a hostile reception at several places. Some anti-renaming activists went to the extent of garlanding the veteran Socialist leader with chappals. However, SM did not lose his cool and tried to engage them in a dialogue with commendable patience. Among the few others who supported us actively were Bapu Kaldate, F.M. (Famu) Shinde and Bapurao Jagtap. Those of my cabinet colleagues who belonged to the Marathwada region were Shankarrao Chavan, Sundarrao Solankhe and Sakharam Nakhate. SM had a good equation with Chavan and so he talked to him about accompanying us in our reach-out effort. 'Chavan has agreed to join us,' SM told me. However, Chavan furnished some excuse or the other and never turned up. He did not want to be seen publicly as a supporter of the re-naming. There was nobody left except us to bear the brunt of the wrath of anti-renaming elements for a long time.

There were quite a few revelations too. Some of the anti-renaming agitators were upset that I had 'singled out' Marathwada to carry out all the 'social experiments'. For instance, the announcement of re-naming was preceded by the appointment of Dr Shankarrao Kharat, a renowned Dalit scholar and writer, as vice-chancellor of the university. 'Could you not have appointed him the vice-chancellor of the University of Pune?' they asked. They were obviously not in a mood to acknowledge his contribution in the fields of literature and academics. There was another section which had no objection to the re-naming but was scared of facing the agitating youth. The latter had drafted letters opposing the re-naming. They carried printed copies of the letters to leaders at tehsil and district levels from the Marathwada region and made them sign on the dotted line. Few could stand up to such pressure tactics.

Marathwada had a long history of animosity between upper-caste Marathas and Dalits. Even the administration was not immune to the malaise. The animosity dated back to the pre-Independence era when the region was part of the Nizam's empire and the Nizam's Razakars, in tandem with several local people from the lower castes, had reportedly committed atrocities. The announcement of renaming provided an excuse for past animosities to spill over, triggering a full-blown conflagration.

Progressive forces in the region were divided on the issue. Some, like Govindbhai Shroff and Anantrao Bhalerao, were non-partisan in their view that renaming was an assault on the identity of the Marathwada region. When I took the decision to change the name 'Marathwada University', I had not reckoned with the strong local sentiment attached to the notion of Marathwada. It is good to remember here that while the rest of the state gained independence in 1947 with India, Marathwada had to wait until 17 September 1948, when the Nizam was overthrown and the state of Hyderabad merged into the Indian union. The Nizam's kingdom covered three broad linguistic entities: there were those who spoke Kannada, those who spoke Telugu and those who spoke Marathi. (To confuse things, there was also Urdu spoken in the Deccan style.) The Marathi-speaking areas had been given the name Marathwada which had become the nucleus of a strong regional identity.

Both Shroff and Bhalerao were held in immense respect, and their stand boosted the morale of the anti-renaming camp. Bhalerao's newspaper, also called *Marathwada*, had always been supportive of the Dalit cause. However, on the renaming issue, *Marathwada* had a different take. Also, Bhalerao was an active member of the Govindbhai Shroff-led Marathwada Vikas Parishad which assiduously pursued a development agenda for the region. This made the task difficult for Bhalerao. While he couldn't distance himself from Shroff, he took a relatively softer stance against the naming issue in his own paper.

Many Congress leaders were anyway peeved with me because I was leading a non-Congress government in the state, displacing their party from the seat of power. As the issue exploded, they spotted an opportunity to embarrass me. In fact, a few of them were complicit in leading the anti-renaming agitation. For instance, my government was aware that Balasaheb Pawar, an influential leader from Marathwada, was actively supporting the anti-renaming agitation. However, there was little that we could do to stop him from doing so at the time.

All this made me realise that it was a tactical mistake to rely solely on leaders of political parties. We should have taken common people, especially the youth, into confidence before the renaming decision was taken. We had failed to gauge the intensity of their anger, however unjustified. When riots erupted, leaders who had supported the decision to rename the university earlier got frightened by the upsurge and did not want to reveal their views on the matter. The administration was left to face the ire of the protestors.

These lessons enabled me to devise a new strategy to break the logjam. The socio-political climate was not conducive for me to take a fresh initiative in the immediate future. But the outline of a possible solution started to take shape in my mind gradually. I was determined to translate it into reality whenever the next opportunity came. The incomplete mission had to be accomplished.

I was out of power from 1980 to 1988. During that period I went all out to re-connect with a cross section of people from Marathwada. I talked to the youth about two things—the rationale behind the renaming of the university and why social cohesion was crucial for the development of Marathwada. In my subsequent stints as chief minister, I kept working at it. There had been four other chief ministers in the intervening period but all of them adopted a hands-off approach to the problem for obvious reasons.

Soon after I began my last term as chief minister in March 1993, I went for swift action. A plan was worked out to resolve the renaming issue by accommodating the sentiments of all stakeholders. Learning from the 1978 experience, I employed a direct approach and sent out personal letters to the sarpanchs (village heads) of all gram panchayats in Marathwada. I also spoke to student organisations and college principals in the region. And finally, we came to a decision that seemed to suit everyone. The university would now be called The Babasaheb Ambedkar Marathwada University. Having done the groundwork with utmost meticulousness, we were ready for the implementation. The decision was announced on 14 January 1994. It was communicated not as a naamaantar (a change in name) but a naamavistar (an extension of the name).

The Dalits were happy because the name of their icon was now a part of the university's name, while those who had fought violently for preserving the identity of the region had no problem with the new nomenclature because 'Marathwada' continued to be a part of the university's modified name.

This time around, the situation was peaceful. In sharp contrast to the general trend of bureaucratic negligence or complicity that was witnessed in 1978, the government machinery was fully geared up now to tackle any untoward developments. Meera Borwankar was posted in Aurangabad as superintendent of police. I was told that she had adopted a zero-tolerance approach towards anything that would disrupt the law and order situation. If a miscreant was caught indulging in violence, she would thrash him in full public view, right in the middle of the road. That helped retain the sanctity of the law, as for men there can't be anything worse than getting beaten up by a woman in public!

We also announced the setting up of four new universities in Maharashtra. That announcement helped defuse any possible reaction to the change in the name of Marathwada university. Thus, Swami Ramanand Teerth University, named after another icon from the Marathwada region, came into being at Nanded. The new university at Amravati in Vidarbha region was named after Sant Gadge Maharaj. An open university named after Yashwantrao Chavan came up at Nashik and Jalgaon became the headquarter of the Uttar Maharashtra university. This time around, Maharashtra was not just peaceful, it was happy.

In retrospect, I feel vindicated. Had we failed to resolve the naming issue, social sentiments in Maharashtra would have simmered with anger for ever. The 'lateral solution' that we came up with reinforced Maharashtra's integrity as a state.

This is how democracy works. It may take time but dialogue is the only way forward. The more you talk, the more you convince people; the more you take them into confidence and work for cohesiveness and inclusion, the better your leadership. I offer this advice to anyone who cares to listen, for I offer it from the benefit of my experience.

Talking about cohesiveness within Maharashtra, I feel concerned that integration within the Vidarbha region is still not as strong as in other parts of the state. This is a collective failure on our part and every time someone raises the demand for carving out a separate Vidarbha state out of Maharashtra, it rankles. For years, the political leadership in the Vidarbha region remained with the upper crust of the society. Brijlal Biyani (Akola), Govind Bhatia (Buldana), Jawaharlal Darda (Yavatmal), Kamalnayan Bajaj (Wardha), Rikabchand Sharma (Nagpur) and Manoharbhai Patel (Bhandara), all belonged to the wealthy class. They dominated the business sector and wielded immense influence over government administration and party structure. They were also the only spokespersons for Vidarbha.

Today, these leaders are no more. However, their legacy continues. It is only in recent years that people from other strata of society have started voicing their independent views and opinions. One needs to hear more from these sections on the real issues that affect the region.

✦ FIVE ✦

In the Opposition

IN JUNE 1980 THE Congress (I) stormed to power in Maharashtra, winning 186 seats out of the 288 in the state assembly. Our party, the Congress (Urs) (which the Samantar Congress had merged into), could muster only forty-seven seats. The Janata Party, our main coalition partner in the state, was crumbling at the national level, triggering widespread disillusionment.

Following defeat the rank and file in the Congress (U) became restless. Chavansaheb was in a mood to reconcile with Indiraji, but I disagreed with him on the issue. When I was away in London our party suffered a major jolt. All but six or seven of our party MLAs crossed over to Congress (I). Those who stayed back included Kamalkishore Kadam, Padamsinh Patil, Malojirao Mogal and Datta Meghe.

Notwithstanding the setback, I witnessed an entirely different scene at the airport when I returned from London. A huge gathering of youths was assembled at the airport to receive me. The mood was upbeat. It strengthened my confidence to rebuild the party with help from grassroots workers, irrespective of the desertions by our MLAs. I got down to the task without any delay.

Power has its own shortcomings. For instance, getting first-hand feedback becomes difficult for a minister, more so for the chief minister. As a result, one often takes decisions without assessing the public mood. Hence, I used the years between 1980 and '85 to mingle with the masses, travelling virtually five days a week, touring villages and towns in every tehsil of the state. The tours were planned as a serious exercise in striking meaningful dialogues with different sections of society, and also to take a close, hard look at the 'system'. This vastly helped me broaden and reinforce my party's political base during that period.

Accompanied by local party MLAs or village functionaries of my party I would visit schools and colleges, government offices and government project sites during the day, meet the intelligentsia in the evening and then chat with the local youth till late into the night. Those were magical days.

There were quite a few lessons for me to learn from my tours. The downtrodden sections of society in the Marathwada region, particularly the Dalit community, had borne the brunt of violence in the wake of my government's decision to rename the university after Dr Babasaheb Ambedkar. During my visits to the affected places I realised that the government machinery had not carried out its responsibility sincerely to control the violence. Worse, it was complicit in some instances. I thought it was my personal failure too because the home portfolio was with me when the riots took place in Marathwada.

The employment guarantee scheme was accorded legal status by my government. While I noticed that it did provide tremendous relief to a large number of disadvantaged men and women in rural areas, I also came across many cases wherein supervisors on various government projects had maintained bogus registers, listing fake names of people working on the site. Huge sums of money were siphoned off, courtesy the inflated lists. There was also a tendency on the part of many of those registered to while away time after marking their attendance in the morning. Here too, certain elements in the government machinery were hand in glove with those indulging in such malpractices. Callousness, alas, is a national curse.

Yet another shortcoming in the system that I came across was the alarmingly low quality of primary schools in many parts of the hinterland. I found during my random checks that students' notebooks were full of grammatical howlers. When I asked teachers about the shockingly low standard of learning they passed the buck to the parents! Many students were first-generation learners and their parents didn't know how to create a conducive atmosphere at home for their children. I found this extremely distressing. Later, I discussed the issue with the well-known educationist Dr Chitra Naik. Failure to combine universalisation of education with quality was the crux of the problem.

My tours also had a positive takeaway of a different kind. Far from the glitz and glamour of big cities there are people who work in their chosen fields with dedication and zeal. Despite the social import of their contribution they are rarely applauded. Not that they hanker after recognition. I met quite a few such souls during those five years.

In Jalna district of Marathwada region, for instance, I came across enterprising farmers employing local resources for water and soil conservation in a big way. I had the same experience in the Nashik district of north Maharashtra. All such observations served as precious inputs when I subsequently worked as part of the government at the state and national level. The bonds struck with progressive farmers during the period have remained strong till date. They keep me up to date with what is happening in reality. It is probably for reasons like these that my views on agriculture and related issues are taken seriously in the country.

My late evening sessions with talented youngsters with a deep interest in literature were equally rejuvenating. Again, compared to those in big cities, the youth in small, often unheard of places invariably come up with literary masterpieces because their expressions are rooted firmly in the harsh realities of life.

Jawahar Rathod was one such poet. His verse made a lasting impression on my mind. Jawahar is no more. In a poem titled 'Paatharwat' (Sculptor) he speaks about the agony of an artist who sculpted an idol for a local temple. The irony is that the upper-caste villagers instal the beautiful idol in the temple with great fanfare, but the sculptor is denied entry into the shrine because of his low caste. Jawahar says in the poem: 'You claim this God is yours. Am I not the one who created Him for you? And yet you prohibit me from coming in?' Listening to the poem in the aftermath of the violence unleashed against Dalits following the renaming of the Marathwada University, I was deeply moved.

Bapurao Jagtap was another young poet with fire in his belly. Although he belonged to the upper-caste Maratha community which had opposed the renaming, he personally supported the renaming decision and penned wonderful poems to promote the cause.

People like Rathod and Jagtap were not directly involved in politics, but I met them from time to time. Fortunately I am good at remembering names and other details too. People are often both pleased and surprised when I address them by their first name, even after a gap of many years. This generates goodwill which has kept me going through turbulent times in my political life.

COLLIDING WITH DATTA SAMANT

Abdul Rehman Antulay of the Congress (I) became the chief minister of Maharashtra on 9 June 1980. Although a dynamic leader who could take bold decisions, Antulay lacked the ability to take people along with him. He had the backing of Prime Minister Indira Gandhi. However, Vasantdada Patil was opposed to him. Antulay sought to placate Vasantdada by inducting his wife, Shalinitai Patil, as revenue minister in his cabinet. That hardly pacified Vasantdada.

Even as dissension within the party came to a boil, the Indira Gandhi Pratibha Pratishthan (IGPP) controversy (also known as the 'cement scandal') exploded. The IGPP was a trust set up by Antulay to encourage talent and art. The trust floated a corpus of ₹5.2 crore, out of which ₹2 crore came as a state government grant, while the remainder was collected as donations from sugar cooperatives and builders. The sugar mills had to pay at the rate of ₹2.50 per tonne of sugarcane they crushed, while builders were asked to contribute a certain amount to the trust against every bag of cement which, being scarce, had to be procured from the government.

Justice B. Lentin of the Bombay high court held Antulay guilty of a quid pro quo between donations to the IGPP and cement allocation. As opposition leader, I launched a blistering attack on Antulay in a speech in the state assembly. Antulay stepped down as chief minister on 12 January 1982.

Around this time the ire brewing among Mumbai's 2.5 lakh textile mill workers came to the fore. Divided across textile unions owing allegiance to the Congress, Communists, Socialists and the Shiv Sena, the Mumbai mill workers were restless because their long-pending demands related to pay hike and bonus were not being met.

The 1947 Bombay Industrial Relations (BIR) Act which recognised the Rashtriya Mill Mazdoor Sangh as the sole representative union of mill workers was another bone of contention. The stage was thus set for the entry of militant leader Datta Samant, even as the textile strike broke the backs of mill workers. Girangao, a hub of chawls and smoke-billowing chimneys of cloth mills situated in central Mumbai, was seething with anger. Samant was known for his aggressive style. Stories of how he would coerce captains of industry into signing a hefty wage hike agreement did the rounds in political circles. True to his credentials, Samant adopted a tough stance right from day one.

Antulay set up a three-member committee to go into the various issues. However, before the committee could complete its proceedings he had to step down. Amidst political uncertainty began the indefinite textile mill workers' strike on 18 January 1982. Three days later, Babasaheb Bhosale was sworn in as Maharashtra chief minister.

Bhosale turned out to be a cruel joke on Maharashtra. Selecting him as Antulay's successor was perhaps Indiraji's way of proclaiming her supremacy in the Congress. Babasaheb Bhosale was a greenhorn. The man couldn't believe for quite some time that he was to head the government. Many stories about why he was handpicked for the coveted post were then doing the rounds. There was one story that Mrs Gandhi chose him to be the Maharashtra chief minister as he shared his second name with Chhatrapati Shivaji, the great Maratha ruler, and the Congress high command thought him to be the warrior king's descendant!

According to another story, when advisers to the Congress high command sat down with a list of party MLAs in Maharashtra, they closed in on the Nehru Nagar assembly constituency in Mumbai. Thus, the high command felt Bhosale had two unmatched qualifications to his credit. One, that he was a 'Bhosale' and, second, that the name of his assembly constituency was 'Nehru' Nagar!

My personal guess was that Bhosale was selected for the chief ministership because he was the son-in-law of veteran Congress leader and freedom fighter Tulshidas Jadhav who was said to be close to the Gandhi family. In the 1969 presidential election Indiraji's candidate, Dr V.V. Giri, had fared poorly in Maharashtra. Of the five or six votes which Dr Giri polled from the state, one was that of Tulshidas Jadhav. That probably tilted the scale in Bhosale's favour.

Bhosale was a nice man who couldn't handle the high pressures of the top job. He had little knowledge of the state and was supremely indifferent to politics and administration. This often found reflection in the comments he made and the odd one-liners he used in situations that warranted seriousness.

The Congress government led by Bhosale—who of course did as he was told by the high command—decided to act tough on the mill issue. The opposition parties in the country, still recovering from the shock of the 1980 poll debacle, cared little for the mill workers' plight.

It was against this backdrop that George Fernandes, the irrepressible Socialist leader and a fine trade union leader who had spent his best years in Mumbai, decided to step into the matter. George and I shared excellent relations. Furthermore, he was on a first-name basis with Shiv Sena chief Balasaheb Thackeray.

Mumbai looked grim in the face of a long-drawn strike. The situation was fast worsening. Samant was not averse to taking the law into his own hands. This, we knew, would spell disaster for Mumbai. It was imperative to halt Samant, to provide an alternative to his destructive leadership. The textile industry was Mumbai's financial backbone. Moreover, it had given rise to a popular culture—theatre, literature and social movements—a sub-text woven into the legend of the city we loved in our different and individual ways.

If the mills collapsed, lakhs of predominantly Marathi-speaking mill workers would become jobless and their families would come to grief. Clearly, the mill strike cast a lengthening shadow over Mumbai and the state as well.

George discussed the issue at length with Thackeray and convinced him to join hands with us to tackle the issue. Thackeray had not taken the Hindutva line then. He was playing his 'sons-of-the-soil' tune. We persuaded him to abandon the Marathi manoos line in favour of the mill strike which had larger ramifications.

George, Thackeray and I held a public meeting at the Shivaji Park ground in Dadar, Mumbai, in November 1982. We announced our plan to intervene in the mill strike. But it was already too late. The strike had killed the mills, and though the youth of the city, those who followed us, were excited by this coming together of political leaders, it was not meant to last. Many Marathi Mumbaikars say even today that had we three stayed together, Maharashtra's politics would have taken a new turn. Who knows? There is no room for hindsight-wisdom in politics.

The Sena turned to Hindutva and teamed up with the Bharatiya Janata Party. That brought to an end my political association with Thackeray, although our friendship continued till the Sena chief's death in November 2012.

SIX

Long March for Farmers' Cause

THE DEMAND FOR REMUNERATIVE prices for farm produce took centre stage in the early 1980s. At that point in time, we were still importing food grains. We were not food sufficient. And yet the farmers were not being paid remunerative prices. Our demand was simple: we should pay farmers enough to make sure that they could till the land and make a reasonable profit. I believe that the going rate was about ₹250 to ₹300 per quintal and our demand was that this be made ₹700. It was double the rate and it sounded unreasonable but that was what it would take to make the government sit up and take note. And so when we hit on ₹600 per quintal, we felt we could make a significant difference to the lives of the farmers.

My colleagues and I decided to organise a long march to press forward the issue. The farmers were going to traverse a 440 kilometre-long path from Jalgaon to Nagpur on foot and we were going to call this march 'Shetkari Dindi', the long march of the farmers.

The usual forms of agitation till then had been dharnas, morchas and bandhs. Anyone familiar with Maharashtra's folk culture will know that the annual pilgrimage to Pandharpur called 'waari' holds a special place in the lives of scores of farmers in the state. In the early part of the monsoon a large number of farmers assemble at the holy places of Alandi and Dehu near Pune and set out on foot to go to Pandharpur (Sholapur district) where Lord Vitthal's temple is located. Men and women form groups, called 'dindis', recite prayers and chant holy songs as they walk. Many more 'dindis' join them at different points along the route. We adopted a similar form for our Shetkari Dindi. It evoked an equally enthusiastic response.

During the day there were only prayers and devotional songs. Speeches on farmers' issues were reserved for late evenings after reaching the last destination for the day. Though attracted to the march because of the dindi form, farmers from villages along the route knew the purpose and were also aware why it was headed to Nagpur where the winter session of the state assembly was in progress.

Many of them greeted us with freshly cooked food and drinking water. The number of participants kept swelling as we approached Nagpur. Villagers would, in a heartwarming gesture, put up arches along the route and sprinkle water to keep the road cool and clean. As we left a village, local residents would come in a huge procession to the last post to see us off, as the dindi continued its walkathon to its next destination.

Women would make as many as 35,000 'bhakris' (rotis) for us. There was only one demand in every hamlet we passed through—'Saheb' (yours truly) should eat 'our bhakri', a request I found tough to turn down. 'Bhakri' and 'vangyaache bharit' (brinjal bharata) was our staple diet during the long march.

I attended the assembly session only twice during its entire schedule and returned to join the march. The show of strength was massive and peaceful. It made national news. This flummoxed the Antulay government.

Yashwantraoji Chavan joined the dindi in Amravati, which is about 165 kilometres from Nagpur. As we reached Pohra village in the forest of Amravati, the police swooped down on us. We were arrested and taken to Bhandara district headquarters. Those arrested included Yashwantrao Chavan, S.M. Joshi, Devi Lal, Karpoori Thakur, Chandrajit Yadav, Surjit Singh Barnala, Harkishan Singh Surjit, A.B. Bardhan and many others. The police turned the dak bungalow into a prison and I and Yeshwantraoji were lodged there, while the others were lodged in Amravati, Wardha, Pulgaon and a few other places. Despite our arrest, the dindi moved on. We were released that night and taken to Nagpur. The next day, we marched to the Vidhan

Sabha. A large number of opposition MLAs joined the dindi in Nagpur, including Rajarambapu Patil and the poet N.D. Mahanor.

It is thanks to the overwhelming response received by the Shetkari Dindi that farmers' issues took centre stage at the national level. Chowdhary Devi Lal and Prakash Singh Badal planned to organise a rally in New Delhi to lend the issue a pan-India canvas. They were impressed by their experience of Shetkari Dindi and they invited me to take the lead.

I toured across Haryana and Punjab with the two leaders to mobilise mass support. We also focused on western Uttar Pradesh and parts of Rajasthan. On a typical day, we would go in three or four vehicles to visit several villages in Rajasthan. There were no rallies, no public meetings. Seated on a string bed, Chowdhary Devi Lal would smoke from a hookah and ask, 'What was the price you got for wheat this year?' After a figure was cited, he would pose the next question, 'Are you happy with the price?' This would prompt farmers to pour out their ire. Encouraged by the farmers' response, Devi Lal would exhort them, in his rugged style, to line up their tractors and march to Delhi for the rally. After gulping down a large glass of milk we would move to the next village.

The Gurudwara prabandhak committees wielded considerable clout in Punjab. My village tours, along with Prakash Singh Badal, were organised by the local prabandhak committees. Since the price for agricultural produce was an issue that hit farmers across states, the response was overwhelming. It was the same story in western Uttar Pradesh and Rajasthan.

The mammoth rally we held at the Boat Club in New Delhi was unprecedented in the history of the capital. Farmers descended in huge numbers on to open maidans and tracts of land from India Gate to the Parliament complex. All credit to Devi Lal and Prakash Singh Badal that they didn't grudge my presiding over the rally though I was several years younger than them. It was an unforgettable experience for me. In fact, the thought of entering national politics came to my mind for the first time after the rally.

All this while, Sharad Joshi's Shetkari Sanghatana had taken up the farmers' cause to launch a series of agitations across Maharashtra. For a decade or so Shetkari Sanghatana had fought for remunerative prices for farm produce in its strongholds of Nashik, Marathwada and Vidarbha regions. The Sanghatana brought into its fold some very effective leaders and aggressive speakers like Madhavrao Khanderao More, Pralhad Patil Karad and Saroj Kashikar. Sharad Joshi's biggest contribution was that he laid down the economics of agriculture in a scientific but simple fashion that could be easily understood by farmers in the country. He also roped in women from the farming family households in huge numbers which was truly creditable. As a result, he could garner tremendous support in Maharashtra, which also created ripples outside the state.

Though Sharad Joshi and I share cordial relations and both of us are firmly committed to the farmers' cause, we could not work together primarily because of his dictatorial approach in the initial period. Totally convinced about his own position on issues, he rarely yielded space to others. There was never any doubt about his commitment to the cause, but his initial decision to stay off electoral politics proved to be his undoing.

Taking to the streets for a cause is not enough. One has to understand that the state administration needs to be shaken out of its stupor and initiate measures regarding the demands, and also implement them at the government level.

Since active politics is the only route to becoming part of the government, shying away from electoral politics does not make sense. Joshi's statement, 'Beat me up with your chappals if I ever enter politics', was thus not liked by many of his followers who began to desert him in the course of time.

This is a problem typical of many people in the voluntary sector. Some of them have been doing excellent work for years, but politics is anathema to them. According to them, 'All politicians are corrupt and are out to loot the people.' This smacks of arrogance. Therefore, while I respect their work, I find their self-righteous attitude unacceptable. Another problem is their reluctance to develop a mass base for their work. It prevents them from taking the issue to its logical end because there is no denying the importance of scale and magnitude in a vast, diverse country like ours.

In recent times the Aam Admi Party (AAP) broke the mental shackles imposed by their 'Guru' and entered politics with full force. Whatever be the party's fate, it must be acknowledged that AAP made a significant impact on Indian politics. Sharad Joshi too eventually shed his initial antipathy to politics and launched his own party, the Swatantra Bharat Party in 1994.

However, while Arvind Kejriwal got his timing right when launching AAP, Joshi's timing did not click. An even more important factor that contributed to AAP's success was its location. Swatantra Bharat Party was based far away from Delhi, in Maharashtra, which was its inherent handicap. As against this the thrust of AAP's activities was Delhi-centric. Anything in Delhi assumes larger-than-life dimensions within a short time. After all, it is the capital of the country. Almost all leading media houses in the country have their head offices in Delhi. This is why a rise in the prices of, say, onion or milk in other parts of the country may not get noticed, but escalating prices in Delhi instantly blow up into a disproportionately big issue. The media plays it 24x7, and Parliament too feels compelled to take note of it.

All governments, irrespective of their party affiliations, therefore, tend to indulge Delhi. This explains why several daily commodities are available in Delhi at a highly subsidised rate. No wonder, many people call Delhi a 'spoilt brat'.

After decades of Jai Jawaan, Jai Kisaan, we still treat our farmers shamefully. We cannot expect of them what we do not expect of ourselves. We expect to pay low prices for food and so we force them, literally, to accept and expect low prices for their grain. Most policy is made in the offices of economists who have never sown a crop, never watched a seed germinate and never wept over the destruction that can be wrought by untimely rain or hail. We do not let farmers impinge on our imaginations until they remind us of their presence, either by scattering onions on the highway or by killing themselves. We need to think of our farmers as the providers of our country and we need to respect them. Or else we will end up in the grip of the major agri-based industries.

SEVEN

The Punjab Tangle

ON 5 JUNE 1984, THE Indian army stormed into the Golden Temple in Amritsar to evict Khalistani militants who were holed up there. The decision to carry out 'Operation Bluestar' was taken by Prime Minister Indira Gandhi. It saw 492 militants killed. Among them was the militant leader Jarnail Singh Bhindranwale. This sparked a series of violent retaliatory actions by Sikh militants leading to Indiraji's assassination on 31 October 1984.

The entire nation was shocked by Indiraji's killing. I rushed to New Delhi to pay homage to the departed leader. Rajiv Gandhi was elected Congress Parliamentary Party leader and took oath as prime minister the next day. Soon after I offered my condolences, he took me aside and suggested that I should return to the Congress. 'Look, Sharad, I kept away from politics all these years but now the situation has forced me into it. Both of us come from the same generation. How long are you going to sit in the opposition? It is high time we started working together,' he said to me. 'I cannot decide on my own. I will have to consult my party on this,' I told him.

In the general elections to the eighth Lok Sabha held in December that year, the 'sympathy wave' gave the Rajiv-led Congress an unprecedented win with 404 seats. The Bharatiya Janata Party was reduced to two seats and, with twenty-eight seats, the Telugu Desam Party emerged as the largest opposition in the Lok Sabha. Our party—Indian Congress (Socialist) or Congress (S), formerly Congress (U)—could win only nine seats, including two from Maharashtra. One of these was my seat, Baramati. Despite the Congress wave sweeping across the nation, I garnered 3,61,618 votes, the second highest tally after Rajiv's 3,65,041 votes in Amethi.

My colleagues in the state unit of Congress (S) were uncomfortable with my being away in New Delhi when elections to the Maharashtra assembly were round the corner. Congress (I) enjoyed complete supremacy and my Congress (S) colleagues felt that the party would be able to hold its ground only if I steered its campaign. So after being member of Parliament for just about three months, I returned to state politics to contest and win my traditional assembly seat from Baramati in March 1985. As expected, the Congress (I) retained power with 161 seats. However, our party could also hold its ground by winning fifty-four seats.

During my brief stint in the Lok Sabha, Rajiv Gandhi and I had several occasions to meet formally and informally. After I returned to Maharashtra, we continued to communicate regularly with each other, sharing views on a variety of issues. There was an informal touch to our relationship. Here was a young man, I felt, who had a strong desire to take the nation on the path of modernity. As we bonded closer for almost two years, I found myself becoming increasingly amenable to his insistence on my 'working' with him.

Then came an opportunity that brought us even closer. The wounds of Operation Bluestar and Indira Gandhi's assassination had not yet healed because of bitterness on both sides. There was a complete breakdown of communication between Akali Dal leaders and the Union government. This did not augur well for restoration of normalcy in Punjab. When I was on a short visit to New Delhi, Union home secretary Ram Pradhan came to see me at Maharashtra Sadan.

'Would you start informal talks with the Akali leaders?' Pradhan asked me. 'I know you have a good equation with [Harcharan Singh] Longowal and [Prakash Singh] Badal...' I was aware that restoring normalcy in Punjab had been accorded top priority by the prime minister and the Union home secretary as well. I had toured Punjab extensively when mobilising support for the farmers' rally in Delhi and had developed an excellent rapport with Longowal and Badal, in particular. Their bonding with the farming community in that state was incredible. So when Ram Pradhan made the request, I was not surprised. But I wanted a clarification before committing myself.

'Does the prime minister want me to talk to the Akalis?' I asked. Pradhan played it safe. 'I shall talk to the prime minister and get back to you shortly,' he said.

After a couple of days, I got a call from New Delhi for a meeting with Rajiv Gandhi. He was visibly restless. Punjab was still simmering because of the anti-Sikh riots that took place in Delhi after Indiraji's assassination, he said, and invited me to play a role in the restoration of dialogue 'in national interest'.

'I haven't thought as yet about how exactly it should be done, but I think you can make a beginning. Ram [Pradhan] also feels you can do it,' he said. I expressed my opinion that Punjab being a crucial border state, it was wrong to keep mass leaders such as Harcharan Singh Longowal, Prakash Singh Badal and Surjit Singh Barnala in jail for a long time. The vacuum created by their absence could prove detrimental to the efforts to restore normalcy.

The Akali leaders were incarcerated at Pachmadhi in Madhya Pradesh. I went there to meet them. They suggested that I should talk to Longowal about what I had in mind. Longowal did not hide his anger. When I brought up the subject of a dialogue with the Centre, he did not talk as a politician, but rather as a member of the Sikh community. The anti-Sikh violence in Delhi had angered him no end. He was particularly furious over the atrocities committed against women and children. It took quite some time for him to calm down.

I kept talking to him for two to three days. Striking a chord with him became easy when I referred to Maharashtra's age-old spiritual and cultural ties with Punjab. Guru Nanak is believed to have travelled extensively in Maharashtra, and Guru Gobind

Singh breathed his last in Nanded. Namdeo, the legendary saint-poet from Maharashtra, had spent quite a few years in Punjab in the thirteenth century and is still revered among Sikhs. Like Maharashtra, the entire nation holds Sikhs in high regard because they have always been in the forefront in the fight for India's freedom and integrity, I said to Longowal. The nation was looking to them again.

Tension began to melt. Longowal indicated that he would consider talking to the government only if the latter was genuine about solving the issue amicably. Before departing, I told the Akali leaders that I would talk to the government about shifting them to New Delhi to facilitate smoother communication.

After I briefed the prime minister and the home secretary about my talks, the Akali Dal leaders were moved to Tihar jail in Delhi where they had frequent interactions with relatives and party colleagues. This helped create a conducive atmosphere for an official interaction with the government. I had told Longowal that Rajiv Gandhi was keen on having a one-on-one dialogue with him without involving other politicians or the administration. I learnt later that such a meeting did take place.

Following a series of discussions between Ram Pradhan and the Akali team led by Longowal, an eleven-point pact between Rajiv Gandhi and H.S. Longowal, popularly known as the Punjab Accord, was signed on 24 July 1985.

However, the Punjab Accord did not receive unequivocal welcome. While those aligned with the Longowal faction were happy, certain sections of Sikh society, especially the youth, felt let down. In less than a month after the signing of the accord, Longowal was shot down, on 20 August 1985, in a gurudwara in village Sherpur, close to his native town in Punjab. This was followed by the assassination of General Arunkumar Vaidya, who was the Army Chief at the time of Operation Bluestar, a year later in Pune.

Pakistan sought to keep the Punjab situation on a boil by

instigating and supporting the militants in various ways. When I later took charge as defence minister in 1991 in the Narasimha Rao government, I realised that much needed to be done to heal the wounds of 1984. Restoring peace and normalcy in Punjab was on top of the Rao government's agenda.

When I visited areas bordering Punjab and Pakistan, my attention was drawn to quite a few things that called for immediate corrective action. Pakistan-based militants used to cross over during the night, set off bombs and commit other disruptive activities across Punjab and sneak back to their safe havens. They camped randomly in houses along the border, forcing families at gunpoint to offer them hospitality. This was routinely followed by raids by the Punjab police on the suspicion that the hosts were supportive of the militants. While the police were duty-bound to follow the militants' trail, the raided families felt victimised by both. This led to a lot of discontent in society.

There were other ill-effects too. Life in Punjab was in bad shape. Rightly called the granary of India, the state had taken to mechanised farming in a big way. All major towns and many villages along the border were thus dotted with tractor-repairing or motor-repairing workshops and outlets that sold a variety of farming-related equipment. Due to the pall of uncertainty, the service providers in these border villages had fled to far-off towns. Doctors and nurses from primary health centres and teachers from primary schools had also deserted their workplaces. As a result, health, education and agrarian services had come to a standstill. The situation had become dangerously rudderless.

After returning to New Delhi, I shared my observations with the prime minister, Narasimha Rao. The government drew up an elaborate plan which was immediately set into motion. Doctors and nurses from the Armed Forces Medical College (AFMC) and its affiliate hospitals were put in charge of primary health services. Likewise, engineers and technicians from the Military Engineering Service (MES) were drafted to run the agriculture-related technical services in villages. There are government-run Kendriya Vidyalayas (KVs) or Central Schools in military cantonments all over the country. Teachers from many of those KVs were deputed to run the schools in the border belt. A security cover was also imperative. Soldiers clad in civilian dress were dispersed in villages with a clear brief. They mingled with the local people, participating in all community activities with an aim to building bonds of mutual trust. They were instructed to neutralise not just cross-border terrorism, but also any oppressive act by the local police.

With the passage of time, these efforts started showing results. Once normalcy was restored in daily life, people felt reassured. Punjab soon regained its rightful place in the progress of mainstream India.

General Sunith Francis Rodrigues, who was the army chief at the time, deserves credit for his major contribution in chalking out the plan and executing it so well. My own role was limited to drawing up the long-term strategy, getting it approved and providing political and other resources for its implementation.

As a rule, the military is kept away from running civilian affairs in our country. The policy is fully justified. But the Indian army's help was taken in Punjab in 1991–92 because the situation was unprecedented and demanded out-of-the-box thinking. However, since the approach was unorthodox, there is no mention of the military's role in any official document.

EIGHT

Merging with the Congress

IN DECEMBER 1986 MY party, the Congress (S), merged with the Congress (I). It was not a spur-of-the-moment decision. The issue had been on my party's radar for more than two years. As I mentioned in the chapter 'Untangling Punjab', Rajiv Gandhi had come up with the merger idea in October 1984 immediately after Indiraji's assassination. Yet, we took two years to decide. There were some reservations in my party on the issue. However, I knew I would be able to convince my party colleagues.

Besides my affinity with Rajiv, there was another, and I would say stronger, reason for me to go with the Congress (I). As I have said earlier, I was always a Congressman at heart. Although my family was aligned with the Left-leaning PWP, I was drawn to the ideology and values of Mahatma Gandhi and Jawaharlal Nehru. Over the years I was convinced that the Congress alone had the will and ability to hold the country together. The Congress believed in pragmatic politics and I shared its belief.

Even when I was on the other side of the fence, that is, when I headed the non-Congress Progressive Democratic Front government in Maharashtra between 1978 and 1980, I never approved of the rabid anti-Congressism propogated by some of my Socialist colleagues.

I broke away from the Congress when I thought that the party had moved away from its basic philosophy. This happened in 1978 and in 1999. We, of the Nationalist Congress Party, strive to preserve the original 'Congress ethos'. My emotional bond with the Congress is strong even to this day. Hence, the Congress Party's deterioration in recent years makes me sad.

Rahul Gandhi is all set to revive his party, but the future, as of now, looks uncertain.

I will forever be a Congressman at heart. But I do not believe in the cult of political 'untouchability' which a number of Congressmen practice when dealing with non-Congress leaders on a personal level. I find any extreme ideological stance, either of the left or the right, singularly distasteful. I like to maintain good personal equations in both camps, left and right. I evaluate an individual not so much on his or her political leanings as on personal qualities. If the balance tilts towards the positive side, I bond with that person.

After he became prime minister, Rajiv Gandhi sent us constant reminders of his invitation to me to rejoin the Congress. My positive response to his efforts to untangle the Punjab issue had brought us close. He got Arun Nehru, the then minister of state for home, involved in the merger discussions. Nehru was Rajiv Gandhi's point man in all matters political. Nehru, in turn, deputed my friend Vijay Dhar, who was working in the Prime Minister's Office (PMO), to discuss the details of the merger with me. Vijay's father P.N. Dhar had been Indira Gandhi's political secretary. Vijay helped speed up things.

National Conference president Farooq Abdulla had been urging me for a long time to re-join the Congress and thus return to the 'mainstream' of national politics. However, Arun Nehru had an entirely different take on the matter. In one of my earlier meetings with him in New Delhi he made it clear at the outset that personally he had no grudges against me. He then went on to add, 'But if you join Congress at this juncture, it will harm both the state of Maharashtra and the Congress party. You have a great following among the youth, especially in the Marathwada region of Maharashtra. Your young followers are pitted against the well-entrenched leadership of the Congress party in various parts of the state. If you return to the Congress, your young followers, in the absence of a viable option, will go to the Shiv Sena. The Sena's influence is currently limited to

Mumbai and Thane. Your return to the Congress will create a space for that party and it will try to strike roots in central Maharashtra as well.'

Taking a cue from Arun Nehru, I undertook a tour of Marathwada to take my party colleagues into confidence before planning the merger rally. After engaging with them in every district of the region I more or less decided to hold the rally in Aurangabad because it was the nerve centre of the Marathwada region.

I must admit that Arun Nehru's political assessment about Marathwada was bang on. Soon after the merger I visited Parbhani, one of the major towns of the region. When I could not spot Jayprakash Mundada, the district president of my party in the pre-merger days, in the gathering of Congress (S) workers, I asked about his whereabouts. 'He has joined the Shiv Sena,' I was told.

When I met Mundada later, he explained, 'What else could I have done? All my years in politics I worked against the Congress leadership in the district. The day I am seen teaming up with Congress leaders, my career will be over.' Mundada later got elected to the state assembly on a Shiv Sena ticket and was also made a minister in the state cabinet. Many such instances in Marathwada proved Arun Nehru right. However, my reasons for re-joining the Congress at that point of time were entirely different and I have explained them earlier in this chapter.

The majority of Congress (I) workers and leaders were in favour of the merger. However, a small faction in the Congress, comprising self-styled 'Indira loyalists', was uncomfortable with the idea. My walking out of the Congress (S)-Congress (I) coalition to head the PDF government in Maharashtra in 1978 still rankled. They voiced their displeasure to Rajiv but he paid no heed. The Maharashtra chief minister at the time, Shankarrao Chavan, was also averse to the idea of my re-joining the Congress, for he saw me as a threat. Senior Congress (I) leader V.N. Gadgil too was opposed to the merger. But neither could do much about it.

On 6 December 1986, the Congress (S) merged with the Congress (I) in the presence of Rajiv Gandhi at a mammoth rally held in Aurangabad. Farooq Abdullah attended the function. The turnout of young Congress (S) and Congress (I) workers was truly remarkable. Rajiv Gandhi's presence at the rally was a signal to intra-party detractors that the merger was happening at his behest.

Much was made of the fact that Rajiv did not mention my name in his welcome speech. The media too indulged in speculation for several days. I attribute this to the Gandhi family's mindset. Whether Indiraji, Rajiv or Soniaji, all Gandhis consider the Congress as their family fiefdom. Contrast this with the large-heartedness of Yashwantrao Chavan who made it a point to mention every local leader by name in his speeches. Chavansaheb knew that such gestures add to the leader's stature and pep up the spirit of local party workers. Chavansaheb truly had a big heart.

Both Indiraji and Rajiv shared another tendency: jumping to conclusions in a jiffy. Without ascertaining facts they believed what they were told. But more of that later.

There are some who think even today that I should not have merged our party with the Congress (I) in 1986. However, I think my decision was correct. The merger decision was taken after considerable deliberation and was born of a genuine feeling that it would be in the interest of the nation at that point in time. So-called loyalists in the Congress (I) party never really bothered me. Loyalty to the Congress's First Family was the only USP of these gentlemen and good women. Hence, they never liked mass leaders or leaders who had risen on their own strength.

Prime Minister Narsimha Rao had to suffer these 'loyalists'. Ditto Dr Manmohan Singh when he was prime minister for two terms. Significantly, both of them had a soft spot for me. The reason could be that I always stood by them in cabinet meetings when they were in the right, even if it meant differing with '10

Janpath' on certain policy issues. Others in the Union cabinet cowered in fear of the First Family: what if the dynasty came to know of their support to the prime minister? I never had such fears.

CM AGAIN

After re-joining the Congress I kept a low profile. But the long-simmering anti-S.B. Chavan sentiment soon came to a boil and many disgruntled leaders began to meet me. Though Vasantdada Patil was by this time the governor of Rajasthan, he continued to take a deep interest in Maharashtra's politics. There was no love lost between S.B. Chavan and him. Whenever Vasantdada came to Maharashtra he would call all of us to discuss the political developments in the state.

When Vasantdada thought the time was ripe to force Chavan out, he invited us to Jaipur. Those present at the Jaipur Raj Bhavan included Shivajirao Deshmukh, Shivaji Giridhar Patil, Ramrao Adik, Shivajirao Nilangekar, Vijaysinh Mohite-Patil and Shankarrao Kolhe. Adik and Nilangekar were chief minister aspirants and said so openly at the meeting. Yet, the unanimous view at the Jaipur conclave was that Vasantdada's would be the final word on the matter.

Vasantdada stunned us with his brief speech. 'I have thought about it in great detail. It is true that Sharad and I had differences which led to great bitterness in the past when he walked out of my government to become the chief minister in 1978. However, times have changed. Today, the political situation in Maharashtra is fluid. The state administration needs to be resurrected. In a situation like this Sharad alone has the capacity to lead the state,' he said. Shivaji Giridhar Patil immediately seconded Vasantdada's view. Although Adik and Nilangekar were disappointed, they eventually agreed to go by the consensus.

After the Jaipur meeting Vasantdada stepped up his attacks

on Shankarrao Chavan. He would come out with frequent statements expressing displeasure with the incumbent leadership in Maharashtra, making it clear that he would not let up till his 'objective' had been achieved. Finally, on 15 October 1987, Vasantdada resigned from the post of Rajasthan governor. Shivajirao Shendge, a prominent leader from the shepherd community in southern Maharashtra, and I hosted a day-long event to mark Vasantdada's seventieth birthday on 13 November in his hometown, Sangli. Congress workers from different parts of the state turned out in large numbers to greet Vasantdada. Amidst birthday celebrations he spoke of the imminent change in the state leadership. Vasantdada's residence, the B-4 cottage near the state secretariat in south Mumbai, became the venue of our meetings.

There was political turmoil at the national level too. V.P. Singh had started drifting away from Rajiv Gandhi. He was removed as finance minister and was given charge of defence. When the Bofors scandal erupted, Singh quit the government and travelled across the country to mobilise public opinion on the issue of corruption in government deals.

Singh himself got elected to the Lok Sabha in a by-election from Allahabad, defeating Sunil Shastri of the Congress. That shook the Congress to the core, and prompted the top leadership to go for changes in the party and its governments in different states.

I was holidaying in Goa at the time. One morning as early as four o'clock, I got a call from the prime minister.

'What are you doing?' asked Rajiv Gandhi.

'Well, at 4 a.m. what else do people do but sleep?' I said jokingly.

'Well, I am working in my office.'

'You have no choice. You are the prime minister. I am a free bird,' I said. After such banter he came straight to the point and asked me to be in New Delhi by evening. Since there was no Goa-New Delhi flight, I had to go via Mumbai. As soon as I landed at the Mumbai airport I noticed that two or three senior police officers, one of them in plainclothes, followed me closely as I walked across from the arrival lounge to the departure terminal from where I flew to New Delhi. Since I had handled the home portfolio earlier I was familiar with the protocol formalities. I had a hazy feeling that I may be asked to lead the state.

It was a little before midnight that I got to meet Rajiv Gandhi. He asked me to take the oath of office and secrecy at 4 p.m. the next day. I was taken aback and pointed out that it was too short a time for me to tie up the loose ends. Also, a lot of formalities had to be completed before I could take the oath.

'Don't worry about all that. You rush back to Mumbai. We shall discuss cabinet formation after your swearing in is done,' replied Rajiv.

On reaching Mumbai I learnt that Chavan had already resigned and other formalities had been set into motion. Thus, on the evening of 24 June 1988, I was sworn in as Maharashtra's chief minister for the second time.

I had extremely cordial relations with Rajiv for a major part of my tenure. We exchanged views on crucial matters, shared our concerns, and once in a while engaged in light banter too. I can recall one interesting experience. Rajiv Gandhi was touring Maharashtra for the 1989 elections and I was with him on the campaign trail. After the last public rally at Sholapur, Rajiv asked me to hop into a small aircraft which was to go to Mhow in Madhya Pradesh. I tried to wriggle out saying that I had a few important engagements lined up the following day in Maharashtra. He brushed this aside, saying that he wanted to discuss something urgent with me, and assured me that I would be flown back in time. He got into the pilot's seat, with me at his side. As we talked Rajiv kept pointing to the terrain underneath to explain the flight route. A little later I noticed that he had changed the course.

'We are taking a short-cut to reach faster,' he said in a matter-of-fact way.

'But we are not supposed to divert from a pre-approved route, are we?' I asked.

'I know. But it's OK. Let us take the risk.'

'What if something untoward happens?'

'We will face it.'

'It may be fine with you,' I said in jest, 'But I have domestic responsibilities.'

At this we both burst out laughing. The landing at Mhow was smooth—Rajiv had, after all, been a successful pilot for years. And I returned to Mumbai by more coventional means to attend to my official (and domestic) engagements.

NURTURING INDUSTRY, CREATING BKC

In my second term as chief minister I decided to accord top priority to Maharashtra's industrial development. The state's agricultural growth was severely constrained by its agro-climatic conditions and although Maharashtra was still the preferred destination for industrialists, one needed to engage them in planning measures and formulating policies to retain the state's prime position.

I set aside two hours every day—2 p.m. to 4 p.m.—for those connected with the industrial sector. They could see me without prior appointment. If an industrialist visited my office by prior appointment and with a formal proposal, I would ask secretaries and department officials to be present so that the proposal could be examined and discussed. If possible, a decision could be taken across the table. This created a conducive atmosphere in the industrial sector.

Gujarat Chief Minister Chimanbhai Patel too was keen on attracting industries to his state. Because of our good equation, we cooperated and competed with each other at the same time. Since Maharashtra had a head start in the sector, Patel would generally divert big-ticket proposals to me, and I reciprocated

My parents Govindrao (Aaba; sitting, second from left) and Sharadabai (Bai; sitting, third from left) with their daughters, sons, sons-in-law and grandchildren. I am in the last row (second from right).

Newly married—Pratibha and I, sometime in 1967-68.

In Baramati in 1960, discussing drought relief work with (L to R) Australian missionaries Hesel Skuces and Edna Wazar, Anantrao Patil and Y.B. Chavan.

With my friends from the Brihan Maharashtra College of Commerce (BMCC) Pune, in 1958. First row (L to R): Abhay Kulkarni, myself and Anand Dalvi; second row (L to R): Sharad Joglekar and B.S. Wani.

Meeting Indira Gandhi when I was the president of the Maharashtra Pradesh Youth Congress (1963-64).

Baramati, 1967: Watching the vote counting process of the first assembly election that I fought successfully. Also in the picture, my representatives, Murlidhar Taware and Shivajirao Bhosle.

Taking the oath (administered by Governor Nawab Ali Yavar Jung) as minister of state in Chief Minister Vasantrao Naik's Maharashtra state cabinet in 1972.

Deep in conversation with the chief minister of Maharashtra, Vasantdada Patil, sometime in the early 1970s.

With (L to R) Bhai Vaidya, Prof. N.D. Patil and Jaganath Jadhav at an informal discussion during the PDF government term in Maharashtra (1979-80).

With K.P. Unnikrishnan and Chandrashekhar.

Agitating for the demands of the Mathadi Kamgar workers, 1981.

At our home, Ramtek, with (L to R) Jaganath Jadhav, Jyoti Basu, and S.M. Joshi in 1980, during my first tenure as chief minister of Maharashtra.

Celebrating 25 years of Geet Ramayana in Pune in 1980, with (L to R) Sudhir Phadke, Pandit Bhimsen Joshi and Atal Bihari Vajpayee.

With Sheikh Abdullah in the late 1970s, when he was CM of Jammu & Kashmir and I of Maharashtra.

With British PM Margaret Thatcher in Mumbai, during one of her visits to India.

Shankarrao Jagtap (speaker of the Maharashtra Vidhan Sabha) and I with Yasser Arafat (Chairman, Palestine Liberation Organization) during one of his visits to Mumbai.

With the World Bank President Robert McNamara in Mumbai, 1978. I have had a long association with the World Bank.

Shetkari Dindi—the mammoth march from Jalgaon to Nagpur for farmers' rights; 1980.

At the rally for Mumbai's textile workers in Shivaji Park, 1982: (L to R) Chhagan Bhujbal, Bal Thackeray, me and George Fernandes.

With Rajiv Gandhi

At the Malegaon Cooperative Sugar Mill during 'galit hangam', the sugarcane crushing season; October 1988.

With the eminent Marathi writer Kusumagraj (V.V. Shirwadkar) and Balram Jakhar (Speaker of the Lok Sabha) at the Jnanpith Award ceremony in Mumbai in 1989.

With Mother Teresa in Mumbai when I was Maharashtra CM, 1990-91.

With Dilip Kumar.

In conversation with Lata Mangeshkar.

In Raigad district in 1989-90 for the ambitious Konkan Railway Project, with (L to R) Madhu Dandavate (Union finance minister) and George Fernandes (Union railway minister).

With the veteran socialist leader Nanasaheb Gore and then prime minister V.P. Singh in New Delhi, discussing the Maharashtra-Karnataka border issue, sometime in 1989-90.

In Nagothane, Raigad District, after heavy rains and floods in the region in July 1989.

With (L to R) Madhukarrao Pichad, Svarupsing Naik and K. Gavit in the predominantly tribal region of Akkalkuwa-Nandurbar in 1990, after there had been deaths due to malnutrition. Following this visit we initiated a special budget for the Tribal Affairs Department. Maharashtra was the first state to do so.

Celebrating Iftar in Mumbai.

With P.V. Narsimha Rao in 1991 at the Congress Parliamentary Party (CPP) meeting where he was elected as CPP Leader.

by sending proposals for small and medium units to his state. The strategy paid dividends to both states.

My dialogue with industrialists was not restricted to big names only. I kept in touch with major overseas players too and during my tours across Maharashtra I made it a point to meet upcoming entrepreneurs. That kept me updated about their problems and future plans.

Around this time, Mumbai, Maharashtra's capital city, was precariously balancing many situations. The textile industry was in the doldrums and the Datta Samant-led strike had brought about the downfall of scores of industrial units in the city. Pharmaceutical companies were in bad shape, while petro-chemical units were preparing to go out of Mumbai. There were several reasons for the decline, the key factor being the high cost of business in Mumbai.

Land prices, wages and transport costs had shot up, resulting in escalated prices of industrial products. This in turn made it difficult for local industries to compete in the national and international market. I came to the conclusion that Mumbai needed a paradigm shift in order to retain its pre-eminence in the business world. The focus should be shifted from production to the finance and service sectors.

Hong Kong and Singapore had made their mark as financial hubs. Mumbai too had the potential to be in the big league. I got down to developing the Bandra-Kurla belt in central Mumbai as a major business hub. As the infrastructure got ready I followed up vigorously with leading banks and financial institutions, both in India and abroad, and got them to set up their units in the Bandra-Kurla Complex (BKC).

There were teething troubles, though. Companies and banks complained that the location was inconvenient. We offered them space at concessional rates. After that everything went on smoothly and before long most leading finance sector brands were ready to set up their offices in BKC.

Today, BKC is one of the world's major finance centres.

Also, this gave a great push to Mumbai's service sector. Several IT units too came up there, and banking and insurance sectors flourished. It is heartening to see thousands of bright young professionals swarming BKC, celebrating Mumbai's never-say-die spirit and superior work culture.

BKC also houses the low-profile, high-value diamond-cutting industry. Earlier, the business was scattered around different places—chiefly in the narrow, congested by-lanes of south Mumbai. As a result the diamond trade could not realise its full potential. We realised early on that tight, well-planned security is the key requirement of the diamond business. After consulting major players in the field we created the necessary facilities in BKC. Today, the diamond-cutting industry in BKC employs over 60,000 people and generates annual revenue to the tune of 11,000 crore by way of exports.

Every city has its own character and credo. History shows us that great cities have to evolve and shed their flab to be in sync with the changing times. If Mumbai could be developed as a financial hub, Pune could take its place in the sun as the key centre of the burgeoning automobile industry. Tata Motors and Bajaj Auto, the two big players, had their production units on the outskirts of Pune, spawning a large number of ancillaries in and around the city. My government initiated measures to attract major global brands as well. Thus, while companies such as Fiat, Mercedes, Volkswagon, General Motors have pitched their tent in Pune, their ancillary units have come up in the neighbouring districts of Kolhapur, Sangli and Aurangabad, generating employment opportunities for young Maharashtra.

It was not just the Mumbai-Pune belt which my government focused on. Nashik and Sinnar in north Maharashtra, Aurangabad and Chikalthana in Marathwada, and Nagpur and Chandrapur in Vidarbha had the potential to develop as industrial centres, and we began work to fulfil this potential. The strategy paid rich dividends and today you will find these cities dotted with industrial units, creating jobs and wealth.

Technical expertise was easily available for these centres. This could happen because of a landmark decision taken in 1983 by Vasantdada Patil, the then chief minister of Maharashtra. He gave the go-ahead to private players to set up engineering colleges on a non-grant basis. This created the necessary infrastructure for imparting technical education in rural and semi-rural areas of the state. After initial hiccups most of these have proved to be a boon to the aspiring youth from Maharashtra's hinterland as well as other parts of the country.

Even after I ceased to be Maharashtra's chief minister I kept up my dialogue with captains of industry, both in India and abroad. Chung Se Yung, chairman of Hyundai, the well-known South Korean automobile giant, was a good friend of mine. I had been persuading him for a long time to start a manufacturing unit in Maharashtra. By the time he decided to visit the state for preliminary assessment, my party had been displaced from power by the Shiv Sena-BJP dispensation. After taking Chung Se Yung to Tata Motors and Bajaj Auto, I introduced him to chief minister Manohar Joshi of the Sena. Joshi took him to Shiv Sena chief Balasaheb Thackeray. I was optimistic about the meeting. However, I was told that things did not turn out as expected during the Hyundai-Thackeray talks.

The Hyundai chairman later told me that he somehow couldn't get the comfort level to begin business in Maharashtra. I passed on the lead to Tamil Nadu chief minister Jayalalitha. Today, Hyundai lives happily in Tamil Nadu.

NINE

'Chandrashekhar Doesn't Change His Mind Three Times a Day'

FRIENDSHIP AND POLITICS DO not necessarily go arm in arm. It's good as long as it lasts, as they say. As long as there is no conflict of interest. A practising politician has to be prepared for any eventuality.

During my long innings in politics I had to wade through several such unsavoury situations. My relationship with Rajiv Gandhi is a case in point. Elsewhere in this book I have written about how we dealt with each other when my government in Maharashtra was sought to be sabotaged in 1990 at the behest of the party high command. Here is another example of how our equations came close to the brink.

After being expelled from the Congress, V.P. Singh went hammer and tongs at the Rajiv Gandhi government on the issue of corruption. In October 1988 Singh merged his party, the Jan Morcha, with the newly constituted Janata Dal which tied up with some other non-Congress political parties and regional parties to form an omnibus alliance called the National Front.

In the November 1989 elections to the ninth Lok Sabha, the Congress under Rajiv Gandhi emerged as the single largest party with 197 seats, while the V.P. Singh-led Janata Dal bagged 140 seats. However, the National Front, backed by the BJP (eighty-five seats), the CPI (twelve seats) and the CPM (thirty-three seats) from outside, formed the government at the centre with V.P. Singh as the prime minister.

The National Front regime couldn't complete even a year in office. Singh couldn't get along with stalwarts such as Devi Lal and Chandrashekhar. This posed a big question mark about the government's longevity right from the start. Then, within days of the government being formed, home minister Mufti Mohammed Sayeed's daughter Rubaiya was abducted by Kashmiri militants. They released her only when the Centre gave in to their demands and released five jailed militants.

Challenges became graver after Singh announced the implementation of the Mandal commission recommendations for backward-caste reservations on 13 August 1990. Two months after this, senior BJP leader L.K. Advani embarked on a 'rathayatra' from Somnath to Ayodhya on the issue of Ram Janmabhoomi, demanding that a Ram temple be built where the Babri mosque stood.

Each was an explosive issue in itself. As the events unfolded in quick succession, Singh's future as prime minister became more and more shaky.

The Congress smelt an opportunity to dislodge him. Both V.P. Singh and Chandrashekhar were leaders from the Rajput community and therefore many attributed their rivalry to the all-too-known intra-community fracas for supremacy. However, it wasn't quite so simple. While Singh, the Raja of Manda, was seen as a representative of the Rajput land-owning royalty, Chandrashekhar was seen as one who identified with the common people from the Rajput community. Notwithstanding Singh's image as a champion of the backward castes (due to his decision to implement the Mandal recommendations), his attitude towards Chandrashekhar often smacked of condescension.

The Congress felt Chandrashekhar had made up his mind to part ways with Singh whose relations with the Gandhi family had, to put it mildly, turned sour. Since Gujarat chief minister Chimanbhai Patel and I had excellent equations with Chandrashekhar, Rajiv Gandhi asked us to hold discussions with him and draw up a strategy.

Chandrashekhar and Devi Lal walked out of the Janata Dal with 52 member of Parliaments in tow, including Mulayam

Singh Yadav, H.D. Deve Gowda, Maneka Gandhi, Yashwant Sinha and Om Prakash Chautala. This left Singh with no option but to seek a vote of confidence in the Lok Sabha. He lost the trust vote and resigned on 7 November 1990.

The splinter group headed by Chandrashekhar had a measly tally of sixty-four member of Parliaments. But the Congress supported him to form the next government. He was to be sworn in as prime minister on 10 November 1990. This was the political scenario when things started going wrong between Rajiv Gandhi and me.

On 9 November, my wife Pratibha, daughter Supriya, my (then would be) son-in-law Sadanand Sule and I went to Delhi to greet Chandrashekhar on the eve of his swearing in as prime minister. He had been our family friend for a long time and had been particularly fond of Supriya since her childhood. 'Uncle, would you join us for lunch after the swearing in?' Supriya asked him.

Pat came the reply: 'Yes, why not? I will come tomorrow.'

The question was innocent as was the answer. But unbeknownst to us, it sparked a misunderstanding between Rajiv and me. People attributed political motives to the 'move' and began to view all subsequent developments through that prism.

Chandrashekhar had a mind of his own and did not care much for diplomatic niceties. Soon after taking oath as prime minister he drove down to the Maharashtra Sadan to have lunch with us. This was unheard of in political circles. The prime minister at Maharashtra Sadan for a private lunch! Political pundits and the media went into a tizzy.

Let me recount another incident to substantiate my point that Chandrashekhar never allowed political considerations to come in the way of personal friendship. The incident happened during his very first visit to Mumbai after assuming office as prime minister. I have a personal driver who has been working with me since 1967. Gama has been more than a driver for me, although he never transgresses the limits of his professional assignment. Because he has put in a number of years as my driver, many of my friends and formal acquaintances know him well.

Chandrashekhar emerged from the Mumbai airport. 'Where is Gama? Call him here,' he ordered as soon as he reached the car. Members of the reception party looked perplexed because they had never ever heard of Gama. However, there was much commotion among members of Gama's fraternity—the scores of drivers of politicians and other VIPs present at the airport. One of them spotted Gama and pushed him towards the prime minister.

'How are you Gama? Good to see you after a long time. Come here,' Chandrashekhar spoke with his characteristic warmth.

Overwhelmed, Gama fumbled for words. The prime minister put his arm around Gama's shoulder and asked photographers to click pictures. To hell with protocol! That was Chandrashekhar for you.

Whenever a prime minister visits Mumbai, he or she stays at Raj Bhavan, the governor's residence at Malabar hill. However, during his Mumbai visits Chandrashekhar would always stay with me at my official bungalow, 'Varsha', whenever I held the chief minister's post.

Neither Chandrashekhar nor I made any attempt to conceal our friendship, even though my well-wishers in Delhi always cautioned me against making our friendship 'public'. This added to the unease of the Congress high command. In any case, the Chandrashekhar government was hanging by a slender thread, surviving solely at the mercy of the Congress party's 197 member of Parliaments. There were enough indications that the alliance would not last long.

On 4 March 1991 Supriya got married to Sadanand Sule in my home town Baramati. In keeping with my credo the wedding was simple—no pomp, no razmatazz. Baramati was literally swarming with people who came from all parts of the state and from other regions as well to greet the newly-weds.

Prime Minister Chandrashekhar, Congress President Rajiv Gandhi, Bhairon Singh Shekhavat, Farooq Abdullah, Janardhan Reddy, S. Bangarappa, B. Shankaranand, Chimanbhai Patel, N.D. Tewari and some industrialists and close friends were present too.

Busy with the wedding preparations, I had no inkling of the latest political developments in New Delhi. All that I knew was that the Congress had been exerting pressure on the Chadrashekhar government in order to undermine it and thus prepare the ground for its own return to power.

Rajiv and Chandrashekhar were seated next to each other at the reception venue in Baramati. As I went up to them I heard Chandrashekhar asking Rajiv what were his plans about going back to New Delhi. Rajiv said he had no particular plans. The prime minister then invited the Congress president to accompany him in his official Boeing. Baramati is about 100 kilometres from Pune. Hence, those who wished to fly to New Delhi had to drive down to Pune to take the New Delhi flight. After some 'gupshup', Chandrashekhar was ready to leave. Rajiv told him that he wanted to spend some more time with my family and that he would join the prime minister in Pune.

For the next two hours I kept getting calls from the prime minister to know if Rajiv had left for Pune. I could see that Rajiv was taking it easy. I, as host, couldn't remind Rajiv to leave for Pune. However, when calls from Pune turned frantic I asked Rajiv what was on his mind. I was taken aback when he said, 'You see, I don't wish to accompany him to New Delhi. You may ask him to go ahead.'

Embarrassed as I was, I had to convey the message to the Pune collector, Shrinivas Patil. It was only after the prime minister's aircraft had taken off from Pune that Rajiv left Baramati. The episode was a clear indication that there was something seriously wrong between the two leaders.

The very next day, Congress members created a ruckus in Parliament, claiming that Rajiv was being spied on by two Haryana police constables posted outside his house. The accusation was unconvincing, even ridiculous, and it threw the political situation in a tailspin.

On 6 March 1991, a livid Chandrashekhar sent his resignation to the president. Rajiv had apparently not anticipated that things would take such a serious turn. He summoned me to New Delhi and asked me if I could placate Chandrashekhar and make him withdraw the resignation.

Knowing Chandrashekhar I was doubtful about my fire-fighting mission. Nevertheless, I went to see him. Chandrashekhar was in his old house and not at the prime minister's official residence.

'What has brought you here?' he asked me in a huff.

'I want to speak to you,' I said.

'Has that fellow asked you to call on me?' he enquired in a rather disparaging tone.

He sensed my awkwardness and was silent. I pressed on. 'There is some misunderstanding. Congress doesn't want your government to fall. Please withdraw your resignation from the prime minister 's post. We would like you to continue.'

He was still seething with anger. 'How could you treat a prime minister in such a manner? This is not about my personal ego. It is about the sanctity of the prime minister's post. Your party president too has held the prime minister's post in the past. Does the Congress really believe that I would depute police constables to snoop on him?'

And then came the parting shot. 'Go back and tell him that Chandrashekhar does not change his mind three times a day. I am not the one to stick to power at any cost. Once I decide on something, I carry it out. There shall be no rethinking on my part. The president may not have accepted my resignation as yet, but he will have to accept it.'

The Baramati episode two days earlier had clearly been a

percursor to the high drama that unfolded in the national capital. Ties between Chandrashekhar and Rajiv Gandhi snapped for good, and the nation stood once again at the crossroads. Fresh elections were announced within just sixteen months of the previous ones to elect the Tenth Lok Sabha.

Clearly, Rajiv Gandhi had propped up the Chandrashekhar government merely as an ad hoc arrangement. He was only buying time so that the Congress could gear up for the next general election.

The rug was to be pulled from under the government's feet when the Congress thought that the time was ripe to call for fresh polls. Earlier, Indira Gandhi had played the same trick on Chaudhary Charan Singh with great success.

However, Rajiv went wrong in his assessment of Chandrashekhar. The Congress's intention was to only humiliate Chandrashekhar and not to remove him from office yet. But Chandrashekhar was made of a different cloth. He believed in calling a spade a shovel. He promptly gave up the prime ministership, and the Congress party's political calculations went haywire.

TEN

A Solution That Slipped Away

ALTHOUGH THE CHANDRASHEKHAR GOVERNMENT did not last for more than seven months, it made during that brief period a serious attempt to tackle the Ram Janmabhoomi-Babri Masjid issue. Bhairon Singh Shekhawat, the BJP veteran from Rajasthan, and I too joined the exercise. However, not many are aware of our efforts for two reasons. One, it was entirely unofficial. Two, it finally came to naught.

The Ram Janmabhoomi-Babri Masjid controversy dates back to the British era. The Babri mosque in Ayodhya had become the subject of dispute in the 1850s, with some Hindu organisations claiming that the mosque stood on the site of a temple that marked the birthplace (janmabhoomi) of Lord Ram and which had been demolished by the Mughals. Post-Independence too the issue kept surfacing from time to time. In the early 1950s the structure was declared to be under dispute by the courts and its gates were locked. In the mid-1980s the controversy took the national centrestage.

An alimony case filed in the Supreme Court by Shah Bano, a Muslim divorcee, was decided in her favour. This was seen by several Muslim organisations as an encroachment on the Muslim Personal Law. In response, the Rajiv Gandhi government moved the Muslim Women (Protection of Rights on Divorce) Bill in the Lok Sabha. Since the government enjoyed a clear majority in the Parliament it was enacted without any difficulty.

The sentiments of a section of the Muslim community were placated because the new Act diluted the effects of the Supreme Court judgement. However, Hindu organisations called it 'appeasement of the minorities'. Then came another twist. On 1 February 1986, the Faizabad district court ordered the unlocking of the gates of the disputed structure in Ayodhya, and within hours the Rajiv Gandhi government opened the gates to allow the 'shilanyas' ceremony for a proposed Ram temple. This was perceived as an attempt to appease Hindu sentiments.

All these developments led to religious polarisation in the country. While some Muslims came together to set up the 'Babri Masjid Action Committee' (BMAC) to safeguard the mosque, some Hindus got together under the banner of 'Ramjanmabhoomi Nyas' to erect the Lord Ram temple. Later, during the eleven-month rule of the V.P. Singh government, BJP leader L.K. Advani took out a 'rathyatra' from Somnath in Gujarat to consolidate public opinion in favour of the Ram temple in Ayodhya. It evoked a big response. The procession was slated to go to Ayodhya, but was halted by the Lalu Prasad Yadav government in Bihar. Though Advani was arrested, the issue continued to simmer even after the V.P. Singh government collapsed.

Prime Minister Chandrashekhar decided to forge a breakthrough soon after he took over. He had a good rapport with Bhairon Singh Shekhawat, who was considered to be one of the 'soft' Hindu leaders of the BJP. The prime minister called Shekhawat and me to deliberate upon a possible approach to resolve the issue. He asked Shekhawat to have closed-door talks with the BMAC leaders. I was asked to do the same with the Ramjanmabhoomi Nyas leadership. This was because while Shekhawat had some rapport with the Muslim community, the Ramjanmabhoomi Nyas was headed by Moropant Pingale, a RSS leader from Maharashtra.

We got down to the task in right earnest. Shekhawat had a series of one-on-one meetings with the BMAC members, while I did the same with Pingale and his close colleagues. A common ground was reached. Then followed a series of joint meetings of all the stakeholders. Shekhawat, in particular, played a major role in bringing both sides to the negotiating table. I learnt that in the process he said a few tough things even to the RSS.

In one part of the structure, as it stood at the time, Hindus offered prayers to a small idol of Lord Ram, while Muslims used the other part of the structure to perform namaaz. Keeping this in mind the solution being hammered out suggested retention of the disputed structure and providing access to Hindus and Muslims from different sides to offer prayers as per their respective religious practices.

It was agreed by both camps to take the dialogue forward so that the long-pending issue could be settled in the near future. Alas, that was not to be. Political developments overtook the process of dialogue. In March 1991 the Chandrashekhar government collapsed after the Congress withdrew its support. If only the government had survived for another six months or so the issue could have perhaps been resolved. The efforts halted with the fall of the government could not be revived.

What happened much later was the demolition of the mosque by Hindu bigots on 6 December 1992 during the regime of Prime Minister P.V. Narasimha Rao. I was defence minister in his cabinet. The home portfolio was with S.B. Chavan, while Madhav Godbole was the home secretary. The BJP and its sister organisations from the RSS clan had started whipping up nation-wide frenzy on the Ayodhya issue. Since the BJP was in power in UP with Kalyan Singh as chief minister, things became tricky.

Even while the Vishwa Hindu Parishad (VHP) and its allies were working towards the 6 December event, we in the central government got engaged in a series of parleys. I pressed for a tough posture on the issue. Godbole was also of the same opinion. But Prime Minister Rao was not in favour of using force. He turned down my suggestion that we should post army platoons at the disputed site as a precautionary measure.

After my suggestion was rejected by the prime minister, I asked the army's intelligence wing to video shoot all developments at the disputed site on 6 December. The film captured various stages of the demolition job accomplished by kar sevaks, including how they were egged on by their leaders.

The demolition exposed Narasimha Rao's weakness as a leader. He certainly did not want the demolition to happen but did not take the necessary steps to prevent it from happening. I tried my best to convince him repeatedly that the kar sevaks would go to any extent to raze the mosque. However, he feared that if the army opened fire, killing some people, it would spark violence across the country. He also cited two things. First, that senior BJP leaders, including Rajmata Vijayaraje Scindia, had given a categorical assurance at a meeting of the National Integration Council that they would not violate the law during the campaign. Second, UP Chief Minister Kalyan Singh had also given an undertaking that his government would prevent any untoward incident at the site.

When we insisted that trusting those leaders would be a risky proposition, Rao said, 'I have full faith in the Rajmata's word. I know she won't let me down.'

Prime Minister Rao, S.B. Chavan and I had an emergency meeting on the evening of 6 December where the home secretary Madhav Godbole narrated in great detail how the mosque was brought down. He also explained how BJP leaders and leaders of other Hindutva organisations, in whom the prime minister had reposed full faith, had played a clear role in the demolition. The prime minister sat through the meeting as if in a daze.

ELEVEN

Revolt in a Teacup

IN 1990, SOME OF the big names in the Maharashtra Congress raised a flag of revolt against me. Apart from a few of my cabinet colleagues such as Vilasrao Deshmukh, Ramrao Adik, Surupsingh Naik, Shivajirao Deshmukh, Jawaharlal Darda and Javed Khan, the rebels included Maharashtra Congress President Sushilkumar Shinde, Shankarrao (S.B.) Chavan, Vitthalrao Gadgil and A.R. Antulay too. Only a few days earlier Shinde had proclaimed publicly that he would never leave my side no matter how strong the opposition ranks were.

The rebels addressed a press conference to declare that they could not work with me any longer because my continuance in office would harm the Congress in the state. They demanded my immediate resignation. The rebellion did not bother me because I knew that although my opponents were acting at the behest of the 'higher ups' in Delhi, they had little support in the party's state unit.

It was finally decided that the issue should be resolved at a meeting of the state legislature party. G.K. Moopanar and Gulam Nabi Azad flew down from New Delhi as party observers. Legislators were sent messages before the meeting that the high command desired a 'change in leadership'. The observers had planned not to take a vote on the issue of leadership change but to have one-on-one talks with the legislators to assess the 'general mood'.

This was the usual ploy employed by the high command to muffle the majority view which was inconvenient to them, and have its own say. However, many legislators made it clear right at the beginning that they would not abide by a decision that was thrust upon them without a proper poll. When the issue was put to vote in the meeting, less than 20 members voted for a change, while nearly 190 MLAs/MLCs stood by me. Sudhakarrao Naik, who succeeded me as chief minister in 1991, played a crucial role in mobilising the legislators' support in my favour. There was a groundswell of support for me even outside the legislature party. A huge gathering of party activists was waiting near the venue to know the outcome of the meeting. When the word went out there were loud cheers all around. But there was also anger against the rebel group.

In fact, the latter had to be escorted to their cars to avoid ugly scenes. Moopanar and Azad went back to apprise the high command of the overwhelming ground support that I had demonstrated. Soon thereafter, M.L. Fotedar called from New Delhi to say that Rajiv Gandhi wanted to meet me. It turned out to be an interesting encounter.

As soon as I entered Rajiv's room, he asked, 'So? What's happening?'

'You know better than me,' I replied. 'Everyone in Mumbai acted quite efficiently as per your instructions. However they, unfortunately, just couldn't muster adequate support.'

Rajiv had no option but to admit his involvement, although obliquely. 'No, no. Something went wrong there. I had just asked them to shake the tree, not uproot it,' he said.

Without making much of it, we moved on.

But I was firm about the removal of Sushilkumar Shinde as state Congress chief. Rajiv did not agree because Shinde's removal would have been seen as a sign of weakness on the part of the high command. I too did not give in. 'How can I tolerate it if the president of the party's state unit himself addresses press conferences demanding the removal of the chief minister?' I asked.

After hectic discussions, it was decided that Shinde would be accommodated in my cabinet, and he would be replaced by senior leader Shivajirao Nilangekar as MPCC president.

When the issue of restructuring the state cabinet came up, I told Rajiv that I would not like to retain the rebel ministers. Not penalising them would send out a wrong signal and this would mar the party's interests in the state in the long run. Rajiv was uncomfortable with my stand and insisted on re-inducting them.

We argued for some time. Finally I said, 'I can understand your difficulty.'

'And what is my difficulty?' he asked.

'They acted on your behalf. How can you abandon them now?' I replied.

After a few moments of awkward silence Rajiv said, 'Ok...Let bygones be bygones. Let's move on.'

I did not make it a prestige issue as I knew the rebel ministers were not to blame much. They did what they did because they were ordered to do so. However, while agreeing to retain them in the state cabinet, I insisted that I would re-allocate the portfolios entirely as per my wish. Rajiv conceded and we concluded the meeting.

A few days later, Sushilkumar Shinde and Vilasrao Deshmukh came to see me. They were like penitent school boys and confessed sheepishly, 'We won't ever repeat this.'

I drew a quick curtain over the episode because as individuals Vilasrao and I shared excellent relations. We had worked together on many occasions in politics and cricket and our families bonded well.

TWELVE

In Defence

THE NINTH LOK SABHA had to be dissolved barely within sixteen months after the 1989 general election. The 'Mandal-Mandir election'—labelled thus because that was the main plank on which the National Front and the BJP fought it—to the tenth Lok Sabha got underway in May 1991. It was stalled midway following Rajiv Gandhi's horrific assassination by militants while he was campaigning at Sriperembudur in Tamil Nadu on the 21st of that month.

The second leg of the election was conducted in June and though the Congress did relatively better in phase two because of the sympathy wave, it still fell short of a majority, bagging 244 seats. The party registered its best performance in Maharashtra, where it won 39 out of the total 48 seats. This was the best Congress tally in any state.

Inevitably, the issue of Rajiv's successor came up. My name was being considered for the prime minister's post in Congress circles, not only in Maharashtra but in some other states too. Though a senior leader, P.V. Narasimha Rao had withdrawn from mainstream politics for health reasons before the election. Given his long experience, there were suggestions to bring him back following the unforeseen exit of Rajiv. Yet, there was a lot of uncertainty. At a meeting held in Hotel Ashoka in Delhi, senior leaders B. Shankaranand and N.K.P. Salve insisted that I should stake claim to the post of prime minister. Party leaders from other states also offered support. Personally I was more circumspect, aware as I was of how such things in the Congress worked. A lot now depended on the inclination of '10 Janpath' which had not revealed its mind yet. But it did that soon.

Self-styled loyalists of 10 Janpath started saying in private conversations that Sharad Pawar's election as prime minister would harm the First Family's interests in view of his young age. 'Woh to lambi race ka ghoda hoga (He will hold the reins for a very long time),' they argued. Among those who played this clever trick were Arjun Singh, M.L. Fotedar, R.K. Dhawan and V. George. They convinced Sonia Gandhi that it would be safer for her to back Narasimha Rao because he was old and was not in good shape. Arjun Singh himself aspired to become prime minister and hoped to succeed Rao soon.

In fact, Singh kept his distance from Rao even after being inducted as the Human Resource Development (HRD) Minister and gradually drifted away when he saw things not working out to his liking. Anyway, once Sonia Gandhi had bought the coterie's 'bring Rao' argument in 1991, the tide turned against me. Congress member of Parliaments for whom allegiance to the Gandhi family was a matter of faith joined the pro-Rao chorus.

Suresh Kalmadi, the party member of Parliament from Pune, was the most vociferous among my supporters. He went all out to mobilise young member of Parliaments from other states and also succeeded in creating a media buzz in my favour. I must, however, admit that the campaign he steered came across as a rather shallow exercise.

A meeting of the Congress Parliamentary Party was convened to elect the new leader. Siddharth Shankar Ray was chosen as observer for the meeting. Even as he announced that there would be no open voting, Fotedar and Arjun Singh re-conveyed the message to the members that 10 Janpath favoured Narasimha Rao. After completing the formality of 'gauging the mood' of all Congress Parliamentary Party (CPP) members, it was declared that Narasimha Rao's lead over me was of 35 'votes'. I know for sure that the outcome would have been different had 10 Janpath not intervened the way it did.

P.C. Alexander was as close to the Gandhi family and Narasimha Rao as he was to me. He played broker and organised a meeting with Rao, saying that we should let bygones be bygones. He knew and I knew that I had been a strong contender but the Gandhi family was not about to let someone with an independent mind get to the prime minister's post. 'The prime minister wants you to join the new ministry', Alexander told me. As suggested by him I had a one-on-one meeting with Narsimha Rao where he offered me the choice of any of the three top portfolios—home, finance or defence. I asked for some time to decide, and later opted for defence. The decision was prompted by the fact that my mentor, Yashwantrao Chavan, had also begun his innings in New Delhi almost thirty years earlier as defence minister.

Narasimha Rao also asked me to suggest a few names to be inducted in the Union ministry. The cabinet accommodated all the six names I recommended and we got back to work.

My knowledge of the defence ministry was limited. So, as was my wont, I consulted a number of veterans and experts in order to update myself on the ministry. Among the naval bases and border areas I visited was Siachen in the Himalayas where Indian and Pakistani troops had been positioned within striking distance of each other for years. I happened to be the first defence minister to go to the world's highest militarised zone. The objective was to boost the morale of our troops who were operating in temperatures well below freezing point. The Pakistani army camp across the border is within sight and there is occassional exchange of fire between soldiers on either side of the border. As I proceeded to the helipad for the take-off for my return journey, there was firing from the Pakistani side. Nothing untoward happened, but the episode gave me a glimpse into the daunting conditions on the glacier.

After visits to the areas bordering China I had thorough discussions with our officers and felt there was room for de-escalating troops on both sides of the border. While the Chinese terrain was on a plateau, our troops were located at a lower altitude and had to climb up the mountain to reach the international border. Even carrying rations to the border was an expensive proposition. Prime Minister Rao was a knowledgeable person on the subject. When I talked to him he gave his opinion in favour of opening bilateral talks with China.

A few days later I got an invitation for an official visit to China. Though the ministry of external affairs and the home ministry were not quite keen on accepting the invitation, the prime minister asked me to go ahead and discuss the de-escalation proposal. After thorough homework on the border situation I led a delegation, comprising defence secretary N.N. Vora and some senior military officers, to China in July 1992.

We had a series of discussions over five days with the Chinese delegation led by China's defence minister, General Chi Haotian. The underlying theme was the need to curtail troops on both sides of the border so that the money thus saved could be better utilised for tackling poverty and unemployment, challenges common to both nations. The Chinese response was positive.

When I conveyed this to the prime minister at the end of the first day's deliberations, he expressed happiness and asked me to continue in the same vein. In subsequent rounds the two delegations prepared a broad framework for troop reduction. Our brief ended there. It was for the heads of the two countries to take it to its logical end at a suitable time later.

Qin Jiwei and I were scheduled to meet and brief the Chinese Premier Li Peng the next day. The destination was not disclosed. We took off at 7 a.m. and after air travel of about four hours, landed at a rather mysterious place near a sea shore. There were hardly any people around but the area was lined with large palatial structures. These served as holiday resorts for top Chinese leaders, I was told.

We briefed the Chinese Premier in one of the palaces. He was satisfied with the details of the five-day bilateral discussions. It was decided that China would extend an official invitation to the Indian prime minister to take the issue forward. (Following a series of confidence-building measures between the two countries, the Indian prime minister was invited to China in September 1993. Narasimha Rao and Li Peng signed a border agreement and three other agreements during that visit.)

After the briefing, Li Peng invited me to join him for a walk on the sea shore. It was a wonderful opportunity to engage the Chinese Premier in an informal talk. Of particular interest to me were developments in the USSR. President Mikhail Gorbachev's introduction of glasnost and perestroika had led to extreme turmoil, resulting eventually in the disintegration of the USSR. Li Peng's response to my query about his personal opinion was immediate and forthright. He felt Russia was already in decline and he squarely blamed Gorbachev for its sorry state. According to him, Gorbachev's biggest mistake was to usher in economic reforms and political openness simultaneously. If he had retained tight political control when introducing the reforms, things would not have spun out of his control.

We then discussed a number of issues in the broad domain of international relations. For me, the discussions proved to be a revelation of the Chinese leadership's focused, hard-nosed approach to world affairs. Li Peng was critical of the double standards employed by the western world on various development issues and was strongly in favour of India and China coming together to protect their own interests. 'We shall not spare any effort to make China an economic superpower and so we would definitely like to maintain friendly ties with our neighbours,' he said. The statement spoke volumes about China's long-term goals and determined approach. Just over two decades later, China has indeed become an economic as well as military superpower. No wonder other world powers feel concerned about China's meteoric rise.

One of the things I started as defence minister was to host weekly dinner meetings for the three service chiefs. While I could update myself on a lot of things during those dinners, the informal nature of interactions also facilitated better bonding among the service chiefs. Such bonding helps when quick responses and coordination are required in times of crisis.

Defence production and sale or purchase of defence material is a sensitive issue the world over. Since arms dealers and their agents are hyperactive in this field, most ministers are scared of being accused of corruption and therefore avoid taking decisions. The bureaucracy too generally tends to drag its feet for fear of being subjected to investigations even after retirement. The problem in India was aggravated in the wake of the Bofors controversy for which Rajiv Gandhi had to pay a heavy political price. But the accusation that the guns were of inferior quality were completely unfounded.

Though the storm subsided in course of time, the Bofors controversy cast a long term negative effect on acquisition decisions. This was a sorry state of affairs. The rapid disintegration of the post-glasnost, post-perestroika USSR posed a peculiar challenge. For years India relied very heavily on the Soviet Union for its defence supplies. Production units of various ancillaries were located in different parts of the unified USSR. Following the break up of the Soviet Union, the locations became parts of different, independent countries. Procuring 'complete' deliveries of defence items thus became a clumsy affair. I therefore initiated the process of looking beyond the erstwhile Soviet Union to fulfil our defence requirements. Narasimha Rao suggested that India should look at the United States for military cooperation. The US Secretary of Defence Dick Cheney welcomed the idea because, as he pointed out when I met him, considering the geographical conditions in the Indian subcontinent, the interests of the two countries converged on many issues. In subsequent years, India and the US drew closer and also signed an agreement for military cooperation.

The work on developing indigenous Arjun tanks had begun long before I took charge of the defence ministry. But it reached fruition during my tenure. Field trials of the tanks were done in Longowal sector of Rajasthan. The high cost of indigenous production of defence material was a serious problem that had to be tackled at the time. I realised that a major reason for the high cost was that production in domestic factories was solely for consumption by the Indian military. For instance, if a factory was asked to produce only 10,000 rifles as against its production capacity of five lakh rifles, the cost per piece would naturally be astronomically high. Take the case of Hindustan Aeronautics Limited, which has production units in Nashik, Bengaluru and Kanpur. Despite its huge infrastructure and high production capacity the company ran into financial difficulties. This was because whenever there was a financial crunch at the Centre, the finance ministry would invariably ask HAL to cut down its production. There were times when HAL did not have an order for aircraft production for two or more years at a stretch.

Tapping overseas markets was the only solution to the problem. Therefore I opened a full-fledged marketing division in the defence production department which started looking for prospective buyers in Asian and African countries. Aggressive strategies by the marketing division resulted in getting substantial orders which enabled our domestic companies to operate to their full capacity. I was also of the opinion that private entrepreneurs should be allowed to enter the defence production market. But I could not pursue this subject much during my tenure as defence minister.

In early 1992 I visited Singapore to secure an order. After my discussion with Prime Minister Goh Chok Tong, he suggested that we could talk further on the issue with his defence minister who said that he would meet me at the golf course the next day. That put me in a fix. I did not understand the game and I told him that plainly. 'Oh, please learn the game. We can talk once you start playing,' he said. We departed on that note. I had a few more engagements after completing which I returned to my hotel. A big golf kit awaited me there. With it was a note from the prime minister. After returning to Delhi I learnt to play golf. Since my daughter Supriya and son-in-law Sadanand were staying in Indonesia and Singapore for some years during that period, I made a few trips to Singapore and played a few games with the Singapore defence minister. The valuable lesson I learnt on the golf course was this: Golf offers you lot of free time during which you can talk in total privacy with the other player. No wonder lot of people in high places all over the world love the game!

In New Delhi my partners on the golf course were mostly top officers from the armed forces or other departments of the government. They never failed to applaud my shots. Even a decidedly poor swing of the golf club by me would evoke 'spontaneous' cheer from the gentlemen officers. That probably spoiled my game. My second valuable lesson on the golf course: If you want to improve your game, as far as possible, avoid playing with your juniors or subordinates.

Another interesting incident that I still recall occurred in the Andaman and Nicobar islands where I visited an Indian naval base. As soon as my helicopter landed I was greeted with the slogans 'Har har Mahadeo' and 'Chhatrapati Shivaji Maharaj ki jai'. It was a pleasant surprise to hear those slogans because they were traditional war cries of the Maratha army of Chhatrapati Shivaji, the sixteenth century warrior king. I certainly had not expected to hear them in a remote place hundreds of miles away from Maharashtra. On making inquiries I was told that some soldiers from the Maratha and Mahar regiments were allotted land on these islands by the British rulers several decades ago. After retirement the families settled there. On hearing about my visit some of them had come to the helipad to greet me the traditional way.

In May 1998 the Atal Bihari Vajpayee-led NDA government conducted five underground nuclear tests at Pokhran, Rajasthan. As a result, the United States, United Kingdom, Canada and some other nations imposed limited sanctions on India. It reminded me of what had happened in this regard during my tenure as defence minister. Advisors to the ministry had informed me in 1992–93 that we were fully equipped to conduct nuclear tests to establish ourselves as a nuclear power in the world. In fact, they were completely in favour of conducting the tests. I took the file to Prime Minister Rao and told him what the advisors had said.

After going through the file he rejected the advice, which I thought was the correct decision in the circumstances that prevailed then. India's economy was in a dire state when the Congress government took charge in 1991. Narasimha Rao had started taking bold decisions but the situation was still quite delicate. Relying on his own excellent reading of international relations, Rao said, 'It will be enough to send out a message to the world that India has the capability to conduct nuclear tests. I don't think it will be wise to actually carry out the tests at this stage. If we do so, we shall invite the wrath of the entire world.'

To elucidate the point, he quoted a practice from his home state of Andhra Pradesh. 'Many farmers from my state live on their farms which are far away from the village. You will invariably find a well-oiled rifle hanging on the wall of their living room. It is rarely used but it still serves the purpose of signalling that the owner of the house is fully equipped to protect himself against any intruders or dacoits. As a nation we too must adopt the same policy.'

✤ THIRTEEN ✤

The Mumbai Bomb Blasts

IMMEDIATELY AFTER THE BABRI mosque was demolished on 6 December 1992, Hindu-Muslim riots tore apart Mumbai's social fabric. Chief Minister Sudhakarrao Naik was in Nagpur for the winter session of the Maharashtra assembly. He should have rushed to Mumbai in anticipation of trouble or at least when the first reports of violence came in. But he dragged his feet and it was only when I chided him that he went to Mumbai after two days. By that time, Mumbai was already in flames. The incidents started in Bhendi Bazar, Dongri, Nagpada and spread rapidly to the northern parts of the city that included Bainganwadi, Gowandi, Kurla, Kalina, Shivajinagar, Bandra, Kherwadi, Behrampada, Paidhuni, Dharavi, Mahim, Jogeshwari and Malwani.

Over a hundred people were killed in the first three days. The mafia and local gangs took over the streets. Naik was shell-shocked and found himself unable to control the situation. The Central government had to send in paramilitary forces. With little sign of the state government gathering its wits, Prime Minister Narasimha Rao asked me to rush to Mumbai and take charge of the law and order operations.

Though the situation was decidedly grave, I was skeptical about going to Mumbai. I thought that Naik, as chief minister, was supposed to enforce the law and my going to Mumbai would certainly cause confusion and misunderstandings. However, the rapid deterioration in the situation forced my hand. I was quite familiar with Mumbai's geography and its social profile. Working round the clock over the next few days I kept a close vigil on police operations. The police raided several places in Santa Cruz, Nagpada, Deonar, Oshiwara and Wakola to seize large stocks of lethal weapons and explosives, which included pistols, guns, choppers, petrol bombs and acid bulbs. That was indication enough of how quickly the situation would have worsened if the government inaction had continued any longer. As soon as the task of regaining control over the situation was accomplished, I returned to Delhi.

However, the peace was shortlived because the state government failed to take follow-up actions to prevent the recurrence of violence. On 7 January 1993, five persons were burnt alive when miscreants set fire to Radhabai Chawl in Jogeshwari. The incident set off another chain of arson and killings. The areas affected this time were Dadar, Parel, Kala Chowki, Worli, Tardeo, Prabhadevi and Byculla. Once again the police had to resort to firing to bring the situation under control. About 2,000 people were killed in the two rounds of violence and although there were no fresh conflagrations after January, tension simmered beneath the surface. The riots also broke Mumbai's financial backbone. Numerous small-scale industries started moving out and cottage enterprises folded up, rendering thousands of wage earners jobless.

These were ominous signs.

The prime minister became increasingly worried over the events in Mumbai since there was no improvement in the ground conditions and held periodic talks with me. N.K.P. Salve, who was close to both Rao and me, came over one day and discussed the Mumbai situation in great detail with me. He then went to meet the prime minister. Rao invited me to his residence to talk about bringing Mumbai back on the rails. The main thrust of his argument was that nothing much could be achieved unless I returned to Maharashtra as chief minister. I was reluctant. But he cancelled all his appointments that day as we kept talking for nearly eight hours. I had thrice been Maharashtra's chief minister and now I was keen on working at the national level. 'If you are keen on replacing the present chief minister, let us appoint a new person in his place. We shall extend him all the necessary support,' I said in an attempt to wriggle out of the situation. However, Rao was adamant and had already made up his mind. Finally, I relented.

When I assumed reins as the chief minister of Maharashtra for the fourth time on 6 March 1993, I was aware that a lot needed to be done to usher in lasting peace. For a start, the state administration needed to be toned up. This was obviously going to take some time. But, in less than a week of the new government taking charge, Mumbai was rocked by a series of bomb blasts, on Friday, 12 March 1993. I witnessed one of them. I was sitting in my sixth-floor Mantralaya office, when I heard a big explosion in the vicinity. Rushing to the window, I saw a commotion near the Air India building at Nariman Point which was less than a kilometre away. Fire and smoke were billowing out of the building. Since I had got reports of a bomb explosion at Bombay Stock Exchange just fifty minutes earlier, it did not take me long to guess that this too was a bomb blast. I wanted to rush to the site but the Mumbai police commissioner advised me against doing so. Within the next hour, reports of bomb explosions came from different parts of the city.

Mumbai was under attack.

Moving swiftly, I called for all the relevant details, which revealed that RDX had been used in the explosions. This indicated a high-level conspiracy because RDX was neither produced locally nor was it available with small-time operators. I got in touch with ammunition factories to ascertain the RDX stocks in their custody. They assured me against any smuggling or movement from their premises. It meant the terrorists had got the explosive material from across the border. Locations of the twelve explosions had been chosen carefully. All of them were either commercial centres or were populated by members of the Hindu community. It was thus obvious that the intention was to set off yet another round of Hindu-Muslim riots.

Before things could turn worse, I rushed to the Doordarshan

studio at Worli to address the people of Maharashtra. I appealed to them to keep calm and discourage rumour mongering. While narrating the day's incidents, I said the explosions had occurred at thirteen places, though the real number was twelve. I slipped in a Muslim-dominated location, though nothing untoward had happened there. This was done solely to create the impression that the explosions had no 'religious' shade. The trick worked. The terrorists' plan to spark off Hindu-Muslim riots through explosions did not fructify.

Later, an inquiry commission was constituted, with Justice B.N. Srikrishna as its head, to probe the Mumbai mayhem. The commission asked me the rationale for 'misquoting' the number of locations of the bomb blasts. I replied that it was my conscious decision, and explained to the commission the circumstances. Justice Srikrishna complimented me, describing it as 'an excellent example of statemanship'.

The next immediate task was to defeat the terrorists' second objective—paralysing Mumbai's life for a long time in order to deal a crushing blow to its global stature. Two things needed to be done. The first was reopening the Bombay Stock Exchange at the earliest. The second was resuming Mumbai's life lines—local trains, Bombay Electric Supply and Transport (BEST) buses and the early-morning transport of milk vans across the city. The prime minister called me from New Delhi to say he wanted to fly down to Mumbai to oversee the operations. However, I pointed out that his visit at that juncture would disrupt the rescue and relief operations. He gracefully agreed to defer the visit. I called a series of meetings of all the relevant agencies to assign specific, time-bound tasks. Everybody—police, other state government departments, the Mumbai municipal corporation staff, railways staff, the telephone department, and so on—pitched in with great determination. They all worked round the clock to put Mumbai back on its feet within forty-eight hours.

By the morning of Monday, March 15, the milk vans were

plying, and the local trains and BEST buses were running on time. Even the Bombay Stock Exchange resumed its work on the stroke of 10 a.m. This was indeed a rare feat in the city's chequered history, and many Mumbai veterans acknowledged this.

After the bomb blasts on Friday, print and television journalists from India and abroad had descended on Mumbai. For two days they sent a series of long dispatches to their respective media houses describing the widespread devastation in Mumbai. None expected normalcy to return in less than seventy-two hours. However, Monday morning gave them a pleasant surprise. Mumbai's resilience became the most discussed subject in the media for several weeks thereafter.

While efforts to bring back Mumbai to normal were on, the police worked extremely efficiently and speedily to track down the culprits. Several places were raided and hundreds of suspects were taken into custody. The investigations revealed the involvement of Tiger Memon, Yakub Memon and Javed Chikna, among many others. They had worked in tandem with Dawood Ibrahim, and had received support from forces in Pakistan.

Large quantities of RDX, guns and ammunition were sent through a sea route to the coastal area of Raigad district and the stocks were stored at a number of places. Among them was a garage in the house of Hindi film star Sanjay Dutt. It was found during subsequent police investigations that an attempt was also made to melt a gun in his house.

Details of Sunjay Dutt's interactions with the underworld and the seizure of arms from his residential premises came as a shocker. His parents, Sunil Dutt and the late Nargis Dutt, were not only popular film personalities, they were also reputed public figures committed to the promotion of communal harmony. Sunil Dutt was, in fact, a Congress member of Parliament from Mumbai. On the other hand, the crime in question was of a very grave nature. The bomb blasts had killed 257 innocent people, injured hundreds more and damaged public property worth crores of rupees. Keeping Sunil Dutt's stature in mind, I called him over to my office and told him about the findings of the investigation. He was shocked and dismayed. 'I shall not obstruct the path of justice. If my son is found to be involved with anti-national elements, please go ahead and punish him,' he said. While I could understand Sunil Dutt's agony as a father, I had no option but to move on with the investigations.

Sunjay Dutt was abroad at the time. His father asked him to return immediately. In April 1993, the Mumbai police arrested him under The Terrorist and Disruptive Activities (Prevention) Act (TADA) as he landed at the Mumbai airport. Sometime later, Sunil Dutt approached me again to ask if the case against his son could be handled leniently. Gauging his state of mind, I explained to him in great detail how strong the evidence against Sanjay Dutt was. He left my office a dejected man. I really felt sorry for him; but I had no other option.

The court cases against Sanjay Dutt went on for a very long time. Following a Supreme Court verdict in March 2013, he was asked to serve rigorous imprisonment for five years.

FOURTEEN

Earthquake in Latur

THE SECOND BIG CHALLENGE in my fourth stint as Maharashtra's chief minister was the earthquake that shook the Marathwada region of the state in September 1993. Getting Mumbai back on its feet in a very short time after the serial bomb blasts in March that year had been a Herculean task, no doubt. But the gigantic rescue and relief operation that had to be conducted in Marathwada was no less daunting. My admiration for the administrative machinery and the people of the state grew multifold after the twin tragedy.

The Ganesh Festival happens to be the most popular event in the cultural and religious calendar of Maharashtra. People from different walks of life participate with great enthusiasm in the ten-day festivities. The celebratory mood is at its peak on the last day when Ganesh idols are taken out in colourful processions for immersion in water bodies all over the state. This puts a lot of strain on the law and order machinery. In 1993, the immersion day fell on 30 September. Since the home portfolio was with me, I kept in constant touch with the officers concerned in order to keep myself updated about the situation in the state. Late in the evening, I learnt about some tension in the immersion procession in Parbhani town of the Marathwada region. Appropriate instructions were given and after being told that the situation there was under control, I prepared to go to bed. It was well past midnight.

Around 3.45 a.m., the window panes of the first-floor bedroom in the chief minister's official bungalow, Varsha, started rattling vigorously. My bed too was shaking. I realised it was an earthquake and rang up the centre that monitored seismic activity at Koynanagar in south Maharashtra. On 11 December 1967 a tremor of 6.5 magnitude had rocked that region, killing 180 people and injuring over 1,500. A big dam is located at Koynanagar and the region is known for frequent seismic activity. My instinct to call Koyananagar was rooted in this history. I was told from the other end that this time around, the epicentre of the tremor was not Koyananagar but Latur, in Marathwada. This was unexpected. So after re-confirming the location of the tremor, I rang up a government office in Latur. The call did not go through. I tried several other numbers there but the result was the same. All telephone lines had gone out of order. I knew it meant big trouble.

I woke up my secretary and asked him to keep an aircraft ready at 7 a.m. to take me to Latur. A wireless message was sent to the affected region that the chief minister was visiting shortly. During transit, I was told that the epicentre of the earthquake was at Killari, which was 43 kilometres from Latur. Since I had toured the region extensively earlier, I was familiar with the location. We landed at Latur at 7.40 in the morning and drove straight to Killari. It was a devastating sight. All houses in and around the village were flattened. Most people had embraced death while asleep. A few survivors were crying out for help from under the debris. Even as we pulled out some people, we were told that the situation was as ghastly in village after village right up to Osmanabad which was about 89 kilometres away. That was proof of the magnitude of the tragedy.

There was no time to waste. The rescue operation had to be launched on a war footing. I summoned collectors and deputy collectors from all neighbouring districts, which included Solapur, Parbhani, Jalna, Beed, Aurangabad and Nanded. Each of them was given charge of the rescue and relief operations of specific villages. The earthquake was followed by heavy rains. Survivors had to be provided with temporary shelters immediately. Tin sheets and other necessary materials were procured from traders far and near. A large number of voluntary organisations had descended from different parts of the state and the country as well. We asked them to run food kitchens for the victims. Public transport buses and other vehicles were deployed to carry various items. About 1,000 doctors, accompanied by para-medical staff, were asked to fan out in the affected villages to provide medical assistance. All this was done in the first forty-eight hours after the earthquake.

Considering the scale of the devastation, I thought it prudent to camp in the affected region to monitor the work. It was an extraordinary step for the chief minister of a state to stay out of the capital for such a long time, but the unprecedented situation demanded an unprecedented response. The decision proved useful. We set up a control room in the state secretariat and put the chief secretary in charge. The control room and my camp in the earthquake-ravaged area were connected with a hotline. Consequently, the entire administrative machinery took a pro-active approach and worked with total devotion. It deserves full credit for the speed and the efficiency with which it accomplished the mammoth task.

I used to visit affected villages in the region to oversee rescue operations. Army jawans and State Reserve Police personnel were deployed on a large scale. One morning I noticed a man, dressed in shirt and trousers, asleep in a bullock cart. Obviously he was not a local resident. When I made enquires, the villagers told me that the person sleeping in the bullock cart was Pravin Pardeshi, then the district collector of Latur. He had been personally involved in relief and rehabilitation operations through several days and nights and, exhausted, he had fallen asleep in the bullock cart. Pardeshi and Bhai Nagrale, the then Osmanabad CEO, set a fine example of how public servants should gear up the state apparatus for the benefit of the people during a crisis. There were many such officers who did commendable work, but remained anonymous.

The earthquake had destroyed virtually all the houses in the affected region. Building permanent shelters for the victims was a prime necessity, but it required huge funds. Dr Manmohan Singh came to the rescue in that hour of need. He was the Union finance minister at the time but had worked in the World Bank earlier. Because he moved fast to secure a loan from the World Bank, the construction work gathered momentum.

Individuals and organisations from Maharashtra and other parts of the country also came forward with substantial aid. The state government took a policy decision at this stage. Since the World Bank loan had to be repaid within a certain time limit, we invested the funds received from the public in fixed deposits so that the loan could be cleared from the interest accrued on the deposits. This spared the state a big financial burden in the following years.

Experts from the Indian Institute of Technology (IIT) Roorkee were summoned to help us rebuild the villages. They came up with several designs of houses to suit the earthquake-prone terrain. Villagers were asked to select models of their choice. There was only one condition that we laid down. We would not allow caste-based housing clusters to come up in any of the villages. As many states in the country, voluntary organisations and corporate houses too came forward to adopt specific villages in the region, we could build about one lakh houses within a year.

The US President Bill Clinton rushed two aircraft to Maharashtra, carrying tents, water cans, medicines and surgical equipment. Other countries and international agencies too pitched in. We were grateful for all the support we got in that difficult time.

Special mention needs to be made of the help extended by the psychiatric department of the Sassoon Hospital-B.J. Medical College in Pune. Led by Dr Mohan Agashe, who is also a well-known stage and film actor, the team from the department camped in the affected region to treat a large number of victims who had suffered mental shock and trauma because of the monumental tragedy.

FIFTEEN

Women's Bill

DURING MY FOURTH STINT as Maharashtra chief minister I had two social issues humming at the back of my mind. First, renaming the Marathwada university after Dr Babasaheb Ambedkar about which I have already written, and, second, bringing in a legislation to pave the way for women's empowerment.

Before I talk about the details of the Women's Bill, however, let me tell you why I feel strongly about the issue. As I have said earlier, I have been greatly influenced by my mother Sharadabai in a number of ways. She was an extraordinarily accomplished and strong woman who was equally at ease at home and in public life.

Even as she groomed each of her eleven children to become 'citizens of substance' in their own right, she joined politics and was elected to the Pune zilla board for over fourteen years. She was as good as many of her male colleagues; in fact, she was better than most. This was during the 1930s and 1940s when women were presumed to be inferior and were denied even basic political rights in much of the world. I grew up with the firm conviction that human qualities were gender neutral. Ever since I joined public life I haven't come across any evidence to prove otherwise.

British Prime Minister Margaret Thatcher is another person who reinforced my belief that women, like men, can play significant roles in all walks of life, including politics, if only they are given an opportunity. Thatcher visited India in 1981 and I was impressed by her confidence and poise when I met her in Mumbai in April that year.

Later, I saw her in action in her own country. Legislators from Commonwealth countries become ex-officio members of the Commonwealth Parliament Association. Besides being able to attend British parliament sessions as observers, they can also avail of other related facilities, including the Parliament's library in London which is stacked with records and literature pertaining to parliamentary democracy in countries across the globe. Unfortunately, very few Indian legislators are aware of the privilege, and fewer still make use of it to enhance their understanding of politics and parliamentary traditions. Whenever I visited London, I would spend a lot of time in the library and also go to the British parliament's visitors' gallery to watch the proceedings. Prime Minister Thatcher's conduct in the House, especially her handling of tough situations, was, to put it simply, awesome.

During one of my visits I happened to witness an incident that made a lasting impression on my mind. The prime minister's visit to Oman had turned out to be controversial. She had struck some official business deals during the tour. Since her son was a member of the official delegation, the opposition had kicked up a row. Her son was a marketing executive in a steel manufacturing company. I was watching the proceedings from the visitors' gallery when Prime Minister Thatcher and Labour leader Michael Foot got into a verbal duel. It sounded almost like Thatcher's inquisition.

'Madam Prime Minister, is it not correct that your son accompanied you as member of the official delegation on your tour of Oman?' Foot asked agitatedly.

'Yes, that is correct,' replied the prime minister, calmly.

'Is it not correct that he is working in a major steel manufacturing company in our country?'

'Yes, that is correct.'

'Is it not correct that he had visited Oman twice before your tour to secure orders for his company?'

'Yes, that is correct.'

'Then it is also correct, Madam Prime Minister, that you used your good offices to get orders for your son's company during the Oman tour.'

'Yes, that is correct.'

The members, who were watching the 'interrogation' keenly all this while, were stunned by Thatcher's answer. As the import of the prime minister's admission sank in, the House was thrown into pandemonium. After the uproar in the House subsided a little, Thatcher rose again to explain.

'What really matters here is that our country got a big order for steel supply because of the business deal we struck during my tour of Oman. I don't think I did anything wrong in using my good offices to ensure that it happened. There is another aspect to the issue. England is currently reeling under economic depression as a result of which a large number of industrial workers may become jobless. Thanks to the supply order procured during my tour, several jobs will surely be saved. Have I committed a crime by doing this? Did I get any personal benefit from the deal? Did my party benefit from it?...If my actions are going to strengthen the ailing economy of our country, I shall keep repeating them.'

There was a deafening silence in the House.

The prime minister's resolute defence of her actions had obviously neutralised her detractors. For me, the Iron Lady's demeanour that day was a valuable lesson in staying unruffled in a raging storm if one's actions are in the public interest. The experience also strengthened my resolve to take effective steps to give women their due. Actually, I had the first opportunity to initiate action in this regard during my tenure as the Union defence minister.

The Indian army hadn't opened its gilded gates to women, barring doctors' posts when I assumed charge of the defence portfolio in 1991. I knew there were limitations to inducting women into the forces. However, I believed there was scope to improve the situation. Soon after taking charge in my office in

South Block, I brought up the subject during talks with senior officers of the ministry and the three service chiefs. The response was lukewarm. The bureaucracy has a time-tested way of handling ministers. Most ministers come to their ministries with certain ideas—some well-founded, many fanciful. Therefore, senior officers just listen to the new minister in the initial phase, assessing how serious and committed he or she is. I knew this from my own experience. So I was not surprised at the administration's non-committal response.

I visited the US in the early part of my tenure as minister for a meeting with my counterpart Dick Cheney, who later became vice-president of that country. After the meeting I was flown in a US defence aircraft to a military base. One thing that struck me during the visit was the number of women officers who were working in different capacities. The entire crew of the defence aircraft comprised women. The military base also had men and women officers in almost equal numbers. The governments of UK and Germany had also been recruiting women in the three services. Even in a country like Malaysia, not part of the 'developed' western world, I found that women were not barred from military service.

Global statistics, which I had had the chance to go through, showed that the frequency of accidents when women were piloting an aircraft was significantly lesser than when men were the pilots. This was generally attributed to the fact that women are more attentive to details than men. I am not a social scientist to comment on the larger import of such findings, but the facts in this case could not be disputed, and they were certainly illuminating.

The defence minister holds weekly joint meetings on Monday mornings at 9 a.m. where the defence secretary, the defence production secretary, the secretary to the ministry of external affairs, and the three service chiefs deliberate on key issues relevant to the working of the defence ministry's different departments. N.N. Vora was the defence secretary. His wife

Usha Vora was also an IAS officer. He was certainly among the finest bureaucrats I came across during my years in office. General Sunith Francis Rodrigues was the army chief, Air Chief Marshal Nirmal Chandra Suri was chief of the air staff, while Admiral Laxminarayan Ramdas was the naval chief. In one of the weekly meetings, I tabled the subject of inducting women in the three services. Vora was supportive of the proposal. The subject was discussed on several occasions, but no conclusion seemed to be in sight. Exasperated at the delay, I set a time limit of three months to arrive at a decision. In the meantime, I secured Prime Minister Narsimha Rao's informal consent. At the end of three months I announced the decision at the Monday meeting. This prompted a comprehensive note laying out the policy which was adopted by the cabinet. An 11% reservation for women in the three services thus became a reality.

About four years after I relinquished my post as defence minister, I ran into Air Chief Marshal (Retd) Nirmal Chandra Suri. I asked him about the women pilots' performance in the Indian Air Force. He was all praise and promised to send me a note. The note he sent corroborated the global statistic I have mentioned earlier. It is heartening to know that today, Indian women are competing and cooperating as equals with males in all the three services.

It was for the first time since Independence that all-women officers contingents of the army, air force and navy walked down Rajpath on Republic Day 2015. In fact, I was overwhelmed to see Wing Commander Pooja Thakur leading the ceremonial Inter-Services Guard of Honour for the chief guest, US President Barak Obama. She did a marvelous job. I am sure it has now become a regular feature. She summed up the spirit very well when she said after the ceremony: 'I am an officer first and then a woman.'

In the first week of January 1994 I started preliminary work to introduce the Women's Bill in Maharashtra. I had a broad idea in mind about the time-frame and the modus operandi for structuring the Bill. For a little over two months thereafter, we worked at breakneck speed to turn the dream into reality.

To set the ball in motion I gave up the home portfolio and took the social welfare department under my wing. This sent out a signal to the bureaucracy that the chief minister was serious about the Bill. I split the social welfare ministry to carve out a separate department for Women and Child Welfare which further narrowed the focus. Chandra Iyengar, secretary of the department, was asked to draft a comprehensive policy. She put her heart and soul into speeding up the process in a streamlined fashion. We decided to involve as many stakeholders as possible at different stages in order to ensure their deeper involvement while shaping the Bill. Facts and figures in the National Crime Record were shared with them. The details were a great eye-opener as they laid bare the extent of oppression women in India were subjected to. If 50% of the country's population was suppressed and kept out of the mainstream, how could we hope to stand up to the developed world where women walk shoulder to shoulder with men in every department of life?

Every step was carefully planned. For a start, a list of academicians and activists was drawn up. It was divided into different categories such as education, health, law and order, and so on, so that each group could discuss a specific topic assigned to it. In all, twenty-one meetings were conducted and I made sure I attended them all. Working papers coming from these groups were shared with relevant departments with a view to preparing the first draft of the Bill. The draft was then circulated among the elected representatives of all parties to get their inputs. The entire process demanded a lot of patience and hard work at each stage but we were at it. With grit, with determination.

The battle was far from over. When the draft Bill was placed before the state cabinet, it met with direct and indirect resistance. Members came up with suggestions and objections on many of the provisions. As a result, the draft kept moving back and forth between the cabinet and the administration. This was a delicate stage. If the political leadership does not show requisite interest and will on an issue, the administration gets frustrated. Many a good initiative of various governments has fallen through because of this phenomenon.

Therefore I was required to display a combination of tact and firmness in response to the changing situations in this particular case. It took eight meetings of the state cabinet for the final draft to be approved. I could see that most of the ministers had got tired of the subject by then and simply wanted to get it over and done with!

The Bill provided for 33% reservation for women among elected representatives in all local government bodies, such as gram panchayats, panchayat samitis, zilla parishads, municipalities and municipal corporations. Since caste-based reservations were already in place, the 33% quota for women was incorporated under different caste categories. The Bill also mandated co-ownership of husband and wife in residential premises allocated under government schemes. Another path-breaking provision was equal succession rights to daughters and sons in ancestral properties, including landholdings.

The last clause was incorporated keeping in mind that women in most houses lived with a sword of insecurity hanging over their heads because they had no legal share in the family property. The enactment of the Bill on the floor of the assembly was the last stage of the process. Since we had ensured participation of different sections of society, including all political parties, during the drafting process, proceedings in the House were running fairly smoothly. At around 10 p.m. that day, I talked to our party whip, took permission of the Speaker and left for home. Around midnight, the party whip telephoned me to say that the Bill had suddenly run into rough weather. Some members, he said, had taken exception to giving equal rights to daughters in family property, and most of the detractors were our own party legislators. I asked one of the senior legislators from that group to come on line. He said many legislators were of the view that the provision on property rights would create rifts within families.

'Why?' I asked.

'After getting married the girl generally goes off to settle in some other village,' he explained. 'If the family land is divided among sons and daughters, the son-in-law would also become a shareholder in the family property. This complication will create bad blood.' That was a typical traditional male response. It called for an oblique approach.

'How many children do you have?' I asked him.

'Three sons, no daughter,' he replied. That gave me an opening to convince him in a way that he would understand.

'Ok, then look at it this way. When you marry off your sons, three daughters-in-law will come into your home. They will get a share in their own ancestral property. Will that not add to your family's assets?'

'Oh, yes!' he said, sounding both surprised and elated. 'It never struck me. Now I understand your point...'

The Bill was passed late in the night by the assembly. The policy document was released by Vice-President K.R. Narayanan at a function held at Nehru Centre in Mumbai on 22 June 1994.

Initially our party suffered some political damage as a consequence of the policy. For instance, we lost an assembly seat in Bhor, near Pune, which was our traditional stronghold. On making thorough inquiries, I was told that some influential families were annoyed because of political reservations given to women in local government bodies. When I broached the subject with the patriarch of a local upper-caste family, he replied, 'How can we accept it? The post of sarpanch has stayed within my family for the last forty years. But, thanks to the caste-based reservations and 33% quota for women in local bodies, a woman from a lower caste may become sarpanch of my village. Do you expect me to approach her with folded hands to get my work done?'

I realised that empowered women in public life ought to be equipped with administrative skills as well. We organised a series of training programmes and workshops for them. Elected women representatives from all parties participated in large numbers in such exercises at Yashada in Pune, the Yashwantrao Chavan Centre, the administrative staff college and the office of local self-government organisation in Mumbai.

In March 2010, the Indian Parliament passed the Women's Reservation Bill reserving one-third of its seats for women. The Bill had been pending for fourteen years and, as we know, the passage was far from smooth. It is a matter of pride for Maharashtra that it set the ball rolling by adopting a comprehensive women's policy as early as 1994.

Another government move that gave me immense satisfaction was the renaming of the Pune University after Savitribai Phule in 2014 during the Congress-NCP regime. The move was more than symbolic because Savitribai's role in improving the condition of women in the nineteenth century continues to be a source of inspiration for all even to this day.

The everlasting effect of the Women's Bill is for all to see. Women have become an integral part of the political decision-making process in local bodies. This has also changed things favourably in other fields, such as dairy, farming, cooperatives and even the service sector in cities and villages.

My heart swells with pride as I see more and more women participating in the decision-making process in the administration, from the grassroot level to the top echelons of government. I am often told that women who function as councillors or as zilla parishad, taluka and panchayat members are puppets in the hands of male relatives—husband, father or brother. However, this is now rarely the case. Today, women have come into their own, and have outgrown the influence of their male relatives. This augurs well for our democracy.

✤ SIXTEEN ✤

Allegations Bizarre and Wild

FOR YEARS, POLITICAL LEADERS who opposed me in Maharashtra worked with the firm belief that to be perceived as heavyweights, they had to take me on. Many of them crossed swords with me on legitimate grounds and with legitimate means. But some resorted to other tactics. At times, they received support from Delhi, especially when I came to be seen as a power centre in national politics. Whether in opposition or in government, my approach was always decisive and pro-active. This resulted in a steady consolidaton of my base within the party and among the masses. Some of my actions apparently hurt certain people's interests; my growing mass base made them feel insecure. And so, they never tired of seizing the slightest opportunity to hit out at me with ill-founded allegations and innuendos. The more serious, even bizarre, the charges they levelled against me, the more attention they got. Some of those who revelled in this game were from the opposition parties. Quite a few were from my own party, the Congress.

To appreciate what I am saying, one will have to understand the roller-coaster nature of Maharashtra's politics from 1978 to 1996. The list of challenges I faced during the period runs long but because I emerged stronger every time, the frustration of my opponents kept mounting. The campaign to malign me was launched against this background.

Let me do a quick recap. On becoming the youngest chief minister in 1978, my government took several decisive steps that triggered a socio-political transformation in Maharashtra. I came to be counted among the frontline leaders in the state. Even after Prime Minister Indira Gandhi dismissed my government in 1980, I managed to get fifty-four of my party's candidates elected to the state assembly. Barring five or six, the rest of them deserted me following Indiraji's thumping win in the seventh Lok Sabha elections. The return of my mentor Yashwantrao Chavan to the Congress was taken as a signal by many that my political career was doomed. But I bounced back. Reaching out to various sections of society across Maharashtra, I re-mobilised enough mass support to get fifty-two candidates elected on my party's ticket in the July 1980 assembly elections.

Responding to Rajiv Gandhi's appeal, I returned to the Congress (I) in 1986 against the wishes of some so-called loyalists from the party. Their discomfiture grew further when I replaced S.B. Chavan as chief minister of Maharashtra in 1988.

An attempt to unseat me was instigated by the party high command in 1990 but it failed due to lack of support among the party legislators. After Rajiv Gandhi's assassination, I entered national politics to become the defence minister in the Narasimha Rao government in 1991 but was again asked by the Congress high command to take charge as chief minister of Maharashtra in 1993. My handling of the disaster caused by the Mumbai bomb blasts and the Latur earthquake that year added to my stature.

Thus it was not surprising that a systematic slander campaign was launched in a bid to chip at my credibility. Gopinath Munde, lately the BJP leader and an aspirant to the chief minister's post, was at the forefront of the smear campaign.

The Janata Dal leader Mrinal Gore also joined the bandwagon by accusing me of land-grabbing. She commanded a lot of respect in the media which gleefully lapped up the allegations she made without any verification. Apparently, newspapers thought that since anything against me was highly 'newsworthy', sensationalising the allegations would fetch them more readers. In fact, Nilubhau Khadilkar, the editor of *Navakal*, a Mumbai-based newspaper, admitted this to me in so many words. No one substantiated the allegations with any evidence. Yet the game continued because it suited them all.

One hazard of being in public life is that people often get swayed by perceptions about you based on untruths, half-truths and wild statements dished out by others who have an axe to grind. When the media laps them up without bothering to do the required homework, the misconceptions get reinforced.

During my innings as Maharashtra chief minister, wild allegations were levelled against me for: i) offering 'patronage' to Hitendra Thakur and Pappu Kalani, both of whom had several criminal cases pending against them, and (ii) my 'links' with Dawood Ibrahim. Let me put the record straight on both counts.

Hitendra Thakur and Pappu Kalani were Congress candidates from Vasai-Virar and Ulhasnagar constituencies, respectively, in the 1990 assembly elections. Both had highly controversial backgrounds and therefore their nomination became a major issue during and after the elections. Stories were planted that they were given Congress tickets at my behest. I campaigned in their constituencies and this too was portrayed as 'proof' of my alliance with them.

Those familiar with how things in the Congress work know that although the party's parliamentary board selects candidates 'officially', the decisions are often influenced by or are left to powerful local party leaders in certain cases. For instance, Madhukarrao Chaudhari's writ ran in Jalgaon district. So if the Jalgaon district Congress unit under his stewardship sent a list of nominees for local constituencies, the parliamentary board would stamp its approval without any discussion. Vasai-Virar and Ulhasnagar assembly constituencies were part of the Thane district where Bhausaheb Vartak and Taramai Vartak were the patron figures in the Congress. The names of Hitendra Thakur and Pappu Kalani were recommended by Taramai Vartak, and as was the practice, they were cleared immediately. I had nothing to do with it.

Now, about why I campaigned in their constituencies. The Shiv Sena-BJP combination had posed a stiff challenge in the 1990 state assembly elections. In fact, it was generally expected that the Congress would lose power. As chief minister I was in charge of the Congress campaign in the state. I travelled across Maharashtra extensively to hold election meetings in a large number of constituencies, including Vasai-Virar and Ulhasnagar. It was a part of the responsibility assigned to me and there was no special favour done to anyone.

Yet another serious but completely unfounded allegation levelled against me during that decade was that I had 'connections' with underworld don Dawood Ibrahim who had a hand in the 1993 bomb blasts which killed 257 people in Mumbai. He has been a fugitive for more than two decades and the issue of his involvement in anti-social, anti-national activities in India keeps surfacing from time to time. It cropped up as recently as July 2015 when the senior lawyer Ram Jethmalani told the media that Dawood was prepared to surrender on certain conditions but I (Sharad Pawar) turned down the offer. The issue being highly sensitive, the media immediately sought my response while my political opponents pounced on it to claim that a 'golden opportunity' to bring Dawood back to India was missed. Let me clear the air.

It is a fact that Jethmalani came to meet me with Dawood Ibrahim's proposal when I was chief minister. He said Dawood telephoned him from London to make the 'offer'. Accordingly, Dawood was ready to surrender and return to India to make himself available for a court trial. Dawood claimed he had no hand in the bomb blasts. The catch was in the conditions he laid down for surrender. He wanted to be kept under house arrest and not in jail because he feared that he would be bumped off in prison. He also had apprehensions about being subjected to third-degree torture during interrogation if he was kept in police custody.

I asked Jethmalani how sure he was that the person who talked to him on the telephone was Dawood Ibrahim. There was room for doubt on this score. Secondly, I said it was ridiculous for a criminal to lay down conditions and a government to accept them meekly. The criminal in this case was accused of hatching a diabolical plan and executing it, causing the death of 257 innocent citizens. I told Jethmalani that I would consult police officers and other relevant people in the government before taking the final decision.

The senior police officers in Mumbai pointed out that Dawood Ibrahim was the prime accused in the case and a warrant had already been issued in his name. The Interpol had also issued a red corner notice. The law just did not permit us to not arrest him when he landed on Indian soil. 'How could we ask our officers to let him off in such circumstances?' they exclaimed. I then took up the issue with Prime Minister P.V. Narsimha Rao and he too concurred with our view.

Since there was complete unanimity against entertaining Dawood's pre-conditions, the issue did not go any further. Jethmalani's 'disclosure' after the lapse of so many years looks to me like nothing more than a publicity stunt.

The obvious objective of the serial bomb blasts was to spark communal riots. But I moved swiftly to keep a tight control over the situation. Not only were there no communal conflagrations, but normalcy returned to the city of Mumbai within just forty-eight hours of the blasts.

A couple of days after the blasts, I got a telephone call from Prime Minister Rao. Advising me to beef up my personal security, he said a senior Intelligence Bureau officer would meet me shortly to share some important information. When we met, the officer played out a recorded conversation which the IB had intercepted. The conversation between a senior military official from Pakistan and their henchman in Mumbai had taken place after the bomb blasts.

Taking the Mumbai person to task, the Pakistani military official said, 'We gave you huge funds. We also trained so many of your boys. The blasts took place as per the plan but we are getting messages that Mumbai is totally peaceful. Things there are going on at their usual pace. Nothing of what we desired is actually happening.'

The reply from Mumbai was: 'When the plan was made, this b*****d Sharad Pawar was not the chief minister. He became chief minister only last week. His administrative capacity is very good. Things would have certainly happened as planned if this man hadn't been in that seat.'

'Then eliminate him,' the Pakistani ordered.

It is thanks to this recording that I realised I was on the radar of Pakistani conspirators.

One of the bomb blasts had taken place near the passport office in Worli. Immediately after the blast, the police had apprehended a Maruti van at the site. Notings in a diary found in the van revealed Yakoob Memon's involvement in the conspiracy. The police raided his house and seized a stock of RDX. Taking a cue from other documents found in the van, the police raided more places. Seventeen passports were seized in those raids. The police hunted down the owners of all those passports and took them into custody. The passports showed interesting entries. They bore stamps in the following order: Departure from Mumbai. Arrival in Dubai. Departure from Dubai within two days. Arrival in Dubai after five weeks. Where were the passport holders during those five weeks? Which was the country that allowed them to arrive and depart without marking their passports? There was little doubt in my mind that it was Pakistan. But we needed more direct proof to be able to accuse a country openly. So we sent a team of investigators to Dubai which verified the dates, flight numbers and lists of passengers who travelled between Dubai and Pakistan during the relevant period. The lists showed nineteen names (including the seventeen in our custody) who had travelled between the two countries without appropriate passport markings.

In a Congress party session in Surajkund which followed soon thereafter, I disclosed this information. The very next day the Pakistani high commissioner called a press conference. Refuting what I had revealed, he made the wild allegation that 'the Maharashtra chief minister' (read Sharad Pawar) had links with the underworld and that he (Pawar) himself had mastermined the whole thing! It was obvious from the Pakistani high commissioner's reaction that I had nailed his country with irrefutable evidence. Unfortunately, however, my domestic political opponents took a cue from the Pakistani high commissioner's statement and started reiterating the allegations with utter recklessness.

A correspondent of the Hindi newspaper *Navbharat Times* went to Dubai around that time to interview Dawood's brother Ibrahim Kaskar. Referring to the Pakistani high commissioner's allegation that I had links with the underworld, he asked Kaskar, 'Do you know Sharad Pawar?' He replied, 'We were born in Mumbai. Sharad Pawar is the chief minister of Maharashtra. Who wouldn't know him?' (For those who do not know, Dawood Ibrahim's father was a constable in the Mumbai police force.) Again, Kaskar's rhetorical question, 'Who wouldn't know him (Sharad Pawar)?' was enough for my detractors to kick up a storm. The BJP member of Parliament from Mumbai, Ram Naik, went a step further to raise it in Parliament. That added fuel to the fire.

The cloud of suspicion seemed to become thicker for conspiracy theorists because a section of Congressmen in Maharashtra came out against me openly. Among them was Sudhakarrao Naik, who succeeded me as chief minister. Later he confessed to me candidly that the 'higher ups' in New Delhi had pushed him into saying and doing many things against me at the time. I knew this all along. But all power within the Congress was traditionally centred around the First Family, the party president and the prime minister, in that order. If the moves against me were instigated there, what was the point in seeking 'justice' from the party high command?

Secondly, I thought it was below my dignity to even react to those wild and patently motivated allegations. I simply did not want to stoop to the level of my opponents. I observed restraint and carried on.

SEVENTEEN

Lavasa and Windmills

MY FRIENDS SAY I am a patient listener and the compliment gladdens my heart. I love listening to people, I enjoy observing the way they think, live and try new things in life or in their profession. The habit, which I cultivated years ago, keeps my mind fresh and alert.

Similarly, tours too—domestic or overseas—have always been a great learning experience for me. My visits to Brazil help me update myself on the latest research in the sugar sector, while meeting the World Bank people adds to my understanding of economic studies conducted around the world. In Britain, I particularly enjoy listening to the debates in the House of Commons and spending time in the parliament library there.

During one of my visits to Britain in the 1980s, a friend told me about the Lake District. Spread over more than 2,000 square kilometres comprising lakes, mountains and forests in northwest England, the holiday destination is known the world over as much for its scenic beauty as for its association with nineteenth-century English writers such as William Wordsworth, Thomas Arnold and John Ruskin. The place is a living example of how human settlements, wild life, farming and forestry co-exist to the benefit of all.

Tourism, however, is the mainstay of the economy. The Lake District attracts over 16 million tourists from all parts of the globe every year. During my visit what struck me the most was the aesthetic, balanced use of the entire terrain. There were big forests interspersed with tracts of agriculture land, dairy units and sheep farming facilities. Excellent connectivity by rail and road catered to the beautifully designed hotels and restaurants that offered a range of cuisines. These were complemented by a number of houses displaying 'Bed & Breakfast' signboards. Impressive education complexes and entertainment parks pointed to a wide variety of tourist clientele.

As I watched the Lake District's splendour, images of the Sahyadri ranges in Maharashtra kept coming to my mind. Almost all tourist destinations in India, especially hill stations, were developed by the British several decades ago. Post-Independence, we have hardly done anything worthwhile to add to the list. There exists a string of dams between Nashik in north Maharashtra and Kolhapur which is at the southern end of the state. They include Kukadi, Chaskaman, Mulshi, Varasgaon, Panshet, Bhatghar, Neera-Deodhar, Dhom, Koyna, Nilwande, Warna and Radhanagari, to name a few. In addition, there are a large number of lakes and reservoirs in this stretch. If developed imaginatively, I felt, the entire region could generate huge revenue from tourism. For a start, I thought one could look at Pune district.

About 40 kilometres to the west of Pune is Varasgaon dam. When the dam was being constructed in the 1970s, residents of affected villages were relocated to new places in the Baramati and Daund tehsils of Pune district. Those who chose to remain moved up the mountains where they built small houses and also started agricultural activity on the slopes. Since it became an unviable proposition for them, the government acquired the land and gave them compensation. Developing a new hill station at the location seemed to me a good idea because of one, easy availability of water, and, second, unproblematic acquisition of land. As chief minister, I asked the administration to assess the possibility of a hill station at Varasgaon and also in the region close to Mahabaleshwar in the Satara district of Maharashtra.

A committee, comprising four MLAs from the region and two government secretaries, was deputed to visit the Lake District and submit a report. The state cabinet approved the report, but it appeared increasingly beyond the government's capacity to actually develop the hill station. On learning that a company named 'Yashomala Developers' had purchased about 5,000-6,000 acres of land in the Varasgaon neighbourhood, I summoned the promoters of the company for talks and suggested that they should develop a full-fledged 'Lake District' in the region.

They expressed inability to handle a project of such a big scale. This was when the name of my friend Ajit Gulabchand came to my mind. Ajit had the vision and drive to execute a project like this one. He came from the illustrious family that owned Walchand Industries. His grandfather Walchand Hirachand started off modestly as a textile trader in Sholapur but through sheer hard work grew to set up one of the leading industrial houses in India. Ajit's own 'Hindustan Constructions' happens to be the second-largest construction company in India.

After I broached the subject with Ajit, he and I drove through the region around Varasgaon for a first-hand feel. I suggested that he could buy the 6,000-odd acres from 'Yashomala Developers' and get going. After a thorough study he said he was excited by the idea. Besides the land with 'Yashomala Developers', he purchased another 4,000 acres in the surrounding area.

In fact, many people from the region approached him on their own about the sale of their land. Ajit commissioned many leading architects and planners from different parts of the world to design a hill station that would accommodate about three lakh people, besides generating tourism opportunities for about 20-25 lakh visitors. Construction work for nearly 25,000 people is already over. In addition to houses for low-income, middle-income and high-income groups, several well-known education institutions in the world such as Ecole Hotelier, Lausanne Christ University and the Educom & Christal House school for economically disadvantaged people have set up their centres at the complex. About 15,000-30,000 tourists visit Lavasa on weekends and vacations. An economic transformation is already underway in the region. While the concept of developing 'smart cities' has found acceptance in the country at present, it is interesting to note that, years ago, the same idea had prompted the inception of the Lavasa project.

Like many other development projects in the country, this one too came under severe criticism from certain quarters. Among the critics were Anna Hazare and Medha Patkar. They started off by alleging that large tracts of land were acquired by deceiving adivasis. The truth is that almost all the purchased land belonged to displaced members of the farming community who had already shifted elsewhere. Since Ajit Gulabchand was an old friend of mine, it was also alleged that I had financial stakes in the project. Again, this was completely untrue because I do not own even an inch of land in Lavasa. Also, less than 3% of the total development land taken from the Maharashtra government has been submerged and the water stored there is utilised in a number of useful ways at the site.

The promoters of the project have given a categorical public assurance that they will not prevent water being drawn from their premises if the city of Pune faces an emergency at any time. One can also notice the massive planting of trees undertaken at the location for preserving the environment. The courts too gave appropriate directions to the government when satellite images of improved greenery were submitted. It is thus not surprising that opposition to Lavasa started lessening when people began visiting the project in large numbers and formed their own opinions. However, the project continues to be used as a tool by my opponents to malign me during election time.

At the government level, environment minister Jayanti Natarajan and Jairam Ramesh posed obstacles to the project during the two UPA governments. But Prime Minister Manmohan Singh was completely satisfied when Ajit Gulabchand made a presentation to him. In fact, he expressed the need for more such projects at different places in the country. After Narendra Modi, as Gujarat chief minister, visited Lavasa, he invited Ajit Gulabchand to develop a similar hill station at Dolera in Gujarat.

What we need to appreciate is that tourism has become a major source of revenue all over the world. India fares very poorly when compared to other nations in this regard. The tourism sector's revenue share in India's GDP is about 6.6% and it provides about 7.7% of the total jobs in the country. Though India has the potential to be among the five fastest growing tourist destinations by 2025, it ranks 65th, shockingly low, in world tourism at present.

If we are serious about bridging the gap, we shall have to shed our traditional mindset and stop opposing everything that appears to be bold and new. I am a strong believer in the creation of new, planned cities. In Maharashtra alone, I believe, there is scope to develop at least twenty new cities like Lavasa. This statement of mine evoked a sharp political debate during elections. However, it was my considered opinion and I would not mind repeating it on any forum. Leaders who truly believe in development politics must inculcate the habit of speaking their mind from time to time. Pandering to populist sentiments will not get us anywhere.

Unless you have an open mind and a will to implement out-of-the-box but fair solutions, it becomes difficult to achieve breakthroughs on several issues. Let me recall another example. During one of my tenures as chief minister, I was on a tour of Satara district in south Maharashtra. I was staying with my friend Vikramsinh Patankar who had a beautiful house in Patan village located in the scenic, hilly surroundings of Koyna dam. Vikramsinh's uncle had housed about 2,000 birds of different species in his aviary and he used to look after them with great love. Chatting with him used to be a real joy whenever I stayed there.

During this particular visit, I was standing in the courtyard when my attention was drawn to the hills in front of the house. The sight was enchanting. I asked Vikramsinh what was at the top the hills to which he said there was hardly anything except some wild bush and a few fruit trees. 'People from neighbouring villages go there to collect firewood and fruit. We don't object to that,' he added. 'Let us go there tomorrow,' I said. I asked my pilot to go to the hilltop and locate a place to land our helicopter.

We flew there the next morning. The pilot had a tough time steadying the helicopter because of the high winds at that altitude. We too had difficulty standing at one place or walking on the plateau. 'We must get the wind velocity measured scientifically. This place would be ideal for setting up a windmill. Why don't you look into it?' I suggested to Vikramsinh.

He got a scientific study done by some reputed institutes in Germany. After they gave the go-ahead signal, he installed four windmills on the hilltop at a cost of ₹2 crore, generating one mega watt of electricity. This was half the cost of power generated by conventional methods. Moreover, wind electricity was pollution-free 'green energy'.

Sometime thereafter I went to Gujarat where I met Tulsi Tanti whose family was looking for an avenue to invest money. Fresh from the success at Patan, I suggested that he could look at the wind electricity business. I helped him find a suitable place to set up an office in Pune. In subsequent years the family installed about 200 windmills in the Patan-Pachgani belt and then went on to expand its business in other parts of Maharashtra and outside.

Suzlon Corporation, owned by the Tanti family, currently happens to be the No. 1 windmill company in India and No. 2 in the field of wind electricity in the world. At present, you will notice a large number of windmills atop hills in the Sangli, Satara, Kolhapur and Ahmednagar districts of western Maharashtra in addition to several hilly areas of north Maharashtra and Vidarbha.

I took my friend Rahul Bajaj to have a look at one of the windmill projects. He installed about 50 windmills to generate electricity for his own industries. It cost him a fraction of the state electricity board's tariff of ₹9 per megawatt (MW). Encouraged by his experience, many other industrialists followed suit.

Thanks to advancements in technology, it is now possible to generate about 2.5 to 3.0 MW of electricity, as against one MW, from four windmills. The improved viability has enabled farmers to earn about ₹100,000 per acre every year from their land as against barely ₹500 which they fetched earlier.

No wonder many farmers from drought-prone areas like Parner, Pathardi, Shegaon and Kavathemahankal came forward to offer pieces of their land for the installation of windmills. When Anna Hazare struck a discordant note saying he would have to be satisfied about any negative effects on the environment in his native Parner village, the local farmers struck down his objections. The environment has remained unaffected and Parner has now become one of the most productive centres of wind energy.

Maharashtra currently generates 300 MW of wind energy, which makes it the leading state in this field in Asia. It has also set an example of how a good concept clicks when it is supported by the will of the government and the people and executed efficiently.

EIGHTEEN

The Enron Soap Opera

THE ENRON POWER PROJECT involved one of the many major struggles I had to wage during my long political innings for something I strongly believed in. In my second term as chief minister, I had decided to prioritise focused efforts for the state's industrial growth. Power, however, was one of the chief hurdles. Ensuring that industrial units got an uninterrupted electricity supply was by any reckoning an uphill task. Domestic power supply too was highly erratic and insufficient. The general perception at the time that Maharashtra was a surplus electricity state was incorrect and the power distribution network needed to be overhauled and thoroughly modernised.

I have been greatly influenced by Dr Babasaheb Ambedkar's thoughts in this regard. We all know him as a jurist and for his pioneering work for the uplift of the Dalits in the country. However, he was also an economist of considerable repute who strongly advocated the cause of infrastructure development. He thought that water, electricity, roads were prerequisites for economic progress. He initiated the setting up of key institutions such as the Central Electricity Authority, and maintained that it was the government's prime responsibility to explore various avenues for power generation. His books, which I procured from the Parliament library, provided me illuminating insights into the subject.

No prizes for guessing that generating electricity requires huge capital investment. In the 1990s, the per megawatt cost of generation was close to ₹4 crore. This meant that the state needed to invest about ₹2,000 crore to generate 500 MW of electricity. Maharashtra lacked the capacity to raise such a huge amount.

There was also another great challenge: the 'clean energy' crusade had begun to take root at the time the world over. This was in sharp contrast to the predominance of high-pollution, coal-guzzling power generation in our country. Hydroelectricity was a good option, chiefly because it was pollution-free and its operational cost was relatively low, but it too required massive capital investment. Moreover, the limited availability of stored water was a major constraint.

Another option was power plants based on natural gas. The control over natural gas in our country rests fully with the central government which, along with the Planning Commission, takes a practical view—and rightly so—on the issue. The laying of pipelines to transport the gas from its source to the power plants incurs huge costs. Therefore, it is a well-established policy to set up power plants in the states where natural gas is available. The only states rich in natural gas production in India are Assam and some of its neighbouring states in the Northeast. Natural gas reserves have recently been identified in Andhra Pradesh as well. As far as Maharashtra is concerned, Bombay High does produce natural gas but not enough to fulfil the state's needs.

After weighing all these factors, I thought of importing natural gas for generation of electricity in the state. Maharashtra is fortunate to have a 720 kilometre-long coast that stretches from Mumbai to Sindhudurg along the Arabian Sea to its west. It was possible to identify a suitable location to set up a gas-based power plant on that stretch.

Secondly, I thought, if the cost of electricity generation was going to be the same for government and private parties, it would be prudent to allow private investment in the power sector, so that the government could divert its limited resources to other sectors such as civic infrastructure, agriculture, education and healthcare. While addressing the Maharashtra Chamber of Commerce way back in 1990, I had strongly advocated that the government must shed its insistence on running enterprises in every field. If private parties were willing to invest in a particular project, I had said, the government must withdraw.

Earlier, I had already allowed a private party, the Bombay Suburban Electric Supply (now owned by the ADA Group) to invest in electricity generation. Long ago, the British government too had invited the Tatas to set up a power generation plant. Each of these initiatives had proved successful. Therefore I decided to take the private investment road.

A government delegation was sent abroad to make an assessment of various private players in the field. Among the companies which made a presentation in the United States at the time was the Enron Corporation. Some companies shortlisted from the preliminary list were asked to make a detailed presentation in Maharashtra. Enron figured in that list too.

Meanwhile, I took charge as defence minister in New Delhi and Sudhakarrao Naik succeeded me as chief minister of Maharashtra. I told him that I was fully convinced about the need for the project but the actual decision to entrust the project at Dabhol to Enron was taken by his government. Four things worked for the Dabhol project. One, the state government was not required to invest any money. Two, importing gas at the site of the project was easy because it was to be located along the coast (Dabhol is a port town in Ratnagiri district). Three, Oman and some other countries had agreed to supply gas at the low rate of one rupee per unit. Four, it was to be a pollution-free 'green energy' project.

Following an agreement between Enron Director Rebecca Mark and the Sudhakarrao Naik government, the project got going. As per the agreement, the Dabhol Power Plant was to be built through the combined efforts of Enron, GE and Bechtel. The project management was to be done by Enron International.

Even while negotiations were underway, the opposition parties in Maharashtra began to politicise the issue. They objected to the entry of foreign companies on our soil, making the specious claim that the Enron project had jeopardised national security. Also, alleging corruption, the Shiv Sena-BJP combine announced that the project would be abandoned if their alliance came to power. 'We shall dump Enron in the Arabian Sea,' they proclaimed. Enron was turned into a major issue in the 1995 state assembly elections in Maharashtra.

The saffron alliance won the elections and one of the first decisions taken by the new government led by Manohar Joshi was to scrap the Enron project. This was a sad development because of the hefty investment made in the project, and as Maharashtra was badly in need of electricity at the time.

We repeatedly cautioned against the scrapping of the project for purely political reasons but the new government would not pay any heed. As expected, Enron Corporation went to court against the government's decision. The issue dragged on for some time. The law department of the state government pointed out that Enron may go to the international court and if the latter upheld the appeal and asked the Maharashtra government to cough up an astronomical compensation, the state would be plunged into deep financial trouble.

The Shiv Sena-BJP government finally saw reason. Chief Minister Joshi, in fact, admitted in public that the charges of corruption levelled by the Shiv Sena–BJP coalition before the election were politically motivated. His government decided to re-invite Enron to run the project. More than 18 months had passed in the meantime. Consequently, gas suppliers went back on the original agreement. Instead of the agreed price of one rupee per unit, the gas price had now shot up to almost five rupees per unit. This meant that for the end consumer, the price of electricity from the project was going to be simply unaffordable. Since the state was not in a position to purchase electricity from Enron at the revised rates, the project work ground to a halt.

Maharashtra thus lost a golden opportunity to get clean electricity at a low price and that too without having to make its own investment. This cast a long shadow on the state's development. In terms of industrial growth it was once far ahead of other states. Following the Enron episode, it could not maintain the pace. Though India had embarked on the path of liberalisation in the early 1990s, the Enron fiasco sent out a signal to the world that we were not a safe investment destination. The image of India in general and Maharashtra in particular suffered a setback, solely because of mindless, destructive political one-upmanship.

Years later, Prime Minister Manmohan Singh appointed a committee under my chairmanship to find a way out of the mess. The Maharashtra chief minister was also a member of the committee. The Enron Corporation made it clear that it was not interested any longer because of the government's haphazard style.

We therefore recommended that we buy out the Enron shares. Ratnagiri Gas and Power Limited thus came into being in 2005 with the Central government buying 70% shares and the Maharashtra government buying 30%. A project which was crucial for Maharashtra's speedy development was all but abandoned at the altar of petty, short-sighted politics in the 1990s. However, I am happy that we did, at least, manage to salvage it in large measure.

I must mention another significant development in this regard. Soon after I took charge as Maharashtra chief minister in 1993, the central government constituted a committee under my chairmanship to draft an energy policy for the country. Union finance minister Manmohan Singh, Union energy minister N.K.P. Salve and the chief ministers of West Bengal, Punjab, Karnataka and Assam were members of the committee. Following an in-depth study, the committee presented the policy draft to the Planning Commission for approval. It was subsequently ratified at a chief ministers' conference. One of our key recommendations was to allow private-sector investment in the energy sector. Notwithstanding the Enron controversy, the policy document drafted by our committee was later widely accepted as a framework across the country.

NINETEEN

The Birth of the NCP

THE THOUGHT OF SHIFTING base to New Delhi had crossed my mind for the first time in 1982 when I was invited by Devi Lal and Prakash Singh Badal to mobilise and preside over a mammoth farmers' rally in the national capital. Thereafter I had a very short stint as Lok Sabha member in 1984 and then a longer one as defence minister in P.V. Narsimha Rao's government. Each of these times, the rigours of state politics drew me back to Maharashtra.

General elections to the 11th Lok Sabha in 1996 finally gave me the opportunity to make the move. The action started almost immediately after I got elected from Baramati to a badly hung House. The BJP emerged as the single largest party with 161 seats. I was then in the Congress Party which won 140 seats. While the Janata Dal got 46, the CPM bagged 32. Various regional parties like the TDP, SP, DMK and others, which had won seats ranging from 20 to 1, got together with the Janata Dal to form a post-poll alliance called the United Front (UF). For two years the nation witnessed extreme political instability as the governments of Atal Bihari Vajpayee, H.D. Deve Gowda and Inder Kumar Gujral collapsed in quick succession.

Following the Congress's Lok Sabha defeat in 1996, Narsimha Rao had to step down as Congress president. He was replaced by Seetaram Kesari. When Vajpayee resigned as prime minister after just 13 days in government, the Congress and Left parties extended outside support to the United Front under Deve Gowda, who was sworn in on 1 June 1996. It was anyone's guess how long his government would last.

Deve Gowda was the Janata Dal chief minister in Karnataka

at the time and was not considered a heavyweight at the national level. Though Kesari had played a key role in Gowda's anointment, he himself was aspiring to the post and therefore did not want the Gowda government to last long. There was stiff resistance within the Congress to Kesari's destabilising moves because the party felt dislodging Gowda would cause another bout of political instability in the country. However, Kesari was on his own trip. He had excess faith in his own ability. Bypassing the internal consensus within the Congress, he pulled the plug on the Gowda government on 11 April 1997. He had acted unilaterally, misusing the power he had as party president.

It was not surprising that Kesari's action evoked a sharp reaction within the party. Many leaders and member of Parliaments, including Margaret Alva and Jaffer Sharif, approached me and insisted that I should stake claim to the prime ministership by displacing party chief Kesari as fast as possible. These functionaries were not really 'close' to me but they assured me of the party's full support if I took the lead. They were also fairly confident of a positive response from President K.R. Narayanan to such a move. Despite mounting pressure from the party member of Parliaments, I chose to keep quiet. Going against the party chief to stake my claim would have split the party. Since I was carrying the 'blot' of 'betraying' Maharashtra Chief Minister Vasantdada Patil in 1978 to lead a PDF government, I did not wish to go through a similar experience now. After I turned down the proposal firmly, Gujral was approached to lead the United Front in Gowda's place and the Congress then renewed its support to the UF government. Gujral took oath on 21 April 1997.

Discontent within the Congress over Kesari's disastrous style of functioning was coming to a boil. When he sought re-election as party president, several leaders decided to oppose him. I was one of them. Rajesh Pilot and A.R. Antulay also threw their hat in the ring, but Antulay later withdrew in my favour. The

Kesari camp was trying to give an impression that his candidature had the blessings of Sonia Gandhi. After a lot of manipulation, he managed to win. However, my objective was to register opposition to Kesari's working style. That objective was achieved.

If the Gowda government survived for ten months, that of Gujral lasted only a month longer! The Jain Commission, which was instituted to probe Rajiv Gandhi's assassination, came out with its report indicting the DMK for its support to the Sri Lankan Tamil militant group LTTE. Rajiv had been killed by the LTTE six years earlier. Since the DMK was a constituent party of the ruling UF coalition, the Congress demanded its removal from the government. When Gujral refused, the Congress withdrew its support and Gujral resigned on 28 November 1997. The subsequent general elections failed to yield a clear verdict once again. The Congress fared marginally better to win 141 seats, while the BJP improved its tally from 161 to 182.

On 14 March 1998, Sonia Gandhi replaced Kesari as Congress president after the Congress Working Committee unceremoniously stripped the latter of the post. Some days before that, A.K. Antony, Ghulam Nabi Azad and I had walked across from the party office at 24 Akbar Road to 10 Janpath to request Sonia Gandhi to assume the party's reins. Former bureaucrat P.C. Alexander played a role at the time. He said to me, 'I know you feel strongly that the Congress must survive the present crisis. But it is obvious you have some reservations about the Gandhi family. In that case, you must forego your personal interests and initiate a dialogue with Sonia Gandhi. When the Congress split in 1978, it had a mass leader of the stature of Indira Gandhi. She could revive the party. It is clear that a man like Kesari will not be able to hold the party together in the present circumstances. You will need some more time to muster adequate support for yourself in the Hindi-speaking belt of north India. You must bring in Sonia Gandhi at this juncture. Only then can the Congress be saved.'

I too had by then come to the conclusion that Kesari's continuance as president would destroy the party. Many senior leaders in the Congress felt comfortable under the spell of 10 Janpath. In fact, they saw the Gandhi family as the only cementing force that could hold the party together. In any case, they invariably acted in tune with the signals they received from there. Therefore, I felt it was better to openly replace Kesari with Sonia Gandhi at that stage.

Though I was among those few who invited Sonia Gandhi to become Congress president, there was little warmth between us. At best our relations were cordial. She relied very heavily on just two or three people for running the party. There was some uneasiness within the Congress that the party had won the maximum number of Lok Sabha seats in 1996 from my home state, Maharashtra.

Against this background, the coterie sought to drive a wedge between me and Sonia Gandhi by pointing out how I had defied Indira Gandhi to form the PDF government in Maharashtra in 1978. The so-called loyalists also drew her attention to the rebellion of some Congress ministers in my cabinet against me in 1990, when I was Maharashtra's chief minister. The fact that the aborted rebellion was sponsored by Rajiv Gandhi meant that Rajiv too was unhappy with me, they argued. All this talk had the desired effect. Sonia Gandhi did not say much but the distrust was evident on her face. It also found reflection in her actions. When she and I decided something through mutual discussion, she would do exactly the opposite. If I selected P.C. Chacko to open a debate on the party's behalf in the House, she would replace him just because he was supposed to be close to me. It is another matter that the same Chacko is now entrusted with the responsibility of the Congress party's revival in Delhi. Apparently the realisation of his calibre dawned on them quite late.

What really took the cake was a shocking amendment to the constitution of the Congress Parliamentary Party which was brought into effect solely to suit Sonia Gandhi. Though she was the Congress president, Sonia Gandhi was not an MP when I was a Lok Sabha member and CPP leader. Soon after she assumed the party's reins, a meeting of the CPP was called while I was away in Mumbai. A decision to amend the CPP constitution was taken in the meeting. Earlier, the CPP leader had to be a member of either the Lok Sabha or the Rajya Sabha and he/she appointed the party leader in the other House. The amendment did away with the condition that the CPP leader had to be an MP. This was obviously done to remove the obstruction in Sonia Gandhi's path. If there was any doubt about the motive, it was quickly dispelled when Pranab Mukerjee proposed her name and it was readily endorsed by all. She then appointed me as the Congress leader in the Lok Sabha and Manmohan Singh as the party leader in the Rajya Sabha.

I was deeply hurt by the decision. Never before in the Congress party's long history had a person become the parliamentary wing's chief without being a member of Parliament. I was a duly elected member of the Lok Sabha and was therefore a natural claimant to the post of CPP leader. I also enjoyed the support of the party's other members in the House. Yet, I was now 'appointed' by a person who was not even an member of Parliament. This unfortunate development put almost too great a distance between Sonia Gandhi and me. The situation was aggravated when she overruled many of my decisions in the Lok Sabha, for instance, by asking some member of her coterie to replace people I selected to speak for the party in the Lok Sabha—the P.C. Chacko case, which I've described above, being one such. The drift was to persist for more than a year before reaching breaking point.

In the meantime, the BJP this time had cobbled together the NDA, comprising the Shiv Sena, the Akali Dal, the Samata Party, the AIADMK and the Trinamul Congress. Some more parties, including the Assam Gana Parishad, the Loktantrik Janata Dal, the Haryana Lok Dal and the National Conference also joined in later. This took the NDA tally to 254 which was still short of the halfway mark in the Lok Sabha. But the Vajpayee government managed to survive with outside support from the Telugu Desam and other smaller parties.

I knew how fragile the government was because it was totally at the mercy of its alliance partners. In April 1999, the AIADMK withdrew its support after Prime Minister Atal Bihari Vajpayee refused to accept certain demands made by the AIADMK supremo Jayalalitha. With 18 AIADMK MPs withdrawing support, the president asked Vajpayee to seek a vote of confidence in the Lok Sabha. The motion of confidence was put to a voice vote. The speaker declared it as passed but we demanded a division of votes because we knew the government was precariously balanced. After the speaker announced that a division of votes would be taken, the Parliament staff took some time to close the doors and activate the voting machinery. During those few minutes I took the Bahujan Samaj Party (BSP) chief Mayavati aside and had a word with her. The BSP had five members in the House and there was intense speculation about what stand it would take. There was palpable tension as the voting ended.

When the electronic display board showed that the Vajpayee government had lost by one vote, everyone got into a guessing game about who voted on which side. Those who had noticed me talking to Mayavati before the voting pressed me to clarify. However, I thought it prudent to keep mum. Even after so many years I am sometimes asked what transpired between Mayavati and me during that brief interaction. Well, let me put it this way: I just impressed upon her that the BSP's interests in Uttar Pradesh would be served better if she voted against the Vajpayee government. Amen!

The full import of the shocking amendment to the Congress Parliamentary Party's constitution came into play at this juncture. Because that amendment enabled Sonia Gandhi to become CPP leader, she was now entitled to have a go at forming the next government. And that was exactly what she attempted to do. The Vajpayee government fell on 17th April and Sonia Gandhi met President Narayanan on 21st April to stake claim with those famous words: 'We have 272 and more are coming.'

Though I was the party leader in the Lok Sabha, she did not feel it was necessary to consult me before going to the president. As it transpired, she did not have 272 seats and the chances of 'more' coming to back the Congress evaporated into thin air when Mulayam Singh Yadav announced on 22nd April that his party would not support the Congress to form the government. The entire episode proved to be hugely embarrassing for the Congress.

THE FINAL BREAK-UP

On the party front, things started going wrong almost immediately after the 12th Lok Sabha came into being. There was already some awkwardness between Sonia Gandhi and me for reasons explained earlier but we had managed to strike a working relationship with her focusing on her responsibilities as Congress president and I carrying out my role as the leader of the party in the Lok Sabha. Before the arrangement could stabilise, an incident occurred that broke my faith even in this working relationship.

Committees comprising member of Parliaments of different political parties are an important element of parliamentary functioning. Depending upon every party's strength in the House, the party nominates members for various parliamentary committees. Following the Speaker's approval, the committees get constituted. As was the practice, I had a detailed discussion with Sonia Gandhi about Congress nominees for parliamentary committees. After we finalised the names, I had the list typed, got her consent and sent it to the Speaker of the Lok Sabha. The next day, Speaker G.M.C. Balayogi called me over to his office.

'There is a problem,' he said. 'I have in front of me two lists from your party.' I was flummoxed. He explained, 'After I received a list of names from you, Congress chief whip P.J. Kurien sent me another list. There is a disparity in the two lists.'

As leader of the Congress in the Lok Sabha, sending the official list to the Speaker was my prerogative. However, since it was an internal issue of the party, I did not discuss it with the Speaker. 'There seems to be a communication gap. I shall revert to you after sorting it out,' I said. After getting a photocopy of the other list, I left. When I confronted Kurien about the second list, he clarified that the list was prepared as instructed by the Congress president. 'What you say is difficult to believe,' I said. 'I am too junior to comment on this. You may please talk to Madam herself,' he replied. I sought a meeting with Sonia Gandhi.

'You and I had a detailed discussion before we finalised the Congress nominees for various parliamentary committees. I submitted the list to the Speaker after you approved it. But the Speaker has now received another list from our party. We need to recall one list. Please ask Kurien to withdraw the list he submitted,' I said.

'You may withdraw your list,' the Congress president replied calmly.

This was not acceptable to me. I was the leader of the party in the Lok Sabha and I had completed all the formalities before submitting our list. Asking me to withdraw the list after all this amounted to a devaluation of the position I held. It was just not right. The incident made me wonder how long I would be able to work in the party. However, I continued carrying out the responsibilities given to me.

After the Vajpayee government fell, elections for the 13th Lok Sabha were announced. The issue of striking alliances with other parties came up in a meeting of the Congress Working Committee (CWC). The AIADMK was unwilling to leave more than six seats for the Congress. I felt it was a humiliating offer for a national party like the Congress. After I voiced my opinion, it was decided that Ghulam Nabi Azad would go to talk to Jayalalitha with whom he was believed to have a good equation. Azad's meeting with Jayalalitha proved futile. The CWC then asked me to go to Chennai. Following our discussion, Jayalalitha agreed to leave 15 seats for the Congress. When I informed the Congress president about the outcome, she expressed satisfaction, saying it was an honourable deal for the party.

On 15 May 1999, the Congress president called a meeting of the CWC. For no apparent reason, she suddenly pulled out a sheet of paper and read aloud: 'I was born outside India. If this becomes an issue in the campaign, how would it impact our party's performance in the election?' She requested CWC members to voice their opinions candidly. Arjun Singh was the first to speak. 'You may be a foreigner by birth but you became a domicile of this country after marriage. You did not leave even after your husband and mother-in-law were assassinated. Just as you embraced this country, the people of India also have accepted you as one of them. For them, you are the 'Rashtra maataa' (the mother of the nation). You alone deserve to lead the nation and the party.' Arjun Singh more or less set the tone of the speeches that followed. A.K. Antony, Ghulam Nabi Azad and Ambika Soni went all out to express their loyalty.

Then came the turn of P.A. Sangma. He was believed to be very close to Sonia Gandhi. So what he said was totally unexpected for many. 'There is no doubt that Sonia Gandhi's foreign origin will be made a big issue in the election. It will be foolish on our part to say there will be no impact if we are criticised for choosing a foreigner to lead us when the party has so many able people. We shall have to devise a strategy to counter that criticism.'

The entire CWC listened to him in rapt attention. A senior member tried to interject but Sangma silenced him immediately by retorting that it would be in everybody's interest if he was allowed to speak without any interruption. When Tariq Anwar's turn came, he concurred with Sangma. After a few others spoke, it was my turn. I said, 'The people of India will not forget that the Gandhi family has contributed a lot to this country. Secondly, a large number of people in the country support the Congress because they acknowledge with gratitude the supreme sacrifices made by Indiraji and Rajiv Gandhi. Therefore we shall be able to counter effectively the opposition parties' campaign against Soniaji's foreign origin. In that sense, I agree with what Sangma said. We must meet the opposition campaign head on. But it will be our gross mistake to presume that the opposition will not campaign on the "foreigner" issue.'

Then I narrated an incident in support of my contention. Some days earlier, I had attended a function in Mumbai University where a girl student asked me, 'In a country of one billion people, why can't the Congress find a leader of Indian origin?' The fact that the question was posed by a member of the young generation indicated that the issue had already reached far and deep. This meant the 'foreigner' issue would take centre stage in the elections. I quoted the incident to underscore the point that the party would have to prepare well to meet this challenge. There was no further debate.

Since Sonia Gandhi had initiated the discussion on the issue, she was expected to respond to the points raised by the members. However, for reasons best known to her, she chose to remain silent. The CWC meeting ended on that uneasy note.

I took the 4 p.m. flight to Mumbai. Journalists were waiting for me at the airport. They told me that Sonia Gandhi had resigned as Congress president. Demonstrations were going on outside the party headquarters in New Delhi. Many women among those assembled there were wailing. Some members of the crowd were raining abuses on Sangma, Tariq Anwar and me, I was told. When journalists asked me for my reaction, I said it was a sensitive issue and so I would not comment before getting all the information.

With more demonstrations the next day, the situation became

tense. The police advised us against going anywhere close to the party office as there was a possibility of a physical assault on us. Sangma, Tariq and I met in Delhi and drafted a four-page letter addressing Sonia Gandhi. Written with restraint, it hinted that the 'foreigner' issue would definitely come up in the campaign for which the party would have to pay a heavy political price. In view of this, we urged Sonia Gandhi to take the immediate initiative of proposing an amendment to the Constitution of India so that the offices of the president, vice-president and prime minister could only be held by natural-born Indian citizens.

Our move was in sharp contrast to the mass show of 'loyalty' which was on full display outside. Soon after our letter was received, the CWC met again to suspend us from the party for six years. Even while the hysterical exhibition of loyalty and support to 10 Janpath continued for a full week, a meeting of the All India Congress Committee (AICC) was called at Talkatora Stadium on 25th May. It dutifully endorsed our suspension.

We came to know later that it was all pre-planned; Arjun Singh had orchestrated the entire episode.

The Congress party ranks across the country were disturbed by our suspension. The reaction was particularly sharp in Maharashtra. Besides P.A. Sangma and Tariq Anwar, senior leaders including Sanat Mehta (Gujarat) and Sarat Chandra Sinha (Assam) came to Mumbai for deliberations. Congress leaders from the second rung in Uttar Pradesh, Bihar, the Northeast, Punjab, Haryana, Gujarat, Goa, Karnataka, Tamil Nadu and Kerela also joined in. Those from Maharashtra included Chhagan Bhujbal and R.R. Patil.

It was decided to form a new party that would promote the original Congress ideology and ethos. The Nationalist Congress Party (NCP) was to be the name of the new party. It was also decided to request the Election Commission to allocate the spinning wheel as the party symbol. The NCP formally came into being at a meeting convened at a packed Shanmukhanand Hall in central Mumbai on 10 June 1999. The excitement was palpable. The meeting adopted the party's constitution and elected office-bearers and members of the national executive. I was elected national president of the party with P.A. Sangma and Tariq Anwar as general secretaries. Bhujbal was elected president of the party's Maharashtra unit.

The public rally that followed at 3 p.m. at the historic Shivaji Park in central Mumbai received an overwhelming response from young Congress workers who had come from far-off villages to express solidarity with the new party. In the following days, the NCP set up its units in other states as well. The new party was duly registered with the Election Commission; but the latter turned down our request for the spinning wheel as the party symbol as it was registered earlier in the name of the Congress (Organisation) party. Instead, the NCP was granted one of our alternative choices, the clock showing 10 minutes past 10, as its symbol. Very appropriate, I suppose, because our meeting at the iconic Shanmukhananda auditorium had started at 10 past 10 on the morning of 10th June that year!

Barely a fortnight later, elections to the 13th Lok Sabha were announced. Although we had little time left for us to work out the poll nitty gritty, the NCP did well, bagging eight seats.

TWENTY

Tie-up with the Congress

THE NATIONAL DEMOCRATIC ALLIANCE (NDA) led by Atal Bihari Vajpayee won 303 seats in the 1999 Lok Sabha election to retain power at the Centre. This prompted the ruling Shiv Sena-BJP alliance in Maharashtra to advance the state assembly elections by six months. The result was a hung assembly. While the Congress and the NCP won 75 and 58 seats respectively, the Shiv Sena bagged 69 seats as against the BJP's tally of 56.

Efforts to form the government did not make much headway for almost two weeks as each party was busy weighing various options. Both the Sena and the BJP sent discreet signals to the NCP, but I was quite clear in my mind that we could never go with either of them to assume office in Maharashtra. On the other hand, the Congress option seemed both prudent and practical. We had parted ways with the Congress after we were expelled from the party. However, that, I thought, wasn't a major hurdle in inking an alliance with the Congress and the latter, too, following a series of meetings, arrived at the same conclusion.

Vilasrao Deshmukh called me and said, 'If the NCP is willing to join hands with the Congress we too can think along those lines.' I told him about the overall consensus within my party. But I knew that such decisions in the Congress were not taken at the state level, so I suggested that he should first get consent from New Delhi and then we could proceed. Vilasrao immediately talked to the Congress high command and called me again in the evening to inform me that he had received the green signal from the party high command.

The next day, Praful Patel and I held a meeting in New Delhi with Vilasrao Deshmukh, Maharashtra Congress president Prataprao Bhosale and Margaret Alva who was the party in-charge for Maharashtra. To the Congress query about setting certain parameters for power sharing, I pointed out that a lot of time had already been wasted. If the two parties got into an exercise of deciding parameters at this stage, new problems could crop up. Instead, I suggested, 'Let us stick to the Shiv Sena-BJP formula of sharing power. As Congress has won more seats, you can keep the chief minister's post.' That set a positive tone to the process and further discussions on distribution of posts got over in very little time.

Vilasrao Deshmukh thus became chief minister of the Congress-NCP government, while Chhagan Bhujbal of the NCP became the deputy chief minister. The assembly Speaker's post was given to the NCP and the Congress got the chairman's post in the legislative council.

I continued my work in the Lok Sabha as a member of the opposition, even as I toured extensively across the country to build the NCP's base. On the morning of 26 January 2001, a major earthquake shook the Kutch region in Gujarat. More than 15,000 people were killed. Bhuj, Anjar and Bachchav tehsils suffered a colossal loss of life and property. On 3rd February Prime Minister Atal Bihari Vajpyee called an all-party meeting in New Delhi to decide on rescue and relief measures for the state. It was decided in the meeting to lay down a long-term policy for disaster management. Sonia Gandhi praised the rehabilitation and reconstruction efforts made by the Maharashtra government, under my leadership, in the wake of the 1993 terrorist bomb blasts in Mumbai and the earthquake in the Killari-Sastur region of the state the same year. The Centre subsequently constituted the National Committee for Disaster Management (NCDM) with Prime Minister Vajpayee as chairman and me as the vice chairman.

Some central ministers and representatives of various political parties were members of this committee. Among them were

George Fernandes, Nitish Kumar, Harkishan Singh Surjeet, A.B. Bardhan, Sonia Gandhi, Mamata Banerjee, Prakash Singh Badal and Mulayam Singh Yadav. Dr A.P.J. Abdul Kalam, who then was the scientific advisor to the prime minister, was also a member of the panel. If one went by the tone of the discussions in the meeting, it was presumed that the actual responsibility would be vested in me.

The committee's mandate was three-pronged: 1) To suggest short-term, medium-term and long-term measures for relief, rehabilitation and re-construction in the earthquake-affected region of Gujarat; 2) To suggest institutional and legislative measures for a long-term strategy to deal with natural calamities in the future; 3) To suggest parameters that would define a 'national calamity'.

I took this responsibility with utmost seriousness because such a step was long overdue. India is a vast, diverse country where calamities of various kinds keep occurring frequently. In the absence of a well-established policy, state governments and other authorities were prone to taking ad hoc measures. Besides being post-facto, their effectiveness often proved to be suspect. Vajpayee had full trust in me. Though he was chairman of the committee, he gave me complete freedom to take decisions. I was accorded a cabinet minister's status, which made it easy for me to plan visits to various places and call meetings of all relevant agencies whenever needed.

Among the countries I visited as part of my work was Japan, which had developed an excellent system to tackle earthquakes. A detailed study of the Japanese mechanism proved to be a crucial input when the committee drafted its report. I also visited the US as parts of that country had been ravaged by a cyclone at the time. The visit enabled me to observe first hand the rescue and relief measures planned and executed there.

The committee submitted its report in just about a year. There was some debate about whether the disaster management department should be under the defence ministry or the home ministry. However, the government accepted the committee's recommendation of clubbing it with the home ministry. The National Disaster Management Authority (NDMA) is now in place and I notice that the committee report has served as the benchmark for a number of steps that the NDMA has taken in the last decade and more.

Consequently, the NCDM won respect and trust in large measure from both officialdom as well as victims of tragedies such as the floods in Himachal Pradesh in 2013 and Jammu-Kashmir in 2014, or the Nepal earthquake in 2015.

It is now mandatory for every state to have a disaster management department. The subject has also been included in the school curriculum with a view to enhancing students' awareness of natural calamities and how to cope with them.

TWENTY-ONE

Battle with Cancer

THE FIRST THING I decided when diagnosed with cancer was that I must devise a strategy to fight and overcome the 'problem'. Certain things in life happen suddenly, unexpectedly, beyond one's control, so to say. There is no point in brooding over them. Most people in such situations get depressed; some simply lose the will to carry on. As far as I am concerned, taking things in my stride is second nature, which I probably inherited from my mother.

Bai had an extraordinary ability to withstand extreme pain or physical discomfiture. Several memories from my childhood bespeak her grit, but one of them stands out the most—the accident that I have referred to earlier. In my native village, Katewadi, there was a peculiar practice in the local community to adopt one bull as God's property. Naturally, feeding the animal was the village responsibility. That was fine. But because of its 'divine connection' no one kept the bull tied or restrained it in any manner. As a result the bull would roam about freely, damage crops or other property and generally become a nuisance. Fed up with its antics, someone shot the bull one night, injuring it badly. When Bai went out in the morning she found the bull lying in a field and tried to bring it some comfort. The angry animal got up, knocked her down and trampled all over her. This went on for nearly 15 minutes. By the time someone rescued her, Bai was grievously wounded. Her right thigh was virtually torn. The leg, we were told, was fractured. In fact, it was much more than a fracture. The bones in her upper leg were almost completely crushed. She was taken for surgery to a hospital in Pune where the damaged bones were removed. As a result the leg became shorter by about six inches. She could never walk without crutches after the incident.

However, Bai's zest for life remained unaffected. She never capitalised on her misfortune, nor sought sympathy. Her demeanour continued to be both stern and caring, as earlier. The will to adapt and learn new things did not diminish. Many years after the mishap my brother Suryakant married a British girl. Bai learnt to speak English so that she could communicate with her daughter-in-law. When one of her sons bought a car—the first four-wheeler in our family—she learnt to drive as well.

Bai's indomitable spirit could not be dampened. As I saw it, the mishap was only a comma, or may be a semi-colon, in her life's march. Never a full stop. The physical handicap was inconsequential. How could I not be influenced by my gritty mother!

During the surgery on one of my cheeks, a patch of skin from my thigh was grafted on the inside. My teeth were removed. A big cotton ball was placed inside the mouth in order to prevent movement of the jaw for about a week after the surgery.

I resolved to beat cancer by simply telling myself, 'I will fight it.' My family, friends and acquaintances were worried, to put it mildly. They were told that I was on borrowed time. Doctors were a tad cautious in their replies. But I knew I was going to win the battle. One of the doctors attending on me was quite young. On checking my medical reports he said that I had only six months of life left.

'What is your age, young man?' I asked him.

He told me.

'Okay, now take it from me. I am going to outlive you,' I said.

This, of course, was a light-hearted remark. The young doctor did not mean ill. Guided by his medical knowledge he was just being truthful. But I too was serious about living long and well. He spoke his truth. I, mine.

It all began when the 2004 Lok Sabha polls were announced. I had begun my campaign. During my poll tour I felt some growth inside my cheek. Dr Ravi Bapat was with me. He accompanies me whenever I am on election tour. He examined my cheek and said, 'We'll have to go back to Mumbai.' Dr Bapat is a very good friend of mine and I trust his advice.

The diagnosis came when the election campaign was already on. My sudden absence would have caused unnecessary speculation and panic in the NCP ranks. I thought it prudent to take senior people in the party into confidence so that they could handle the campaign efficiently when I was away. A meeting of senior NCP leaders from all over Maharashtra and other states was called in Pune. Only a handful of them were aware of my illness. Others were plain worried about what I was going to say. I kept it straight and simple. Taking care that things wouldn't turn sentimental, I told them about the diagnosis and the impending surgery. I also explained clinically the various post-surgery possibilities. Everyone was stunned but no one panicked. Since I was going to be hospitalised for a few days all key leaders were assigned specific responsibilities to ensure that the campaign did not get derailed. The meeting ended with a firm resolve to carry on undeterred.

As soon as the doctors at the Breach Candy hospital in Mumbai gave me permission, I started monitoring the campaign from my hospital bed. A few days after I was allowed to go home I flew down to Kolhapur, Aurangabad and Nagpur to address election rallies. As my constant companion, Dr Bapat took great care of my medicines and diet as prescribed by Dr Sultan Pradhan.

The show went on as planned.

During the surgery my cheek had been cut up and repaired, my teeth had been taken out. After the surgery, the series of chemotherapy sessions I had at Apollo Hospital near Delhi peeled off the surface of my tongue and lips, causing excruciating pain. Even as simple a task as sipping water became an ordeal. I couldn't sip water without my mouth being anesthetised.

I must thank Dr Ravi Bapat and Dr Sharadini Dahanukar

for planning and monitoring my medication. I owe a huge debt to Dr Sultan Pradhan too. His great skills put me back in action. When we consulted the doctors at the Sloan Kettering hospital in New York, they strongly recommended Dr Pradhan's name. He is by far the best doctor for oral cancer, they said. I was thus put in safe hands.

After the elections we formed a government at the Centre with Dr Manmohan Singh as prime minister and I chose the agriculture portfolio in his cabinet. Every morning I would be in my office at Krishi Bhavan. I would work till 3 p.m. From Krishi Bhavan I would drive down to Apollo Hospital for chemotherapy.

A strong will power alone carries you through when your physical condition is fragile. If you keep thinking about the physical pain all the time you will find the pain gets much worse. Instead, you concentrate on the work at hand and that helps you forget the pain. I did precisely that. My strategy was simple: Don't mope or worry, don't dither, take the medicines on time and concentrate solely on work. The strategy worked.

The chemotherapy sessions were painful but I never skipped my office. Clearance of files and attending meetings on time was a routine I followed uninterruptedly. As soon as my physical condition permitted, I started meeting visitors, either one-on-one or in delegations. No politician can avoid interacting with people. This was something I enjoyed the most. I am told often that I am a good listener. It is a self-taught skill developed over the years. Every visitor comes with a unique issue to discuss or get resolved. And there are always so many of them awaiting their turn to meet one. Therefore listening to each of them in all seriousness and going straight to the operative part of the problem in question is crucial.

Also, I don't wait for visitors to come to me. Whenever I have free time or even during travel, I interact with a lot of people from different backgrounds. This practice has resulted in improving my ability to grasp diverse situations and people.

The skill to anticipate something correctly and come up with a solution quickly leaves the visitor satisfied, and saves my time.

I went to the Sloan Kettering Cancer Center in the US for follow-up treatment after the surgery. Dr Mehta was my doctor. He asked me to visit the Center every three months. However, noticing a steady improvement in my health, he curtailed my visits progressively to one in six months and, then, one a year. 'I am satisfied with your health report. You need not come here again,' he told me on my last visit.

The importance of prompt medical assistance and will power can hardly be overstated. Two years after the cancer ailment, I began to feel uneasy during a meeting in Krishi Bhavan. 'Anything wrong, Sir?' asked Radha Singh, the agriculture secretary. She immediately took me to the Ram Manohar Lohia hospital where blockages were located in my coronary arteries. I asked the hospital to go ahead with surgery without further loss of time. However, the blockages disappeared before I was wheeled into the operation theatre. But stents had to be implanted when the problem recurred after six months.

In December 2014, my pelvic bone suffered a fracture when I slipped in my house. Doctors told me after the orthopaedic surgery that it would take some months before I could start walking, and that too with a walking stick. Belying all speculations, I started to walk within a fortnight of the operation. The walking stick soon became a thing of the past.

Lifestyle is an important issue which many politicians generally ignore. After being diagnosed with oral cancer I gave up the old habit of chewing mouth fresheners containing tobacco. I am glad that the Congress-NCP government in Maharashtra clamped a ban on all tobacco products.

Politics demands full-time involvement and entails a wide variety of activities, including administrative work, touring, public relations—all at one time. The high degree of multi-tasking calls for an ability to manage tensions which in turn comes only from a disciplined lifestyle. I have been a stickler in this regard. I get up early and never miss a walk. I don't eat anything between my regular meals. The diet is low on chilli, spices and oil, but I drink a lot of water during the day. Taking rest too is an important factor but because of a disciplined lifestyle, I can do with very little sleep. When needed, I can immediately go to sleep even during a thirty-minute helicopter ride so that I am fresh and alert on landing.

Talking about cancer, I lost two of my colleagues in politics to the dreaded disease in recent years. Former Maharashtra Chief Minister Vilasrao Deshmukh died of liver cancer in August 2012. Long before he took seriously ill, his pale face indicated that something was wrong with him. I remember having mentioned this to him on a couple of occasions, however, he brushed it aside, saying that he had by choice lost some weight which may have caused weakness. When I visited his son Reitesh's wedding in February that year, he tried to get up from his seat to greet me, but could not rise. When I asked him, his answer was the same. I still feel Vilasrao would not have succumbed so soon to his ailment had he not chosen to ignore the alarm signals.

R.R. (aka Aba) Patil, former deputy chief minister of Maharashtra and NCP leader, died at the age of 57 on 16 February 2015. He was suffering from oral cancer, but kept it a secret till things were completely beyond redemption. The secrecy he maintained was to such an extent that it took a lot of effort on our part to find out which hospital he was admitted to. By the time we located him, the disease had advanced to the last stage and Aba had decided not to fight any more.

I saw Aba Patil evolve as political activist and later as a leader. He was remarkably good as rural development minister during the Congress-NCP decade-long rule in the state. He was honest and was deeply steeped in ground wisdom.

I had to seek his resignation as home minister following his controversial remark over the 26/11 attack on Mumbai. There was such uproar over his statement that I had no other option but to seek his resignation. However, he was later reinstated as home minister and continued his good work there till the 2014 assembly elections which saw the end of the Congress-NCP regime.

I was deeply pained by Patil's untimely death. My heart goes out to him when I think that he probably concealed his illness from all so that the party wouldn't suffer during elections. He was deeply devoted to the NCP, with which he had been associated since its inception in 1999.

TWENTY-TWO

At Home in Agriculture

IN 2003, THE RULING NDA started preparing for the 14th Lok Sabha elections in the belief that it would retain power. Riding on the slogan 'India Shining', the government advanced the elections by six months and paid heavily for its overconfidence. The Congress, on the other hand, played its cards with guarded optimism and decided to fight the NDA by sewing up a broad coalition.

One evening, Congress president Sonia Gandhi stepped out of 10 Janpath and walked down straight to my 6 Gurudwara Rakabganj home for talks. This certainly was a warm gesture as we were meeting officially for the first time after the birth of the NCP. It wasn't too difficult to fathom why Sonia Gandhi visited my house. With a slump in the NDA's popularity she saw an excellent opportunity for the Congress to lead a coalition government at the Centre after the elections. And she didn't mind making the first move. I responded positively to her proposal for a united front to take on the NDA. We fought the elections as allies.

The NDA lost power, winning only 181 Lok Sabha seats, including the BJP's tally of 138. Improving its tally, the Congress bagged 145 seats, but the UPA fell short of the halfway mark as it won 218 seats in all. The Congress strategists pulled out all stops to gather more allies. Pranab Mukherjee and Manmohan Singh came to my house requesting support for the Congress to form the government. The Left parties led by the CPM offered external support to the UPA. However, the Congress, Mukherjee said, wanted the NCP, the DMK and the National Conference to be part of the government. In view of the post-election arithmetic in the Lok Sabha our party had already decided to accept the Congress offer when it came. We thus got down to discussing the portfolios.

'What is your preference?' Pranabda asked me.

'Agriculture,' I said without any hesitation.

Pranabda looked surprised and relieved too. He quickly nodded in approval. I could see why. Home, finance and external affairs are the most coveted ministries in any government and Pranabda may have been worried that I would demand one of them. However, I was of the view that it would be in the fitness of things if the largest party wanted to retain key portfolios, and I had no intention of embarrassing my visitors.

Manmohan Singh was of course more than happy with my choice, though for a different reason. Aware of my abiding interest in agriculture he knew that I would not spare any effort to do justice to the job.

'I have a pre-condition, though,' I said. Pranabda became a little anxious. 'I would like food, animal husbandry and water resources to be clubbed with the agriculture ministry,' I said. The practice so far had been to allocate these departments to different ministries. Each ministry had its own priorities which often ran at cross purposes. This invariably led to incoherence in government policies affecting some very good initiatives.

Manmohan Singh saw my point and agreed immediately. Pranabda's astuteness came into play at this juncture. While there was no problem to clubbing the food and animal husbandry departments with agriculture, he had reservations about water resources too being added to the agriculture ministry. 'Your home state Maharashtra has long-pending water-sharing issues with Karnataka, Andhra Pradesh and Gujarat. If this department is clubbed under your portfolio your actions and statements on the issue will always be susceptible to criticism. It will also create problems for the government,' he argued. I thought he had a point. What I liked was the way he put it. The quintessential Pranabda, who could say 'no' with sophistication.

No wonder he was the UPA regime's trouble-shooter whose task was to bail out the government or the party during times of crisis. Pranabda suggested that instead of water resources, the food processing department should be clubbed with the agriculture ministry. I had no reason to disagree.

Selecting the parliamentary leader was a slightly awkward issue for the Congress. While Sonia Gandhi was the party's No. 1 leader, the Congress wanted to play it safe this time because of its embarrassing experience in 1999. As we have seen, after the Vajpayee government collapsed by a single vote that year, Sonia Gandhi had unilaterally declared that she had the support of 272 members in the Lok Sabha. Going a step further, she had even staked a claim with the president to form the next government. What happened subsequently caused a huge loss of face for the Congress because Mulayam Singh Yadav refused to give a letter of support to the Congress.

However, this time around they were determined to avoid a repeat of the 1999 episode. The Congress leadership sought prior approval of all its allies. On behalf of the NCP I made it clear to the Congress emissaries that selecting the Congress leader, who would most likely become the prime minister, was entirely that party's prerogative and I had nothing to say about it. Then, following the Congress's request we gave them the letter of support.

Everything seemed to be going smoothly when politics in New Delhi took a dramatic turn. Sonia Gandhi was unanimously elected leader of the Congress Parliamentary Party on 16 May 2004. A few days later she took everyone by surprise by turning down the parliamentary leader's post, citing her 'inner voice' as the reason. This caused an upheaval in the Congress party and also unsettled its allies. The CPI-CPM wanted to know about the composition and the character of the government under the changed circumstances. The general secretaries of the two parties, A.B. Bardhan and Prakash Karat, suggested during talks with me that I should discuss all issues with Sonia Gandhi. Speculation was rife in political circles and the media about the cause of her 'renunciation'. When I spoke to her I could sense that the 'foreign origin' issue had something to do with her decision to turn down the post of prime minister. She apparently thought the issue would crop up again and anytime, and that would obviously put her in an awkward situation.

It was also said at the time that there was resistance within the Gandhi family to her becoming the prime minister because the family had already lost two of its members (Indiraji and Rajiv) because of the political decisions they took as prime ministers.

During our talks after turning down the parliamentary leader's post, Sonia Gandhi said that a suitable mechanism should be set up to ensure smooth coordination across UPA constituents and efficient functioning of the coalition government. The genesis of the National Advisory Council (NAC), which came into being on 4 June 2004 to guide the UPA government, and which Sonia Gandhi headed, lay in this proposal.

Many were surprised that I should opt for the agriculture ministry and retain it for ten years (2004-2014) in UPA-I and UPA-II. This calls for an explanation. Whatever happens in the field of agriculture directly affects more than 60% of the Indian population, besides influencing practically every sector of the economy in a variety of ways. I was confident that I would be able to contribute significantly in this crucial sector. I am a born farmer and all issues related to agriculture have been a subject of passion and study for me down the years.

In 2004, the agriculture sector was far from healthy and this, I thought, was an opportunity for me to put my expertise and experience to good use and try to set things right.

It had been almost four decades since the country witnessed the 'green revolution' that made India self-sufficient in agricultural production. C. Subramanyam was the agriculture minister in Indira Gandhi's cabinet. Annasaheb Shinde was the minister of state, while Shivraman was the agriculture secretary. The Indian Council for Agriculture Research (ICAR) was headed by Dr M.S. Swaminathan. The combination of a well-planned government policy, hands-on leadership in the ministry, able administration and involvement of research institutes yielded stunning results.

Later, Babu Jagjivan Ram too provided a firm direction to the agriculture ministry. Unfortunately, the ministry failed to keep pace with changing times thereafter.

Barring the 1984–89 period when Balram Jakhar was in charge, no agriculture minister could enjoy a full term of five years till I took over in 2004. After 1990 the sector that contributed 17.5% to the national economy and created 54.6% of the total jobs suffered the most. The agriculture growth rate touched the low point of 1.92% in 1996–97. The NDA regime under Atal Bihari Vajpayee which preceded UPA-I also did not give this sector the serious attention it deserved.

The scenario was dismal but I felt I would be able to bring about a turnaround in agriculture if I could get a team of my choice in the administration. Bureaucracy plays a very important role in a government's ability to deliver. I needed a good team. Manmohan Singh gave me a free hand to choose my officials. My technique was simple. First, place the right people in the right place. Second, brief them without any ambiguity about the government's expectations when implementing policies. Third, give them full operational freedom. I never interfered in their work.

For years my practice has been to update myself constantly about various aspects of agriculture. I would be constantly at it, going on field visits, visiting research centres in India and abroad, and interacting with scientists to understand key issues. I continue to do so even today.

Bureaucrats have their own way of making a slightly premature assessment of newly appointed ministers. They have a mechanism to gauge the new minister's knowledge and depth of interest. I am sure they must have done so in my case too. There is reason for me to believe that I acquitted myself creditably. As a result I never came across any 'attitudinal problems' on the part of the bureaucracy. Once the ministry's agenda had been set, the entire team put its shoulder to the wheel.

If the gap between policy makers and those who implement the policy can be mitigated, it yields exemplary results. That is why I kept a focus on updating my own knowledge base in agriculture. I interacted informally with domestic and international experts from different institutes, went through research papers and visited places where innovators in agriculture were at work. This helped me form considered opinions on key issues which I shared with colleagues from different arms of the agriculture ministry.

My priority was to re-energise the Indian Council for Agriculture Research. Underperforming research organisations cause long-lasting damage. Since ICAR was the backbone of Indian agriculture we, for a start, focused our attention on addressing its problems. The ICAR umbrella covers some important research institutes in the country. Among them are units in Kerala and Maharashtra that specialise in fisheries, a camel research institute in Rajasthan, an institute that carries out research in grapes, onions and garlic. There are many more focusing on specific crops, fruits, soil and water.

The ICAR has a total of 5,000 posts for agricultural scientists. As many as 500 were vacant when I took charge of the ministry. This had affected the ICAR's work badly. A scientific and agricultural scientists recruitment board was set up by inducting retired top scientists from across the country. The board was given a free hand to recruit the best available talent with just one mandate—the recruits should be in the age group of 35-45 years. This ensured that while the new work force had some prior experience, it would be active for at least a decade or more.

The second thing I did was to enhance the international

experience of our agricultural scientists. Such exposure is critically important in the era of global competition. The Food and Agriculture Organisation is a United Nations body with a number of centres across the world. For instance, there is one at Hyderabad which conducts research on pulses. Irrespective of their locations, these centres typically have scientists coming from about 10 to 20 countries. They are drawn based on a specific quota allocated to each continent. Since international experts in a particular field work together in such a set-up, it updates them on the latest scientific breakthroughs and worldwide developments. That in turn enables them to shape and modify the research work back home. Keeping this in mind I created a system that offered our scientists an opportunity to work for about three months every year in these FAO centres.

The third reform pertained to the actual working of the 80-plus institutes under ICAR. As a result, constant interference from the agriculture ministry was curtailed and they were given complete operational freedom. Every institute was asked to present an annual work plan along with its financial requirements. Once the plan and the budget were approved, there was no dabbling in their functioning by my ministry. This system induced tremendous enthusiasm which soon reflected in the performance of all the institutes.

When India and the United States signed the atomic energy deal, some other bilateral agreements were also underway. One of these agreements provided that the US would share its research findings in agriculture, food and other areas with India. As part of the deal, the US also offered milk and milk products. We learnt that the cows whose milk was being used were reared on cattle feed that contained meat. Now this was explosive in our domestic context! I conveyed to my counterpart in the US that keeping in mind the sensitivity of the Indian population about anything related to the cow, we would not be able to accept the products they were offering. The US secretary for agriculture sent me a nasty letter, saying if that was the case, it would not share findings of the latest research on the subject with us. The US probably expected us to cave in after the refusal. But I sent back a communication that we could not accept the agreement in its present form. This response generated some heat in that country. In the meanwhile I convinced the prime minister and the cabinet that the people of India would simply not accept the thought of a cow that consumed non-vegetarian food. The cabinet decided to abandon the proposed agreement.

Excepting this episode, we got into research-related bilateral agreements with a number of institutes and countries. With Dr Mangala Rai and then Dr S. Ayyappan as its director, the ICAR put in a sterling performance after that. Scientists' self-esteem was restored, operational freedom to individual institutes and giving more depth to the foundation for research virtually breathed new life into the apex body of Indian agricultural research.

One immediate benefit of the efforts was the timely availability of genuine good quality seeds of various crops to Indian farmers. This came as a big relief to the agriculturists who were perpetually deceived by suppliers of fake or sub-standard seeds.

The ultimate objective of research is the public good. If there is no sharing of research findings, the objective cannot be achieved. I noticed extreme reluctance in our scientific community to exchange research findings with others. 'You will have to shed this attitude if you expect to know the research outcomes from other parts of the world. It has to be a two-way process,' I told them. The research findings in ICAR institutes were also made available at an appropriate stage to private parties for a price. This benefited all stakeholders, including farmers.

A major factor that yielded spectacular results in agricultural production during 2005-2014 was the strong policy and institutional support that was given to the sector. The minimum support price (MSP) for agricultural produce is a tricky issue.

Any increase in the MSP of food grains, milk, meat and fish leads to a rise in the consumer price index, driving up inflation. No government is comfortable with the political fallout from a rise in the prices of essential commodities. Therefore governments in the past, primarily under pressure from the finance ministry, had never increased the MSP of these products by more than five to ten rupees at a time. I took the issue head on and pursued it doggedly to its logical end within the government. I argued that farmers' morale and their interest in their vocation could be maintained only if they were adequately compensated for their toil and investment in agriculture. If the cost of inputs in farming had gone up, the MSP should also go up in appropriate measure. When we increased the MSP for wheat by an unprecedented ₹60 per quintal, it resulted in a remarkable growth in wheat production in Punjab, Haryana, Madhya Pradesh and western Uttar Pradesh the very next year. It was the same story in the case of other crops.

We also introduced the concept of bonus in farm prices. The Food Corporation of India (FCI) procures food grains from farmers in different markets. Private traders also do the same. We asked the FCI to procure food grains at prices higher than those offered by private traders. This 'bonus' diverted a large number of farmers from private traders to the FCI. As a result, all FCI warehouses in the country filled up within three to four years.

The progress made in the case of oil seeds and pulses was also significant but it fell short of the requirement. Pulses are protein-rich and therefore form an important ingredient of Indian food. But the harvesting cycle for pulses is almost seven to eight months. Second, the productivity is not very high. Therefore farmers don't show much interest in the cultivation of pulses. Our per capita consumption of edible oil is higher than other countries and so the domestic demand is also high. But here again we have not yet succeeded in meeting the demand through indigenous production.

Earlier, our annual import bill for these two items was one lakh crore rupees (₹40,000 crore for pulses and ₹60,000 crore for edible oil). Increase in indigenous production of oil seeds and pulses during my tenure brought it down to ₹45,000 crore. This was a big support to the national economy. But we have a long way to go still.

Our domestic horticultural production was another weak area, unbecoming of a country bestowed with an amazingly wide range in climate and soil type. The low production, in turn, is reflected in the low consumption of fruits. This was my next target.

As Maharashtra chief minister in 1988 I had brought fruit cultivation under the employment guarantee scheme (EGS). As per the modified scheme, the state government offered specified wages to farmers even if they cultivated fruit trees on their private farms. It made EGS more productive for the government. There was an overwhelmingly positive response from the farmers because it boosted their family incomes. The production of the Alfonso mango in the coastal belt (Konkan) of Maharashtra grew multifold, while the Marathwada and Vidarbha regions in the state registered new highs in the production of sweet lime and orange respectively. Even farmers from chronically drought-affected regions took to pomegranate cultivation in a big way. This made Maharashtra the number one state in horticultural production in India.

I launched the National Horticulture Mission (NHM) in 2005-2006. It aimed at developing the full potential for horticulture in individual states across the country. The idea was to augment the production of state-specific produce that included fruits, flowers, vegetables, plantation crops, cashew nuts, spices, medicinal and aromatic plants.

Like the grape producers association in Maharashtra, we set up individual national-level associations for grapes, oranges, pomegranates, apples and so on. They were provided offices and other infrastructural facilities by the ministry for the first three years. A national-level meet of two or three days for each of these associations was also initiated. These meets provided a platform for select farmers from different parts of the country to present their success stories. The participants also engaged in question-answer sessions with officers from my ministry and with agriculture scientists on a variety of issues ranging from productivity to marketing. This encouraged the younger generation of farmers to take to horticulture. Young farmers from all over the country are keen to learn new technology and they possess a flexible mindset which is required to try out innovations in the field.

The NHM has accelerated horticultural production in India significantly. With the standard of living going up, more Indians have started consuming fruits. These two factors have filled fruit cultivators' coffers. The impact is most visible in some of the so-called 'BIMARU' states, the northern states that have traditionally underperformed economically. While litchi production in Bihar has shot up, the production of mangoes in Uttar Pradesh has also shown a remarkable increase. Like the Alfonso from Maharashtra, litchis from Bihar are now in great demand in international markets.

The 'second green revolution in eastern India' that we launched made a big difference to national food security. Punjab and Haryana have been traditionally known as our granaries because of their high production of wheat and rice. But both crops consume large amounts of water. As a result, the water table in both the states has sunk to an alarming 150 feet. On the other hand, the availability of water in Assam, Odisha, West Bengal, Jharkhand and Chhatisgarh is far better. We encouraged paddy cultivation in these states by providing high-quality, high-production seeds and fertilisers to local farmers. Credit facilities were also made easy to avail. The efforts paid rich dividends. These states became major suppliers of rice to other parts of the country. India is currently also the number one exporter of rice in the world.

Madhya Pradesh made major headway in wheat production. Chief Minister Shivrajsinh Chauhan offered an MSP higher than that of the Union government. This enabled his state to compete with the traditional leaders, Punjab and Haryana. In fact, the wheat from Madhya Pradesh is of a very high quality and is in demand overseas as well. As an exporter of wheat, India now ranks second in the world.

As these other states made their mark in the production of wheat and rice, many farmers from Punjab, Haryana and western Uttar Pradesh shifted to the cultivation of oil seeds and pulses.

New varieties of cotton and sugarcane were developed and introduced during my tenure as agriculture minister. Maharashtra, Tamil Nadu, Karnataka and Andhra Pradesh became major cotton producing states and we became the second-highest exporter of cotton in the world. In sugar exports too we rank second after Brazil.

During informal talks on the sidelines of FAO meetings, delegates from the developed countries used to say to me, 'You are a dangerous nation. When your domestic production of food grains falls, your massive imports shoot up the prices in international markets. And when you have a surplus production, your large exports make the prices tumble.' Their fear was sparked by fairly high levels of agricultural production in our country. In one particular year, the deficit in India's international trade was completely offset by our agricultural exports. This had never happened earlier.

The breakthroughs we achieved in agriculture helped elevate India's international stature as well. The world stopped looking at our country as one that always sought patronage for waivers and subsidies. In fact, we were able to offer help to other countries. Shortage of food is chronic in many African countries. Since the US was their main supplier, the supplies were often laced with a political agenda. Prime Minister Manmohan Singh called a meeting of all African nations at Vigyan Bhavan in New Delhi to discuss their problem of hunger. At the end of the meet a number of bilateral agreements were signed. India's export of food grains to these countries gave them breathing space. This did a world of good for India's image.

During a visit to Bangladesh, President Pranab Mukherjee assured the hosts of rice exports from India. It made our position a little awkward because the domestic production that year was not high enough to accommodate the additional export requirement. However, since our word was given, we managed to fulfil the export order. Diplomacy and financial aid are the obvious mainstays of international relations. It was established during those ten years—2004-15—that agriculture too could be a major tool in international diplomacy.

Loan waivers are a contentious issue in agriculture. In principle I believe writing off any loan is not the right thing to do. But looking at the Indian situation in the year 2007-2008, several factors convinced me that a different approach was necessary. Nearly 64% of the Indian farmers were found to be in debt and had gone virtually bankrupt. Droughts, excessive rains, sub-standard seeds and delays in supply of fertilisers over the years had hit them badly. The interest on loans taken from private lenders and banks had piled up. The burden of the debt did not allow them to avail fresh institutional credit. This had dampened overall sentiment among agriculturists. The total burden of debt was to the tune of ₹67,000 crore rupees.

After studying the issue from various angles I came to the conclusion that there was no option but to write off the loans. Agriculture was stunted and it could not be revived in the absence of fresh investment. Unless farmers were freed of the burden of debt they would not be able to get fresh institutional credit. My proposal for the loan waiver generated intense debate in the cabinet. P. Chidambaram had strong reservations. As finance minister he was fully justified. Presenting the broad picture I explained in great detail how extricating agriculture from the debt logjam would benefit the overall national economy. Members of the cabinet had generally come to respect my understanding of agriculture by then, so they went by my word. Though Chidambaram was apprehensive, as any finance minister would be, the farmer in him appreciated my point after a thorough discussion and gave his nod.

The proposal was approved. On 29 February 2008, Chidambaram announced the package that included two components: waiving of loans and a one-time settlement for small and medium farmers. Categorical instructions were sent to all public sector banks, rural banks, scheduled commercial banks and authorised lending institutions to ensure that the scheme was implemented by 30 June 2008.

The loan waiver announcement was received with great jubilation by the farming community in the country. There were some murmurs of dissent in uninformed urban areas but that was understandable. More needed to be done now. The rate of interest on fresh loans was an important issue. For five or six years I had been urging for lower interest rates on farm loans and had succeeded in bringing them down from 12% to 4% in stages. After the loan waiver announcement I spoke to the chief ministers of various states requesting them to do something more on the issue of interest rates. Karnataka took the lead. Kerala, Tamil Nadu, Maharashtra, Punjab, Haryana and several other states announced a zero per cent interest rate if farmers repaid loans up to ₹3 lakh in time. This led to a massive capital investment in the farm sector and eventually resulted in a sharp rise in agricultural production.

In order to improve the per-hectare productivity of various crops across the country, the ministry introduced an element of competition among states. A level playing ground was created wherein states were clubbed in accordance with their prevailing levels of production for a particular crop. For instance, Punjab, Haryana and Madhya Pradesh were bracketed in one group for wheat. States lower down in the order were clubbed in another group. The same system was followed for other crops so that all the states in the country could be covered. The awards given ranged from ₹5 crore to ₹10 crore.

The competition prompted all states to pay more attention to the issue. When Chhatisgarh won the top prize in rice productivity, newspapers in that state came out with special supplements for nearly a week to celebrate the achievement. Besides Chief Minister Raman Singh of Chhatisgarh, chief ministers Navin Patnaik of Odisha and Nitish Kumar of Bihar took a personal interest in enhancing agricultural productivity in their respective states. Narendra Modi, as Gujarat chief minister, focused on oil seed production. All of them achieved commendable results. The phenomenal rise in agricultural production received international recognition. India won gold medals from the International Rice Research Institute (IRRI) Centre in Manila for its achievements.

Another important aspect that we addressed during my time as the country's agriculture minister was that of genetically modified (GM) crops. The debate over GM crops remains inconclusive not just in India but all over the world. It needs to be noted that the developed countries make rampant use of GM seeds on their own soil but take a strong position against their use in India. They pour in large funds to support anti-GM campaigns and exert pressure in various ways. Some people in our country are also opposed to GM crops. I chose the line of least resistance by focusing on a non-food item like cotton. A particular kind of larva destroys the cotton bud from within in the blooming stage of the plant. This often poses a major threat to the crop. But in the GM variety, an internal mechanism within the plant kills the larva before it can cause damage. To begin with, we imported GM cotton seeds from the internationally known company Monsanto, and followed that up by quickly developing GM seeds at the Cotton Research Institute in Nagpur. Mahyco, an Indian company, also succeeded in developing GM cotton seeds. As a result imports came down drastically.

This initiative evoked strong criticism in the media. Though some self-styled environmentalists raised hell, farmers in India did not bother. Since the farmers' sole focus was on increased productivity, they went for GM cotton seeds and thus managed to save at least ₹4,000 per acre. The share of GM cotton in domestic production reached almost 94% and India became the second-largest cotton producing country in the world. Adopting a firm posture on the issue, I made an unambiguous statement in the Parliament in favour of GM cotton. That stand neutralised the resistance substantially.

However, the opposition to genetically modified food items continues to be very high in our country. This poses obstacles in conducting experiments in the production of rice.

The opponents of GM technology rushed to the Supreme Court which banned the use of GM seeds for all crops except cotton. The apex court went further by giving an inexplicable ruling which prohibited further research and trials in that area. It summoned officers from the agriculture department to issue a stern warning in this regard. Trial plants developed from GM seeds had to be uprooted; we had to abide by the Supreme Court's verdict. This came as a big blow because research and development work in many other crops was close to a critical stage at the time. Scientists working on GM varieties of oilseeds actually broke down in front of me when they had to simply abandon their work because of the court decision. I honestly believe that India lost a big opportunity to assert itself as a prime agricultural power in the world due to that unfortunate development.

However, we pressed ahead with other research initiatives where there was no dispute. There are 84 agriculture universities in the country. They are staffed by a large number of agriculture scientists and possess large tracts of farm land. Like the 80 research centres of ICAR, these universities too had immense potential for research and development. What they lacked were funds. I impressed upon ICAR to release more funds for them. The universities also started receiving substantial aid from a corpus that had already been set up for their development. Like their counterparts in ICAR centres, scientists from universities were regularly sent overseas to work in research institutes. This boosted their morale.

Many agriculture universities have 100-200 acres of land. We asked them to use the land as demonstration farms and open them up for farmers. Thus farmers learnt about new varieties of crops and different techniques of cultivation. Literature in local languages was made available. Visitors also started buying seeds for new crop varieties from the demonstration farms. It served a dual purpose. The bond between universities and agriculturists strengthened. Second, agriculture universities did not just remain centres for training scientists; they also became 'vocational centres' for farmers in the real sense.

We also broke the old monopoly enjoyed by Agriculture Produce Marketing Committees (APMCs) in order to liberalise agriculture trade. The immediate objective was to rejuvenate the agro-processing sector and diminish the agents' role in the marketing chain. Agro-processing enterprises were thus allowed to bypass APMCs and buy raw material directly from farmers. This became a win-win situation for both. Besides getting authentic guidance from agro-processing units regarding cultivation practices, farmers also received higher and assured prices for their produce from those units. This encouraged contract farming and ensured a supply of adequate quantities of raw material to the processing units. Farmers' response to the liberalisation process has been overwhelming.

The National Advisory Council (NAC) was mandated to help or guide the UPA government on policy matters, and it had views on many issues of governance. There was some merit in the criticism that it often worked as an extra-constitutional authority undermining the Union Cabinet. However, the hallowed body kept my department at an arm's distance. If I differed with it on any issue relating to my departments my opinion was taken as the final word without much ado.

Unfortunately, this was not the case with portfolios under Congress ministers. There were occasions when even Manmohan Singh and P. Chidambaram differed with the NAC because they felt that its stand did not make sound economic sense. But if Congress ministers got a message that a particular decision had to be made because it had the NAC head Sonia Gandhi's backing, they fell in line without much discussion.

I had an intense tussle with the NAC on provisions under the Food Security Bill in the year 2013. Our differences occupied a lot of media space in the latter half of UPA-II. Though I concurred with the NAC in principle on supporting the needy, I was not in favour of the blanket distribution of food grains at absurdly low prices that it insisted upon. I argued that offering food grains at such low prices would rob the measure of its social value. I also argued that the heavily subsidised prices would lead to malpractice. Many undeserving people would buy grains at one to three rupees a kilo and sell them in the black market at a higher price, I pointed out. This was exactly what happened in several instances later.

Earlier, very few fair price shops across the country procured their full monthly quota of grains because many of their registered customers were economically well-off and did not buy grains from these shops. After the food security scheme was introduced, the shops suddenly started procuring the full quota! This obviously meant that the bulk of the procurement was sold off in the black market. Manmohan Singh and Chidambaram also shared my view but the balance finally tilted in the NAC's favour for reasons I have already explained. I had used the word 'jholawallas' to describe the NAC members. This evoked a sharp reaction but I had done that intentionally so that Sonia Gandhi would know the kind of people she had chosen as advisers.

We as a nation are faced with a big challenge pertaining to the judicious and equitable use of water for irrigation. Indian farmers, by and large, feel most comfortable when they see trenches in the field brimming with water. This mindset needs to change. Israel has set an example by discontinuing the practice of irrigating the entire farm land. Farmers in that country use drip irrigation techniques to provide water only to the roots of plants. This not only avoids wastage of water but also protects soil texture from the ill effects of flood irrigation. We shall have to emulate this practice, failing which skirmishes over water supply will escalate in various parts of our country.

During my tenure as agriculture minister we introduced the Rainfed Mission. Karnataka and Andhra Pradesh were among the first few states to benefit from the initiative.

The food supply chain in our country, running from the farmer to the end consumer, requires substantive intervention by the government. Nearly 30% of agricultural produce in India suffers damage during transit. This accounts for a loss of about ₹40,000 crore. In developed countries this wastage does not exceed 3% to 5%. The solution lies in building a string of cold-storage facilities along the route. The charge of the agro-processing industry was given to me in the last year of my tenure. I got cold storages included in the priority list of credit supply, spoke to heads of banks and ensured extension of loan for the building of cold storages at 3% interest rate. I wish the charge of the agro-processing department had come to me earlier. A lot more could have been accomplished.

In the last official meeting of UPA-II a resolution complimenting the government for its various achievements was passed. The agriculture ministry finds a special mention in the resolution. When my friends from the Congress talk about the UPA's performance they too mostly speak of how well the agriculture ministry performed. Although they scrupulously avoid taking my name I am happy that President Pranab Mukherjee and former Prime Minister Manmohan Singh have always been liberal with praise, wherever it is due.

TWENTY-THREE

Groups of Ministers

PRIME MINISTER MANMOHAN SINGH adopted the system of Groups of Ministers (GoMs) and Empowered Groups of Ministers (EGoMs) to handle several important issues which had the potential for long-term impact on the country. There were more than 50 such groups working at different points in time during the ten years of UPA-I and UPA-II. The system worked very well when there were sharp differences within the cabinet on a particular issue or when a subject demanded in-depth, dispassionate thinking.

In the cabinet system of government that we have adopted from the British, some differences on policy issues crop up from time to time. The minister in charge of the relevant portfolio is expected to answer the members' queries. He or she may also invite the secretary of the department to provide additional inputs when required. Even after all this, serious differences often persist. Under such circumstances Manmohan Singh recommended that the issue should be entrusted to a GoM. The chairperson and members of the GoM were then appointed through a government notification. The GoMs would meet any number of times with a view to arriving at a cogent, well though-out policy on the issue at hand. It would also involve the bureaucracy in discussions, which did not happen in the cabinet system of decision making. The recommendations of the GoMs would then come up before the cabinet for final ratification. Because of the elaborate process that had already been undergone, the cabinet would generally give its nod to the GoM draft without much discussion.

On certain issues it was thought necessary to consult not just the bureaucracy but also experts and other stakeholders outside the government. Such issues were handed over to EGoMs. Since the latter were not straitjacketed, decisions made in this manner had a lot of depth. The process was more mature, broad-based, realistic and transparent. It certainly enhanced the quality of governance. Pranab Mukherjee and I headed most of the GoMs and EGoMs during UPA-I and UPA-II. P. Chidambaram also chaired a number of these groups.

One of the most important GoMs under my chairmanship was the one mandated to formulate India's pharmaceutical policy. Not many people are aware that Indian pharma companies have a significant presence in the international market. Our companies are major suppliers of generic medicines in the United States, Russia, South Asia, Brazil and Africa. The committee under me decided to give a boost to this sector by promoting liberalisation, attracting investments and encouraging research activity. Three stakeholders had to be factored in. Vocal, aggressive non-government organisations (NGOs) which focused solely on low pricing of medicines was one group. These NGOs occupied a lot of space and time in the print and electronic media. The second stakeholders were those who sought to protect the interests of manufacturers. The least visible was the third group which comprised researchers.

The importance of improving the availability of medicines and keeping their prices within reasonable limits certainly could not be denied. But there were other related issues too. Supporting research activity in this field was critical. The average time span between the commencement of research and launching the final product in the market was about seven to eight years. The process was cumbersome because various tests had to be conducted at different stages in order to ensure that the final product was safe for human consumption.

Obviously, this entailed huge costs which needed to be loaded on the market prices of products. Keeping the long-term interests of the sector in mind this was a correct approach. But some

NGOs were simply not prepared to accept the reality. Since the NGOs' stand was a populist one, taking a firm decision was a tough call for the government.

It is thanks to Manmohan Singh, who had faith in my ability to take unpopular but sensible decisions, that he made it a practice to pass on all such tricky issues to a GoM under me. This suited my friends in the Congress for a different reason. If the decision displeased people and invited criticism in the media, they could easily wash their hands off the decision. The refrain would be: 'We too don't subscribe to the decision but we are helpless because it is taken by a partner in our coalition.' Ignoring these irritants, our GoM took firm decisions because we believed they were in the long-term interest of the domestic pharma sector.

The results of our decisions can be seen in the expansion of some of our pharma companies in recent years. Jawaharlal Nehru had recognised the need for laying the foundation of this sector years ago. The trigger was Kasturba Gandhi's death. When Nehru visited Aga Khan Palace in Pune to pay his last tributes, he was told that Kasturba could not get the required medicines in time. He then set up a number of factories, the Hindustan Antibiotics Limited at Pimpri, near Pune being one of them. All these companies were, of course, in the public sector. When the government of India opened the domestic market to foreign manufacturers these public sector companies declined. For long, Indian markets continued to be dominated by overseas companies. Those from Switzerland had the largest share. Our GoM decided to re-structure the policy in a way that would enable Indian manufacturers to compete with their foreign counterparts in a fair manner. We did not make any monetary concessions but ensured that there would be no unwarranted obstacles in the expansion plans of Indian companies. This spawned a number of success stories.

Two and a half decades ago, Sun Pharma was a small manufacturing company. It now boasts manufacturing units in

16 countries, including the US, Russia, Pakistan, Bangladesh, Brazil, Australia and China. Dilip Shanghvi, its founder, is currently counted among the richest people in India. Emcure Pharmaceuticals is yet another company that spread its wings impressively in developing, producing and marketing its products internationally.

At present, India is the second-largest manufacturer of medicines in the world. Within the country Gujarat tops the list among manufacturers. Maharashtra is at number two.

TWENTY-FOUR

Looking Ahead

POLITICS AND GOVERNANCE

Democracy and multi-ethnicity are India's two qualities that I find fascinating. Ours is a subcontinent of unparalleled diversity. We as a people have shown remarkable resilience in the face of many upheavals—social, political—over the last 65 years. That should be a matter of pride for every Indian and this, I think, augurs well for the country's future.

Today, the BJP enjoys a clear majority in the Lok Sabha. This has happened after years of fragile coalition politics and has on the one hand generated the hope of a stable regime and on the other, triggered fear of authoritarian rule. To understand why I am saying this we will have to go back in time for a quick recap of the past.

Thanks to its pre-1947 legacy, the Congress party accommodated and nurtured different streams of thought for years and, as a result, faced no major political hurdle till 1967 when Dr Ram Manohar Lohiya and Choudhary Charan Singh mobilised forces under the Samyukta Vidhayak Dal (SVD). The banner came as an alternative to the Congress chiefly in the Hindi belt—UP, MP and Bihar.

The SVD experiment proved to be unstable and a resurgent Congress, buoyed by victory in the Bangladesh war of 1971, re-established its national supremacy. This was followed by the Emergency when the Congress digressed from the path of democracy and was subsequently rejected by India in 1977. The Janata Party rule that followed was as shortlived as the SVD, and facilitated the Congress's return to power.

For the next two decades, the country witnessed smooth power transitions, with the Congress and other parties switching places in rotation.

Unlike all the earlier coalitions, the NDA under Atal Bihari Vajpayee could complete its full term from 1999 to 2004 only because of Vajpayee's towering personality and accommodative style of functioning. In many ways he was a 'Congressman' in the BJP. Following the UPA's ten-year rule, of which I have spoken earlier, we now have the BJP and its allies in power, with Narendra Modi as the prime minister. The most striking feature of the Narendra Modi regime is that for the first time in the BJP's history, the entire parliamentary party transcended the RSS straitjacket to stand firmly behind one man. Just as Congressmen used to say of Indira Gandhi, many present-day BJP member of Parliaments admit openly, 'We are here because of Modi.' This was not the case even when Vajpayee was at the helm.

Modi's style of functioning has caused many worries. Ruling with an iron hand in a single state like Gujarat is one thing, but the same technique cannot be replayed for a long time when you are running the country. Political power has a tendency to concentrate in a few hands and once that happens, it does not take much time to become corrupt. Nor does it last long, as world history has shown us time and again.

Today, the BJP and the Congress are the only two parties that enjoy a pan-Indian presence and both seem to be suffering from what is being called by commentators 'personality cult politics'. It is not a healthy sign that the BJP should hold on to Modi's designer kurtas, while the Congress politics revolves only around Rahul Gandhi.

As things look at present, it will be an uphill task for the Congress to stand up as a formidable alternative to the BJP at the national level. To be able to turn the tide, the Congress has no option other than to take smaller and regional parties along. But for that to happen, it will have to create confidence among its prospective allies that it would run the coalition in the same spirit that Vajpayee showed. Manmohan Singh did exhibit this ability during the UPA's ten-year-long rule. However, let's not forget that the Congress of today is a lot weaker than it was in the UPA era.

The BJP's popularity graph, which peaked in 2014, has begun to come down. Unless it takes quick corrective measures, the party will find it difficult to retain power for long. The setback that the BJP suffered in the Bihar assembly elections of October–November 2015 has underscored this fact. There is no denying the fact that the BJP's mainstay is the large number of dedicated, hard-working people in the RSS-BJP parivaar. But, it must also be noted that the BJP could expand its reach only when it showed willingness to be flexible about Hindutva, its core ideology.

The rapid rise of the Indian middle class over the last two decades is another factor that has worked in the BJP's favour. As people from the lower strata of society graduated into the middle class, their resistance to BJP ideology faded. Yet, even this constituency may be lost. The Indian middle class now takes certain freedoms for granted, but the BJP has still not been able to project itself as a liberal outfit with a pluralistic outlook and inclusive agenda.

At the other end of the spectrum are the Communists who refuse to have a re-look at their ideological moorings despite a changed world. Consequently, they have been reduced to rapidly shrinking pockets. After losing power in West Bengal and Kerala, they are holding on to it only in Tripura at present.

More than 20 years have passed since the Communist regime in the erstwhile Soviet Union collapsed. Chinese Communism has modified itself to align with liberalisation and the market economy. Though the Communist party in that country continues to maintain a tight hold on all affairs, it has definitely moved away from its traditional economic policies. The Communists in India discard the Chinese model, calling it unsustainable. The evidence of the success of this model points to the contrary, notwithstanding the hiccups along the way. Communism did hold a lot of attraction among the Indian youth when I was barely out of my teens. That glamour is fast eroding. The Gen Next is enamoured of democratic values and a liberal economy, and they do not think Communism will lead them to a better life.

Since the Indian comrades are unwilling to acknowledge this fact, I am afraid they won't be able to retain their status as pressure groups in the coming years. On the social front, the Communists are known and respected for their progressive outlook. It is sad that the reduction in the Indian Communists' political strength owing to their out-of-sync economic stand has also reduced their say in the social sector.

Most regional parties in India have come a long way since their inception. Though they still talk of regional identities, their politics actually revolve around individual leaders rather than an ideological pivot. J. Jayalalitha of the AIADMK in Tamil Nadu and Chandrababu Naidu of the Telugu Desam Party in Andhra Pradesh are examples of how a leader with mass appeal and proven administrative skill can achieve success in elections. Since people at large now accord more importance to the rulers yielding material results than anything else, ideological issues have taken a back seat.

Even a party like the Akali Dal in Punjab, which has a distinct religious identity, seems to have read the writing on the wall. In Bihar, the Janata Dal-United—JD(U)—of Nitish Kumar did make a shift from identity politics to the politics of development. However, in Bihar and Uttar Pradesh, issues related to social change still hold popular appeal. As I see it, regional parties in different parts of the country will continue to hold their ground even while they seek to align with the national mainstream. The 2015 Bihar elections, in which Nitish Kumar's (JD)U and Lalu Prasad Yadav's RJD came together to defeat the BJP, were a good illustration of this. Vajpayee showed that it is possible to balance national needs with regional aspirations. That model ought to be emulated in the future.

As the voters have come to expect 'result-oriented' politics from all parties, political dynasties everywhere now have short 'expiry dates'. There is no denying that leaders belonging to 'political families' have an initial advantage over others in their respective parties, but they too have to deliver on their promises, failing which the voters do not think twice before voting them out of power. Chandrababu Naidu, for instance, was known as N.T. Rama Rao's son-in-law when he entered politics. However, he has survived and grown because of his work, and his current standing in state and national politics is entirely of his own making.

All political parties, whether national or regional, have started feeling the pressure to deliver 'material results' to their electorate. Most people still go to leaders to get their individual problems resolved. But citizens in general now expect overall economic development without caring too much about political ideologies. This in turn has driven home the need to create some kind of mechanism for the capacity building of the political class in our country. Development issues have become complex in the wake of liberalisation and globalisation, while socio-economic disparities are leading to conflicting expectations and though advancements in technology have come as a big boon, the need for politicians to enhance their understanding of various subjects has become far more acute than earlier.

Most political parties have stopped grooming their workers the way they should. There are only a handful of exceptions. The Communist parties lay special emphasis on training their workers in their own way. The RSS-BJP, at the other end of the political spectrum, has set up an institute called Rambhau Mhalgi Prabodhini (RMP) near Mumbai which is engaged in research and training its cadres. I notice that BJP members of Parliament and members of the Modi government also make use of RMP as a valuable resource base. Such attempts, however, are few and inadequate in our political arena.

I know of an institute in South Korea that has been engaged for several years in the training of Korean politicians and bureaucrats. The institute educates them on a wide range of subjects that include the Constitution of South Korea, its political system, problems of poverty and unemployment and efforts being made across the world to resolve them, customisation of those models to suit Korean requirements, and so forth. Because the Korean political class and bureaucrats pass under the portals of this institute, they tackle various issues on the basis of a common understanding. This makes decision-making faster and implementation smoother. As is evident, the high-quality work culture has percolated to their private sector too. The training institute is owned by the government but is run on an autonomous basis and its head enjoys a status almost at par with that of the prime minister.

If we want to attempt something similar in India, we shall obviously have to structure it to suit our democratic system. Teaching governance is easier but tackling varying ideologies under a common programme is another matter. Therefore we will need to accommodate the ideological aspect in the efforts for capacity building of our politicians and bureaucrats. Some people talk of the need to have a 'guided democracy' in India in order to speed up our development process. That is neither desirable nor workable. Guided democracy entails restricting people's fundamental rights which in turn may lead to excesses as we witnessed during Emergency. A better way is to inculcate a high sense of responsibility among people across the board. Many private sector companies in India have been successfully implementing multilateral leadership programmes. We must take a cue from this and encourage the public sector to emulate them. In due course of time, I am sure, the efforts will yield the desired results.

There are a few things that call for our immediate attention in the meantime. With the government withdrawing from several areas of economic activity, the private sector has started playing a bigger role in India. This has brought in new dimensions to the responsibilities vested in the political leadership and the bureaucracy. While they are required to handle all public private partnership (PPP) projects on the basis of a common understanding, the need for efficiency and transparency in the process has grown multi-fold. Such transactions are prone to wrongdoings as is evident from the Louise Berger projects in Goa. This makes people suspicious of all PPP projects and that is an unfortunate thing from a long-term perspective. When baseless allegations of corruption are levelled either out of ignorance or for political reasons, decision makers in the government and the involved private parties lose heart to carry on.

The Enron Corporation withdrew from its power generation project in Maharashtra after wild allegations were made in 1993. Consequently, precious years were lost before the government stepped in with additional investment to produce electricity and that too at a much higher rate than what Enron had offered. Such occurrences ought to be avoided.

Another issue that troubles many public projects is that of engaging consultants. Most projects involve complex technologies and economics. Decisions in such cases cannot be left to bureaucrats, political leaders or even the people at large who lack the necessary know-how. Domain expertise is absolutely critical for making the right decisions and therefore the tendency to bow to unjustified 'public pressure' needs to be curtailed in such cases. Having said that, one must also not ignore the fact that many so-called experts have their own hidden agenda when they offer consultancy. Only a well-informed and alert administration and political executive can steer clear of such hidden agendas.

We have failed to develop a political culture that should take important economic issues beyond petty political considerations. Since all political parties have now come to taking turns on the treasury benches and in the opposition, we need to work on this in all seriousness. The political tussle between the BJP and the

Congress on the General Sales Tax Bill and the Insurance Bill in recent months was an example of economic sense becoming a casualty at the altar of political exigencies. The BJP put up a strong resistance when the UPA tried to push those bills. When the sides switched after the 2014 elections, the Congress stalled the parliament proceedings to prevent the BJP from introducing the same reforms. Both acts were irresponsible and must be avoided in future.

The judiciary invariably plays a prominent role when the political class paralyses the decision-making process or when the executive arm of the government is weak. In either scenario, affected people are left with no other recourse but to approach the courts. The judiciary was decidedly proactive during some parts of P.V. Narasimha Rao's tenure as prime minister, and later during the UPA rule when Manmohan Singh was at the helm. Such a thing did not happen when a strong leader like Indira Gandhi headed the government. One may recall how upset Lok Sabha Speaker Somnath Chatterjee was at one point during UPA-I due to the perceived encroachment by the judiciary on the rights of the Parliament. But as I said, it would be wrong to blame the judiciary alone in such matters.

The media, the fourth pillar of democracy, has assumed immense clout of late. Every time complaints of sensationalism or distortion increase against television channels and newspapers, some people talk about imposing restrictions on the media. I do not approve of it because it is neither desirable nor practical. No media outlet can afford to compromise on its credibility. It is due to advanced technology, big private investments and easy availability of communication gadgets that the media have pervaded people's lives at present. It is also true that certain media outlets lose their balance on occasions under the influence of their investors or due to market competition. But with the passage of time, I am sure, things will cool down, aberrations will reduce and the media will focus better on preserving its credibility and prestige in the public eye.

AGRICULTURE

I do not have the slightest doubt about India's potential to become the world's food basket. What stands in the way of realising that potential is the absence of a comprehensive approach. Keeping the larger picture in mind, I initiated several measures in this direction during my ten-year tenure as agriculture minister at the Centre and we achieved much during the period, but the effort needs to be carried forward with determination.

The 'comprehensive approach' demands synergy across available agricultural land and irrigation water in our country, farm technology, processing of agricultural produce and marketing of the finished goods. These elements directly influence the national economy besides elevating the living standard of farmers, making agriculture sustainable.

We as a nation shall have to reduce the burden of manpower on our agriculture. I was severely criticised for saying this earlier. 'How can the union agriculture minister ask members of the farmer community to take up other professions?' some people asked. The critics never bothered to understand why I said so. I continue to stand by the statement and would like to explain it here. At the time of Independence, 80% of the Indian population was dependent on agriculture. It has now come down to around 60%. But while the population has grown five-fold since Independence, the total land mass has remained static. Thus the number of dependents on agriculture actually increased in real numbers. Now consider it at the micro level. The average per capita land holding in our country had always been low when compared to the developed world. In a typical family with multiple offspring, it kept sliding with successive generations to reach a point where agriculture became totally unviable due to the abysmally small size of the cultivable land in each farmer's possession.

The problem has been aggravated with growing urbanisation

which necessitated big portions of land being acquired for developing infrastructure such as housing complexes, industrial estates, roads, dams, ports, airports, bridges and so on. Take the case of Palam airport. Surrounded by farm land some years ago, it is now a part of Delhi's urban landscape. What stands as a busy metropolis called Navi Mumbai today was nothing but acres of paddy fields. The Jawaharlal Nehru Port Trust and the Rashtriya Chemical Fertiliser factory at Thal Vaishet in Raigad district of Maharashtra transformed the very face of the neighbourhood.

One finds the same phenomenon spreading across India. It only underscores the point that shrinking agricultural land will not be able to support an increased number of agriculturists.

It may sound a little far-fetched but the real solution to the problem lies in convincing farmers to send their children for higher education. For example, if two or three out of four children in a typical farmer family go for higher education and enter different vocations, the financial status of the entire family improves and farming also becomes sustainable. This phenomenon must be scaled up. Countries like Bangladesh or Sri Lanka where the proportion of dependents on agriculture is still around 75-80% are languishing at the bottom, while Japan, Canada, Australia and the US (the per capita land holding in the last two countries is exceptionally high) and other affluent countries around the world have barely 4-12% of the population dependent on agriculture.

Some states like Assam, Bengal, Bihar, and Odisha are rich in water resources when compared to Karnataka, Maharashtra, Gujarat, Telangana and Andhra Pradesh. This is a challenge as well as an opportunity for the planners. Rational crop planning at the macro level and educating individual farmers in improved farm practices will yield the desired results. In a democratic set-up like ours, farmers cannot obviously be compelled to go for specific crops. But the farmers are aware of market requirements. So it would be prudent to allow market forces to influence the farmers' choice of crops. Farmers also have a deep understanding of the agro-climatic conditions of their respective regions and make their decisions accordingly. Thus high-rainfall states opt for paddy cultivation just as Punjab prefers wheat out of choice. It is only where water is in short supply or the soil is not conducive to growing conventional crops that cultivators take the risk of attempting new crops.

The more than 80 agriculture universities and other research institutes in our country are engaged in research on farm practices and new varieties of crops. The average age of scientists working in these institutes is between 35 and 45 years. In the years to come, this young force will be a very big asset for the agriculture sector.

Let me give you an example. The Vasantdada Sugar Institute (VSI) near Pune, of which I am the chairman, has been doing excellent work on sugarcane for several years. The scientists there are currently developing a particular variety of the crop wherein short sugarcane stems would be grown in a greenhouse for three months before the onset of the monsoon and then taken to open fields for further growth. The research will shortly reach the stage of field trials. If the experiment succeeds, it will curtail water usage for sugarcane by at least 30%. Since the sugar sector is an important element of India's rural life in a variety of ways, the success of the VSI experiment will also benefit the national economy.

Increasing the per-acre productivity of agricultural produce is going to acquire immense importance. Therefore, blanket opposition to the introduction of new varieties of crops does not make sense. The present agriculture minister has spoken strongly for preserving traditional crop varieties. While there is no dispute about that, it must not translate automatically into resistance to genetic upgradation of crops. I have discussed the issue of GM crops in the chapter 'At Home in Agriculture', so let me just point out one interesting thing in this regard. Opposition to GM crops in India often receives direct or tacit support from countries where GM products have been consumed for many years. We import edible oil worth ₹60,000 crore rupees from the US, Argentina and Brazil. It is GM-based. Many corn varieties consumed in our country are also GM-based. One must understand that no GM crop is permitted to be introduced in our country unless it has passed through rigorous seven-year trials and is certified as 'safe'. If every possible care is taken before a particular GM breed is allowed, I do not see any point in opposing it. Let it be noted that China, which faces the same kind of population pressure as we do, has not banned GM products. It is high time we re-visited our stand on the issue.

Traditional crop varieties and organically grown crops are certainly important and they should have their rightful place in the market. But they will not be able to feed our billion-plus population as their productivity per acre is low. Secondly, they are unaffordable for a large number of people. Hence the ideal thing to do would be to make available both traditional/organic products and their hybrid/GM varieties and leave the choice to the consumers. This is important also because of the changing food habits in our society. The consumption of cereals, pulses, vegetable and fruits has grown multifold and therefore the pressure on production has also gone up.

Our performance in fishery is not commensurate with the long coastline that we are blessed with. Most of what we produce is consumed domestically. This also explains why 55% of our gross national fishery production is from inland water sources and only 45% is from the sea. But this sector is important because a large number of women are actively involved in this field. While the men folk go out for actual fishing, women handle other operations like processing and marketing. In an otherwise male-dominated society, this is a welcome sign of women empowerment.

A year ago, India was the world's largest producer of rice and was number two in the production of wheat. If we consider the fact that people in many countries across the world are moving away from agriculture, then we stand an excellent chance to become a major player in this field. For that to happen we shall have to focus much more on enhancing the quality of agricultural produce and making farming remunerative. This can only be done through a substantial infusion of agriculture credit. It was to the tune of ₹80,000 crore in my last year as agriculture minister and needs to be increased further.

Agriculture insurance also calls for reforms. At present, insurance facility is available on only certain crops and for villages or clusters as a whole. If individuals are allowed to insure their crops, it will serve as a big boost. Prices of agriculture produce are a contentious issue that pitches farmers and urban consumers against each other. This calls for maintaining a delicate balance because even though city dwellers expect low prices, agriculturists would not stay in their profession if it did not assure them a standard of living comparable to their urban counterparts. The government will also have to calibrate its priorities for agriculture and industry. More than 60% of our population is in the agriculture sector and it constitutes a sizeable section of the market for non-agricultural products and services. Low priority to agriculture would directly affect the purchasing power of those consumers. Obviously that in turn would hit the sales of all kinds of commodities.

I do not see corporate farming taking root in our country at least for some more years to come. But contract farming has already come to stay. In states like Punjab, big corporate houses sign contracts with farmers and buy their produce at fixed prices. The farmer is provided seeds, fertilisers and loans, the cost for which is adjusted against the prices offered. This benefits both parties. The decades-old cooperative sugar sector in Maharashtra is another example of contract farming with sugar factories and sugarcane growers as the contracted parties. The biggest hurdle in corporate farming taking root is that farmers in our country are mentally opposed to giving up their land to someone else. They would rather keep it within the family.

Only when farmers start getting more remunerative occupations outside agriculture on a large scale will they agree to sell land to corporate houses.

SOCIAL FABRIC

With more than 50% of the Indian population under the age of 25 at present, we pride ourselves on being a 'young nation' with a potential to compete with the developed nations of the world. By 2020, the average age of citizens in China and Japan, the two Asian giants, will be 37 and 48 respectively while that of Indians will be around 29. That will certainly be a huge 'population dividend', provided we tackle the challenge wisely.

It brings me back to the oft-repeated theme of educating our youth. The onus is on planners who will be required to open up a broad spectrum of career avenues by imparting skills and knowledge to the huge mass of young aspirants. In many countries not all opt for higher studies. After attaining a certain level in education, many boys and girls choose to learn skills required for various vocations instead of enrolling for advanced education. We too shall have to move in that direction but the youth will respond in really big numbers only when there is a significant rise in the earnings and social status of 'skilled' professionals. At present, only a few niche segments like marketing offer financial security and social status to candidates who have not done their post-graduation or more.

The Information Technology (IT) sector has become a big magnet for most young men and women at present. But in my opinion, the current boom will start deflating in another 10 to 20 years, primarily because wealth creation in the IT sector is not based on production of material goods per se. China is making headway in IT but it is also laying emphasis on the production sector. That will make sense for us, too, in the longer run. However, the Chinese model dictates that sections of people should do certain kinds of jobs, which cannot be done in a democratic set-up like ours. We shall therefore have to go for a policy of incentives and penalties in the job market.

Liberalisation of the Indian economy 25 years ago resulted in increased movement of people across different states in our country. In the first 10 to 15 years, it caused social unrest in some pockets where local people thought outsiders were encroaching upon 'their' territory. The tensions between 'sons of the soil' and 'outsiders' spilled into different walks of public life, giving a new dimension to identity politics. I do not expect this phase to last long because the pace of in-migration is now being matched by that of out-migration in most places in India. Secondly, 'sons of the soil' politics becomes counter-productive when the number of in-migrants at a place crosses a certain threshold among the electorate.

Perhaps the most urgent issues of our social life as a nation are, and will continue to be, those of equality and harmony. How prudent is it to persist with the policy of reservation for backward sections of society in the era of globalisation? This question is sometimes raised at different forums with the argument that job reservations tend to affect the efficiency of governance and this becomes a handicap because globalisation does not compromise on quality of service. Well, the effect of reservations on quality of service may be a reality in the initial stage but the situation definitely improves with the passage of time. Let us presume for a moment that doing away with reservations will facilitate better governance. But will it also not cause immense social strife? Will that, in turn, not affect the economic progress of the society as a whole? More importantly, will it not be grossly unjust and unfair in our social milieu?

While I am totally in favour of persisting with caste-based reservations in the job sector, I also feel that reservations should be restricted only to the entry level. Thus, inducting a candidate in service through a caste-based reservation quota is fine, but the quota system should have no place when it comes to giving promotions. All promotions must be given strictly on the basis of merit. This is because there is a feeling among the youth that absence of merit-based promotions will have a dual effect: i) it will definitely affect quality of governance; ii) it will also induce a sense of frustration in the administration.

Caste is a highly sensitive issue in Indian society and therefore a lot depends on how sensible, mature officers behave with their colleagues irrespective of their social backgrounds. I have come across officers of both kinds—those who never miss an opportunity to pass snide remarks against colleagues from 'lower castes', and those who take utmost care to encourage and support their 'lower caste' colleagues. May the tribe of progressive officers increase!

The issue of Hindu-Muslim relations is an equally urgent and sensitive one. The path to improvement of these relations is through education and economic progress. It is long and arduous, but there is no other option. Hardliners on both sides often complicate the problem, but fortunately common people in the two communities listen to the voice of sanity, and education and the possibility of economic progress will only strengthen such maturity.

Ushering socio-religious reform in any community is a slow process which is prone to occasional setbacks and is anything but linear. All efforts in that direction, however well-intentioned, need to be made keeping the sensitivities and problems of the communities in mind.

Hamid Dalwai, founder of the Muslim Satyashodhak Samaj, was a close friend of mine. He died young and in fact spent his last days in my official house, Ramtek, when I was chief minister of Maharashtra. I respected him a lot for his commitment to reform and his courage but I always argued with him against launching a frontal attack on regressive customs in his community. A better way, I felt, was to focus on education and improve the economic conditions of the people.

The percentage of Muslims doing jobs in the public and

private sector is abysmally low. This is not a healthy sign. If the mainstream job market fails to accommodate the youth from the community, they will seek recourse elsewhere. While populist measures, like the ones Mulayam Singh Yadav sometimes takes, must be avoided, there is no denying that members of the Muslim community should get due opportunities in the job market. The late H.N. Bahuguna had taken a proactive but cautious approach in this regard when he was UP chief minister.

At a time when extremist organisations are playing havoc with our social climate, the leadership from all communities will have to step forward and guide society on the path of restraint and progress. If that happens, the present upsurge of extremism will definitely subside. The greater responsibility to safeguard the social fabric, of course, falls on the majority community.

This reminds me of an incident which goes to show how healthy the religious sentiments were among the common Hindu and Muslim people in our country till some years ago. There was this person called Aman Momin who hailed from Kolhapur in South Maharashtra, working in the United Nations office in New York. Despite being in the US for many years, he had retained his heavy Kolhapur accent when he spoke Marathi. Whenever I visited the UN office he would regale me with hilarious anecdotes from the past. Here is one of his narrations in his own words:

> After completing school education in Kolhapur, I went to a college in Pune and graduated in Arts. Since I was the first graduate from the Muslim community in town, my parents asked me to distribute sweets. Rasul Khan was a prominent community leader who owned a bicycle shop in the neighbourhood. As I offered him sweets, he asked, 'Kya seekha?' (What did you study?)
>
> 'Chacha, maine BA pass kiya'. (Uncle, I did BA.)
>
> 'Bahot achha. Lekin matric jarur hona. Samjhe?' (Very good. But you must also do your matriculation. Is that clear?)
>
> Rasul Khan's innocence was manifest again a few years later.

> After my graduation I took a job in Mumbai and stayed at a place on Mohammed Ali Road. During those years, I came in contact with Muslim League activists from the neighbourhood and decided to set up a branch of the party on my return to Kolhapur.
>
> I called a meeting of my community members in Kolhapur to share my intention with them. There was no dissenting voice. How could there be? I was not only the most educated among them but also one who had spent some years in a big city like Mumbai in a high-paying job. Obviously I was a very 'wise man'! Whatever I said was accepted as gospel truth. Of course, nobody understood a thing about politics and everybody was clueless about what Muslim League meant. They said in a chorus—'League nikaalnaa hai? Nikaalenge. Usmein kya badi baat hai?' (You want us to set up a League? We will set it up. What is so difficult about it?)
>
> Rasul chacha intervened. 'It is a tradition in Kolhapur to offer prayers to Goddess Ambabai before starting anything new. We must go to the Ambabai temple before starting the League.' Everyone agreed. We promptly took a procession out to the temple so that a Muslim party could do well. After offering prayers to Ambabai, the procession started on its way back.
>
> Rasul chacha was happy but he had a genuine doubt. He took me aside and asked, 'Beta, tu bola League nikaalna hai. Lekin udhar Rajarampuri mein ek Shivlinga hai na. To aur ek League ki kya jaroorat hai?' (Son, you said you want us to set up a League. But there is already one Shivlinga in Rajarampuri locality. Why do we need another League?') Poor chacha did not know that League was not linga though the two words sounded a bit similar!!

How I wish that simplicity and innocence return.

Today, we live in troubling times. We seem to be waging a war of attrition against our minorities. Consider the ban on beef. Maharashtra has had a ban on cow slaughter since 1976 when the Maharashtra Animal Preservation Act was passed. But to extend this to all bovine species is to attack the most

Being sworn in by President R. Venkatraman as Union defence minister in 1991.

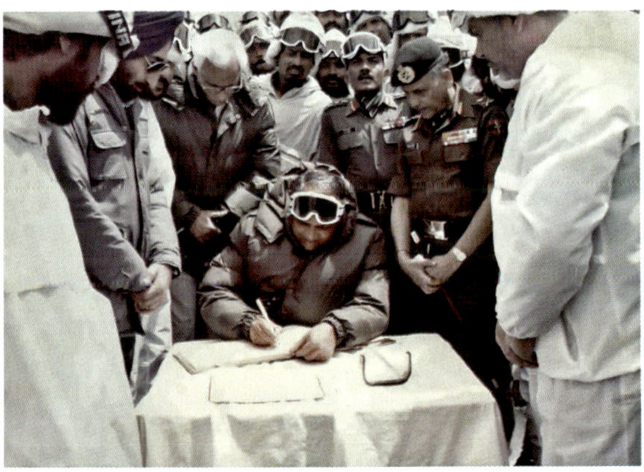

As defence minister (1992-93) at the Siachen glacier with defence secretary N.N. Vora (above) and soldiers of the Indian Army stationed there (below). I was the first defence minister to visit Siachen.

On a visit to the southernmost part of the country, Indira Point, in Andaman Nicobar, as Union defence minister (1992-93). I was accompanied by the then navy chief Admiral Ramdas (second from right).

Left: As Union defence minister at Bombay High, participating in a naval exercise.

Above: With my wife Pratibha, dedicating a ship to the nation.

With the US defence secretary Dick Cheney in Washington DC, 1992.

With Dr. A.P.J. Abdul Kalam. Our long association started in 1991 when I was the defence minister and Dr. Kalam was defence advisor to the government of India.

With China's defence minister Quinn Jewai in Bejing, 1992-93.

In Killari in September 1993 during my ten-day stay there after the devastating Latur earthquake.

With Sonia Gandhi.

The meeting at Shanmukhanand Hall, Mumbai in 1999 where the founding of the Nationalist Congress Party (NCP) was announced. In the picture with me are Chhagan Bhujbal, Tariq Anwar and several other colleagues.

Hosting Bill Clinton for breakfast at my Mumbai residence, 2000.

Sharing a light moment with the renowned Marathi writer P.L. Deshpande.

With sitar maestro Pandit Ravi Shankar in New Delhi, 1992.

With the CEO of Intel, Craig Barrett, and his wife, Barbara, during their visit to Baramati in November 2006 to review the education joint venture between Vidya Pratishthan College and Intel.

Receiving a doctorate at the Lawrence Technology University Michigan; 18 May 2008

At the swearing-in ceremony of the UPA-2 government, 22 May 2009. I am with Pranab Mukherji, Manmohan Singh, Sushil Kumar Shinde, Ghulam Nabi Azad, Kapil Sibbal and Murli Deora.

With P. Chidambaram and Farooq Abdullah.

Receiving the Best Parliamentarian Award from President Pratibha Patil in 2007 in the centr hall of Parliament. Also in the picture are (L to R) Prime Minister Manmohan Singh, Vic President M. Hamid Ansari and Speaker of the Lok Sabha Somnath Chatterje

With Hillary Clinton at the Indian Council of Agricultural Research, Pusa; July 2009.

With US President Barack Obama in New Delhi during his first visit to India in 2010.

Being sworn in as Union minister for agriculture by President Pratibha Patil;
22 May 2009

On a visit to Mizoram when I was minister for agriculture in the Manmohan Singh government. I am accompanied by the Mizoram CM Lal Thanhawla.

With Prime Minister Sheikh Hasina of Bangladesh in Dhaka during an official visit as India's minister for agriculture, 2009.

Praful Patel, Sonia Gandhi and I at a rally in Bhandara district during the 2014 Lok Sabha elections.

At the Samata Melawa—NCP rally for social justice; Mumbai, 10 June 2011.

With President Pranab Mukherji during his visit to Baramati to inaugurate a new college building of Vidya Pratishthan; 19 January 2014.

On my grandson Vijay's 13th birthday in January 2015, with my granddaughter Revati, wife Pratibha, daughter Supriya, grandson Vijay and son-in-law Sadanand.

The entire family gets together for Diwali in Baramati. It is a tradition we follow religiously every year.

affordable protein sources of two communities: the Dalit and the Muslim.

If we look at the history of which foodstuffs have found subsidies in our country, we will find there is no protein source on the list. We have subsidised carbohydrates in the form of rice and wheat; we have oils in the form of cooking oil of one sort or the other; we have sugar and kerosene. But even pulses have never been on the Public Distribution Services (PDS) list. This has meant that the price of dal and lentils has never been protected, and the farmer is almost inevitably paid more for wheat or rice. Now let me add one more layer to this. Dal takes six months to grow. Rice or wheat takes four months. When a farmer can sow and reap three crops a year and be paid more for each one of them, why would she or he plant two for which there is no governmental price support? No wonder demand outstrips supply and the result is the inhuman price of ₹200 per kilo that our poor are now expected to pay for dal. With the end of buffalo meat, what will the poor eat as protein?

This is worrying, but what is even more frightening is the way in which anyone seems to be empowered these days to take the law into their own hands and punish what may not even be cow slaughter. In many other ways, too, if you belong to a minority community, you are marked. This threatens the very fabric of our nation. The idea of India as an inclusive state was not just the Congress view. There was no doubt in the minds of the majority of our nation's founding fathers that we were a mosaic and our diversity was never to be threatened. It is imperative that we ensure it never is.

INDIA IN THE WORLD

In the chapter 'At Home in Agriculture', I have talked about the potential of our agriculture sector not only to become a major player in the international market but also to promote our diplomatic interests. BRICS is an excellent platform where India can meaningfully engage with Brazil, Russia, China and South Africa in two areas—the exchange of technology and the exchange of scientists. During my term as agriculture minister, India entered into bilateral and multilateral agreements with the member countries of BRICS and there is enough scope to take the thread forward. Since all the member countries of BRICS have long coast lines, we must also explore the possibility of developing our fishery sector with their collaboration.

I am happy that Prime Minister Narendra Modi is making concerted efforts to reach out to several countries across the world, including the BRICS members. However, I must also point out that some of his domestic actions were not in tune with those efforts. His absence at the President's Iftaar party for two consecutive years since coming to power sent out a wrong signal across the border. He would do well to remember what Atal Bihari Vajpayee had said: 'One can choose one's friends, not one's neighbours.' Shahryar Khan, the former foreign minister of Pakistan, is a good friend of mine. 'We had no issues with Vajpayee or Manmohan Singh, but we can't understand Modi,' he told me once. I believe there is room for improvement here. The importance of sending the right signals to and engaging meaningfully with Pakistan and other neighbouring countries cannot be overstated.

The prime minister must also be more careful while making statements about domestic issues when he is on foreign soil. Some of his recent speeches in foreign countries smacked of indiscretion and were rightly criticised in India. Modi would do well to remember that he represents the entire nation and not a particular political party when he is abroad.

International sanctions against Iran have been lifted following the US-Iran nuclear deal. This has created an opening for India to enhance its trade with Iran. There exists a lot of potential to export wheat and industrial products to that country. There is also considerable scope for Indian construction companies and corporates to do business in the region. India's proximity to Iran and Saudi Arabia will obviously make Israel uncomfortable. But if these ties are going to benefit us we must ignore Israel, should it make any noise.

The African continent offers immense scope for India to acquire land on long lease and practise agriculture there. In fact, Englishmen have been growing coffee in several African countries for many decades, and Chinese companies have invested heavily in land in many parts of Africa. But the government of India took a policy decision during the UPA regime not to acquire land in any foreign country for commercial reasons. Manmohan Singh had a point when he explained, 'Nobody really likes to part with one's land to anyone else. If we acquire farm land in African countries, it will benefit them monetarily. But their feeling of happiness will definitely make way for unhappiness, if not anger, when, after some years, they find us growing rich by exploiting their land. It will spoil our relations forever. Just as Indians feel exploited by the British, the Africans will feel exploited by us.'

Land for cultivation is also available in Argentina and some countries in South America, but for the reasons explained above, we are not looking in that direction. However, some Indian agriculturists, primarily from the Sikh community, have acquired farm land in those countries in their individual capacity. This trend among private individuals is a positive one and will continue.

TWENTY-FIVE

People

I HAVE REFERRED THROUGHOUT this book to people whom I have interacted with closely over the years. However, some personalities deserve special mention and I will talk briefly about them in this chapter.

Y.B. CHAVAN

I am often described as the 'protégé' of Yashwantraoji Chavan and I must say that I am proud of the epithet. I have always been a Congressman at heart and the major credit for this should go to Yashwantrao Balwantrao Chavan. Y.B. Chavan was a true and dedicated Congressman who paid the price for his convictions when the party drifted from its ideals.

I was a student in Pune's BMM College when Maharashtra was carved out of the erstwhile bilingual state of Bombay (as it was then known) and Chavansaheb was the separate Marathi state's first chief minister. The birth of Maharashtra had followed a long and spirited mass movement spearheaded by the Samyukta Maharashtra Samiti with stalwarts such as Acharya Atre, S.A. Dange and S.M. Joshi who later fired many salvos at the new chief minister. Chavansaheb faced the adversity with grace and restraint.

Those were difficult days for the Congress Party and for Chavansaheb too. He was walking, as it were, on a razor's edge, trying to defuse the Gujarati-Marathi face-off on the one hand and standing up to the calumnious campaign launched by his political rivals, both within and outside of the Congress.

Soon after he took charge as chief minister, Chavansaheb

decided to pay a visit to Fort Shivneri, the birthplace of Chhatrapati Shivaji. Some of us in the college decided to be there to listen to him. We furiously cycled our way to the fort in excitement—a 93-kilometre-long journey from Pune—because it was his first public appearance after being sworn in as chief minister of the new state.

Chavansaheb was a highly cultured person. So was his politics. The speech he delivered at Fort Shivneri reflected his concerns and his resolve to redefine Maharashtra's destiny. There was a ring of sincerity to his voice which touched our core. Thereafter we never missed a single speech of Chavansaheb's. His words brought to us his thoughts, his thoughts shaped our young minds.

The famous bhajan of Sant Tukaram—the legendary saint-poet of Maharashtra—'Jethe jaato tethe tu maaza sangati/ Chalaveesi haati dharooniya' sums up my deep bond with Saheb and my respect for him. He always walked with me, he held my hand as I took my first faltering step in the public life of Maharashtra.

Chavansaheb was closely aligned with Nehruvian politics. I too was influenced by Panditji's thoughts. As college students we witnessed how hard he was trying to translate Panditji's vision into reality. Pioneering work was done under the new chief minister's leadership in the fields of industry, education, literature, art and culture. Moreover, Chavansaheb always came across as a warm person. There was no way I could have escaped his influence. I soon joined the Congress.

Chavansaheb never concealed his admiration for Nehru. His statement that he considered Nehru to be more important than Maharashtra triggered a ruckus in the state. The Samyukta Maharashtra Samiti leaders dubbed him a traitor. However, Chavansaheb was made of sterner stuff. He refused to buckle under pressure. With his characteristic calm, he explained that Nehru alone had the vision and the spunk to preserve the nation's integrity.

Nehru was not amenable to the idea of linguistic states. Hence, convincing him on the contentious issue was a Herculean task. However, the creation of Andhra Pradesh in 1956 as a linguistic state after a fierce struggle by Telugu-speaking people from the Madras Presidency considerably weakened the Centre's position on the issue of linguistic states. A poor show by the Congress in the 1957 elections was a clear indication that people in the bilingual Bombay Presidency were angry with the party. After Indira Gandhi became Congress president in 1959, Chavansaheb started a dialogue with the Centre through her.

As the movement for a separate Marathi state reached its peak, he cautioned Indiraji that continued refusal to accede to the popular demand would push the entire Marathi-speaking population away from the Congress. This was neither in the interest of the nation nor the party. Indiraji took it up with Nehru and succeeded in changing his mind. That cleared the way for the creation of Maharashtra state on 1 May 1960.

True to the Congress culture, Chavansaheb chose to keep a low profile when he differed with the party leadership. During such times he expressed himself openly in the party forum but he never went to the extreme of breaking away from the party. He was a gentleman to the core and a stickler for maintaining decorum. In a field crowded with opportunists these qualities proved to be a bane. However, Chavansaheb neither cared about the consequences nor regretted being true to his principles. I cannot help recalling two incidents to prove the point.

In response to a call from Prime Minister Jawaharlal Nehru in the wake of the Indo-China war of 1962, Chavansaheb quit as chief minister of Maharashtra to take charge as defence minister, a portfolio he went on to hold for four years. Before accepting Nehru's invitation, however, he told the prime minister that he would need a 'go ahead' from just one person, his wife Venutai.

India's victory in the 1965 war against Pakistan was the high point of his tenure. Following a ceasefire the Soviet Union hosted a summit meeting of the two nations at Tashkent for a peaceful resolution of the conflict. Chavansaheb was a member of the Indian delegation. Prime Minister Lal Bahadur Shastri and Pakistan President Ayub Khan signed the famous Tashkent agreement on 10 January 1966. Hours later, Shastri passed away due to a massive heart attack. The next day, Chavansaheb, along with Swaran Singh and others, brought his body to India.

Even as the nation mourned its beloved leader and Gulzarilal Nanda took charge as acting prime minister, the Congress leadership went into a huddle to discuss Shastri's successor. Chavansaheb was undeniably one of the front-runners for the post. Thanks to the victory over Pakistan, his popularity was at its peak. His deft handling of the defence portfolio after the 1962 China war had already earned him credit as an able administrator. Morarji Desai also aspired to the prime minister's post, but the mild-mannered Chavansaheb was certainly a more acceptable leader.

One evening, senior Congress leaders from Maharashtra, including Kisan Veer, Abasaheb Kulkarni and N.K.P. Salve assembled on the lawns of his house in New Delhi. Though a junior at the time, I was quite close to Chavansaheb and was also part of the group. After assessing the political situation in the country and within the Congress, everyone impressed upon him that the time was ripe to stake claim to the prime minister's post. Chavansaheb agreed to think over it positively. However, he said, 'I must consult Indira Gandhi before taking a decision.'

When I heard that I involuntarily blurted out, 'Oh, we know what the outcome will be.' Chastising me for the 'indiscretion', he explained the rationale behind his asking Indiraji. Maharashtra would not have become a separate state if Indiraji had not used her good offices with Prime Minister Nehru in 1959-60. Secondly, he owed his own entry in national politics to the invitation from Indiraji's father to take over as defence minister in 1962. 'I feel it is my duty to talk to Indiraji at this juncture,' he said before leaving.

We waited anxiously at his place after he left. He returned from Indiraji's house after some time but looking at him one couldn't guess as to what had transpired in their meeting, till he told us. 'I told her that there was a lot of pressure on me to stake claim to the prime minister's post. But my relationship with her family took priority and therefore I thought it prudent to inform her before moving further,' he explained. And what was her response? 'Well, she heard me out patiently and then said she would revert after thinking over it.'

Unable to contain my disappointment, I blurted said, 'It's all over...I know what she will revert with.' I was again sharply rebuked for the comment. The group resumed chatting animatedly but the mood was dismal. Then came the telephone call from Indiraji. Chavansaheb went to the neighbouring room to take the call. He returned after a few minutes.

'What did she say?' we asked impatiently.

'She said she was thankful for my good words about her family and also for updating her. She has decided to stake claim to the prime minister's post and expects my continued cooperation.' Supported by Congress President K. Kamraj, Indiraji became prime minister on 24 January 1966. Chavansaheb lost it by a whisker.

Was that a case of misplaced courtesy on Chavansaheb's part? Well...

The second time Chavansaheb was close to becoming prime minister was in July 1979. The Janata Party government under Prime Minister Morarji Desai started to cave in under its own pressure. Indira Gandhi, though not a member of Parliament, was on a comeback trail. While she headed one faction of the Congress (called the Congress [I]), the other faction (the Congress [S]) had leaders such as Devraj Urs, Chavansaheb, S. Karunakaran, Brahmanand Reddy, Deokant Barua, A.K. Antony and Priyaranjandas Munshi. As leader of the opposition in the Lok Sabha, Chavansaheb tabled a no-confidence motion against the Janata government. Charan Singh, along with 85 member of

Parliaments, quit the Janata Party to form a new outfit called Janata Party-Secular. George Fernandes and Madhu Limaye also resigned, forcing Morarji Desai to step down. The situation became extremely fluid because no party had enough numbers in the Lok Sabha to form a government on its own.

A lot depended on what stand President Neelam Sanjiva Reddy would take. It was at this juncture that a Congress (S) delegation met the president. The president indicated to us that Chavansaheb was in a position of advantage to stake a claim to forming the next government.

Chavansaheb refused to jump in the fray. Instead, the Congress (S) and the Congress (I) both supported Charan Singh though he had only 64 member of Parliaments of his own. He became the new prime minister and Chavansaheb, the deputy prime minister. The government lasted for barely three weeks because the Congress (I) withdrew support even before a motion of confidence could be tabled in the Parliament.

Indira Gandhi swept back to power in the 1980 general elections with her party winning 353 seats as against a meagre 13 seats of the Congress (S). Chavansaheb was distraught. 'People of the country have given their mandate in favour of what they think to be the real Congress. Indiraji has won the popular approval and we have been rejected,' he said to me. He was inclined to realign with Indira Gandhi but I was dead against the move. I could see his restlessness growing as the days passed.

It had been our practice to meet at the Rayat Shikshan Sanstha office in Satara every year to commemorate the death anniversary of Karmaveer Bhaurao Patil, the legendary social activist and educator. On 9 May 1981, Chavansaheb, Kisan Veer and I went to Laxmanrao Patil's house for lunch after the anniversary function was over. It was there that Chavansaheb told us about his decision to join the Congress (I).

Kisan Veer and I opposed it vehemently. We pointed out that Indira Gandhi had strayed from the traditional framework of the Congress party. She had made it a policy to instigate her cohorts to undermine those who enjoyed mass support. We reasoned for a long time but it was futile. Emotions ran high. People like Ramrao Adik and Nasikrao Tirpude in the state Congress (I) often spoke insultingly about Chavansaheb. How could we work with such men, we asked. But nothing seemed to change his mind.

We feared Chavansaheb would get completely isolated in the Congress (I). Such, now, was the culture of that party. Unfortunately, we were proved right. Chavansaheb wrote to Indira Gandhi, saying that the people of the country had acknowledged her party as the real Congress and therefore he would like to join the Congress (I). Ignoring Chavansaheb's stature and seniority, Indiraji informed him that the letter would be placed before the Congress Working Committee for its consideration. The humiliation continued for three months before he was admitted into the party.

The titan's autumn days were sad. He led a lonely life in New Delhi. No leader from the Congress (I) would visit him. I, however, made it a point to go to New Delhi fairly regularly and spend time with him. We spent hours chatting about developments from various fields in Maharashtra. There was a marked decline in his health after his wife Venutai passed away. His eyes would well up at the slightest provocation. Watching him in that state was painful. On 25 November 1984 his health deteriorated drastically. I decided to rush to New Delhi with a team of doctors from Mumbai. As we were about to leave for New Delhi, came the news of his death.

All that he left behind as his personal property was a modest house in Karad and 5,700 books on a variety of subjects. Each book had his handwritten notings in the margins. There was jewellery worth ₹87,000 and a plot valued at ₹1.25 lakh at Uruli Kanchan, near Pune, which he wanted to be utilised for a social cause.

Chavansaheb dedicated his entire life to the Congress. But

there still isn't appropriate acknowledgement of his contribution at the party level. However, soon after his death, many of Saheb's friends, associates and followers came together to set up a trust in his name. Founded on 17 September 1985 in Mumbai, the Yashwantrao Chavan Pratishthan conducts numerous activities, including lectures on development issues, empowerment workshops for women, youth and the handicapped, cultural programmes and so on, round the year.

MORARJI DESAI

When I became a minister in 1972 in the Vasantrao Naik government in Maharashtra, one of the first things I did was to study how my predecessors had handled various issues in earlier years. I spent hours going through the files and was struck by the notings made in the margins of the papers by Morarji Desai when he had been in charge of the various departments. The notings reflected his deep knowledge of public affairs and his vast administrative experience. There was absolute clarity, not a word more, not a word less. I sought to follow the example all through my tenure in the state and central governments.

Morarjibhai was elder to me by 45 years. Also, he was a stern person with a sharp tongue. Although I had cordial relations with him, I knew how tough it was to convince him about something that he disagreed with. He was the prime minister when I led the PDF government in Maharashtra with his Janata Party as one of my alliance partners. Whenever he visited Mumbai, I used to go to the airport to receive him as protocol demanded.

During those days my government had relaxed restrictions on liquor distribution in Maharashtra. I knew well that Morarjibhai, the strict Gandhian that he was, would be unhappy with the decision. As we sat in the car on our way back to south Mumbai from the airport during one of his visits, he expressed his displeasure with the relaxation of liquor restrictions. I tried to put up a defence but he was adamant. While I was saying something on the subject, I casually touched the left side of my chest with my hand. He noticed it immediately and asked me what was wrong.

'Nothing much. But there is a slight pain in the chest,' I said.

The old man was concerned. 'Don't take it lightly. I will tell you a simple remedy. You must try shivambu therapy,' he said. Shivambu means self-urine therapy. There are many people who believe that urine has excellent medicinal properties and consuming it regularly keeps one fit. As a staunch believer in shivambu therapy, Morarjibhai used to advocate it to anyone who cared to listen.

For the next half hour, he educated me on the benefits of shivambu, forgetting everything about the liquor issue. That was a relief!

A few days later, he came to Mumbai again. I knew he would ask me what I was going to do about reviewing the decision on liquor distribution. By now I had become wiser about wriggling out of the tricky issue. As soon as we sat in the car at the airport, I brought up the topic of shivambu therapy.

'Morarjibhai,' I said, 'thank you very much for suggesting the therapy. I have been practising it regularly since then and I have actually started feeling better.' He was very happy to hear that and kept telling me about some more benefits of the therapy throughout the remaining journey.

His government fell shortly thereafter. When I learnt that he had decided to settle down in Mumbai, I went over to meet him. He led a spartan life and I knew he did not own a house in Mumbai. I offered him a flat in Oceana, an apartment complex in south Mumbai, from the state government quota. He turned down the offer, saying he had ceased to be a government functionary and therefore was not entitled to the accommodation. I tried to convince him for a long time but failed. Exasperated, I said, 'Are you going to live on the pavement?

How will that look for a man who has been chief minister of the state and prime minister of the country?'

'Rubbish. I would rather dive into the Arabian Sea. No. I won't live on the pavement. That would be an encroachment on public property. I would never do that,' he retorted.

After much cajoling, he finally agreed to move into the Oceana flat on one condition: his heirs would not inherit the property and the government would take possession of the flat as soon as he passed away. He expired on 10 April 1995 at the ripe age of 99. As he had wished, the flat was back in government possession within days of his demise.

P.V. NARASIMHA RAO

P.V. Narasimha Rao is one leader who, in my opinion, deserved much more recognition and respect than he actually received in our country. It is being gradually accepted—somewhat grudgingly, though, in certain circles—that Rao should be given a very large share of the credit for turning around the Indian economy in the 1990s.

Rao became prime minister when the Indian economy was in a precarious condition. However, he had an excellent grasp of critical issues and also possessed the necessary courage to set the liberalisation process in motion. Manmohan Singh, the then finance minister, is widely and rightly lauded for presenting a landmark budget that year. But it would not have been possible for Dr Singh to break new ground without the firm political backing of his prime minister.

I remember the uproar created by Rao's decision to omit the word 'Socialist' from an economic resolution in one of the meetings of the All India Congress Committee. The departure from the traditional party line was a bold decision, but Rao stood unmoved amidst the raging controversy.

The reason why Rao's exceptional contribution to the nation's progress was not applauded was probably due to the fact that he, well, didn't belong to the Gandhi family. He came from a modest background.

A man of extraordinary intelligence, Rao was fluent in Telugu, Marathi, Kannada, Bengali, Gujarati, Hindi and English. When I was the defence minister in his government, we used to often converse in Marathi. During that period, I was witness to his deep understanding of international relations. Another quality that struck me was his ability to take along with him people from different walks of life while running the government. Although I had contested against him for the prime minister's post, he didn't hold it against me. We got along well.

Our relationship went back to the days when he was the national general secretary of the Congress and I was secretary of the party's Maharashtra state unit. He hailed from Andhra Pradesh, but was closely linked to the Marathwada region in Maharashtra as a follower of Swami Ramanand Tirth who led a movement against the Razakars in the two neighbouring states. The Razakars were a private militia which resisted the integration of the princely state of the Nizam with India, and instead, wanted it to accede to Pakistan. They were also responsible for brutal murders, rapes and torture of people from the Telangana and Marathwada regions.

Post Independence, Rao was active in Andhra politics but moved to New Delhi after the rise of N.T. Rama Rao in that state. I was in the Congress (S) when the Congress nominated him to contest a Lok Sabha election from Ramtek in the Vidarbha region of Maharashtra. He won the keen fight, defeating Shankarrao Gedam of our party. 'I hope I shall never have to fight an election against an opponent like you,' Rao said later. Subsequently, we were in the same party and he made it a point to take me with him for his election campaigns.

He was an astute politician who made all his moves deftly and after deep thought. This was often made fun of. It was joked that in the case of Narasimha Rao, not taking a decision was also a decision. I don't think that was a correct evaluation of Rao. When he wanted something done fast, his decisions were quick.

ATAL BIHARI VAJPAYEE

Atal Bihari Vajpayee could blend politics and poise with effortless ease. Though ideologically there was no common ground between us, I always found him to be a highly cultured person who genuinely believed in democratic values and the parliamentary system. Interacting with him was a pleasure.

Atalji was the first leader without any connection with the Congress to head a government at the Centre. I was leader of the opposition at the time. He could run the NDA government for a total of six years because he recognised that Indian polity had undergone a major transformation and the days of one-party government were over. Regional parties were treated with respect and given their due for the first time during his tenure. His unique working style carried him through despite a number of odds. He had a fine sense of right and wrong. And a delightful sense of humour too.

Certain key posts like those of the chief vigilance commissioner or the Central Bureau of Investigation director are filled after consultations between the prime minister, his senior cabinet colleagues and the leader of the opposition. Attending those meetings with Atal Bihari Vajpayee, L.K. Advani and Jaswant Singh was a pleasure because Atalji discarded partisanship and took the decisions purely on merit.

A typical meeting would start with the prime minister sitting with his eyes closed and none of us saying a word for the first few minutes. After a while, Atalji would slowly open his eyes, cast a thoughtful look at those present, and ask, 'Aaj ki meeting ka prayojan kya hai?' (What is the agenda for today's meeting?). Jaswant Singh would then explain that the meeting was convened to select a candidate for a particular post. Atalji would again look at each of us and ask, 'Aap ke man mein koi hai?' (Do you have anyone in mind?). If all of us agreed on a name, the meeting would get over quickly. If we differed, the prime minister allowed us to debate on the merits and demerits of individual candidates for a few minutes and then call for a tea break. On resumption, he would again listen to us for a while and announce his decision.

I remember a meeting when Advaniji and I just could not agree on a particular name. After hearing us out patiently for some time, Atalji intervened in his inimitable style. Turning to Advaniji, he pointed towards me and said, 'Lalji, hum log satta mein abhi aaye hain. Inko satta ka humse zyada tajurba hai. Inka kehna maan lete hain.' (Lalji, we have come to power only recently but these people have a long experience of running a government. Let us go by what he says.)

Atalji was much more open and progressive in his outlook compared to his colleagues from the RSS parivaar. He used to be in a very light mood when away from the hurly burly of domestic politics. I have fond memories of the time when I was a member of a delegation led by him to the United Nations. Once the day's work was over, we used to spend lot of time chatting on a variety of subjects. It was great fun to listen to him as he regaled us with anecdotes from his ideological fraternity. No wonder his popularity cut across all party lines and ideological barriers.

BIJU PATNAIK

Bijuda, as we called him, may have been older than me by 24 years but our close bond completely belied the age gap. His elder son Prem (elder brother of Odisha Chief Minister Navin Patnaik) and I had a common friend in Lalit Mohan Thapar and the three of us used to often meet at Lalit's house in New Delhi. Lalit, as is well known, was the head of the Lalit Thapar group of companies that owned many industries, including Crompton Greaves, BILT, JCT Mills and the Ballarpur paper mill. It was through Prem or Guddu, his pet name, that I came in contact with Bijuda who took an instant liking for me and, in fact, treated me like his son.

He was a truly amazing person. A towering personality with qualities of both head and heart. Starting off in the Royal Indian Air Force during British rule, he joined the Indian freedom struggle and carried out many hazardous operations on Pandit Nehru's instructions as a skillful, daredevil pilot. He set up the Kalinga steel company and an aviation company. While both companies were doing well, Bijuda sold them off to raise money when he decided to enter national politics.

Bijuda was very close to Indira Gandhi whom he fondly called 'Indu'. However, they parted ways following Indiraji's stand in the 1969 presidential election. When Emergency was declared in 1975, he was arrested and put in jail. I was a Congress minister in Maharashtra at the time and used to suggest to Indiraji that Bijuda should be freed at the earliest.

After he was released in 1977, he wanted a short break from politics. He asked me to accompany him to Kashmir where the two of us spent about ten days going on long walks and chatting about everything under the sun. Listening to him was such an enriching experience! He told me about the two adventurous missions he had carried out in 1947. The Independence struggles in India and Indonesia were at their peak. President Sukarno wanted to send his associate Sultan Sjahrir to attend a conference organised in Delhi, but found it difficult to do so because Indonesian air space was dominated by the Dutch. Knowing Bijuda's courage and expertise, Nehru entrusted the task to him. Bijuda and his wife flew in a Dakota to Java and managed to pick up Sjahrir and fly back to India via Singapore. The Indonesian government later acknowledged Bijuda's contribution to their freedom struggle by conferring on him honorary citizenship and the country's highest civilian award as well.

The second mission Bijuda carried out was in October 1947

when Nehru asked him to fly Indian soldiers to Kashmir where raiders from Pakistan were playing havoc. The PMO had given specific instructions to him not to land in Srinagar if the enemy was anywhere in sight. Bijuda flew dangerously low to ensure there were no raiders around and then landed at the airport. I just couldn't stop marvelling at the man's extra-ordinary courage as I listened to the anecdotes.

A forthright attitude was evident in everything Bijuda did. I remember his speeches and interventions in the chief ministers' conferences during 1978-80 when he was heading the Odisha government and I was the chief minister of Maharashtra. Even a stern Morarji Desai, seated in the prime minister's chair, could not cramp Bijuda's plain-speaking style in those meetings.

GEORGE FERNANDES

Before I met George Fernandes, my impression of him was merely that of a fire-spewing unionist. Known for his oratory and aggressive working style, he had shot to fame as a 'giant killer' after he defeated Congress stalwart S.K. Patil from Bombay south in the 1969 general elections. He was a darling of the powerful taxi drivers' union in Mumbai, as a result of which he wielded a lot of clout in the city.

The popular story was that George would just have to stand, with his arms wide open, in the middle of the busy Hutatma Chowk (Flora Fountain square) in south Mumbai and taxis and BEST buses would screech to a halt for a strike! Such was George's charisma.

George's stature as a militant leader grew further when he successfully organised a nation-wide railway strike in 1974. My impression of him changed rapidly after I started interacting with him directly during 1978-80 when he was the Union railway minister in the Janata government and I was the chief minister of Maharashtra.

I noticed that George's trade unionism was more than matched by his prolific reading. His house was littered with books on a wide range of subjects and he could easily rattle off paragraphs or comments from any of them. He has been ailing for the last few years and it is really sad to see a man so full of life now bedridden. In his heyday, he could travel for days at a stretch and was a true warhorse. All of this was reflected in the way he carried out responsibilities in public life. One of the finest parliamentarians in our country, he also excelled as minister of railways and defence in two different governments. We grew close despite the fact that we belonged to different political parties which were mostly rolling up their sleeves against each other.

There are many claimants to the credit for making the Konkan Railway a reality. But according to me, George's contribution was the most noteworthy. He was the Union railway minister when I, as Maharashtra chief minister, called a meeting in the Maharashtra Sadan in New Delhi to discuss the feasibility of the project. Though George agreed that the project was crucial for the states of Maharashtra, Goa, Karnataka and Kerala, he pointed out that the Union government did not have the necessary funds.

'We shall pick up some of the costs,' I said.

'And who is "we"?' George asked.

'The four stakeholder states,' I replied.

He asked me to assess the possibility of raising the funds and revert to him.

After getting a nod from the state cabinet in Maharashtra, I roped in Pratapsinh Rane, Virendra Patil and E.K. Nayanar, the chief ministers of Goa, Karnataka and Kerala, respectively. While Goa and Karnakata agreed to contribute their share, Kerala pleaded helplessness for want of funds. Maharashtra loaned the additional amount to overcome the problem. Besides the Union government funding, the Konkan Railway Corporation also raised money by floating bonds in the open market. It happens to be the only railway project in the country where state governments are stakeholders. George played a crucial role in the entire long-drawn process.

Most of George's erstwhile colleagues found his decision to join the NDA government under Atal Bihari Vajpayee unpalatable. However, he was very clear about why he had chosen to chart a new political course. Economic development of India was now the key word for George and he did not mind tying up with the BJP, despite its Hindutva agenda, because that party, he thought, was best suited at the time to take the development agenda forward. 'What about the RSS hardliners?' I asked him once.

'Oh, don't worry about them. I know they will bark but not bite,' he replied confidently.

THE GANDHIS

The Nehru-Gandhi dynasty is the strongest glue that has kept the Congress party going for decades and the reasons are obvious. Five generations of the family have not just been in the forefront of national politics, they have also been at the helm of the Congress party. Motilal Nehru was the party president way back in 1928, while his son Jawaharlal dominated Indian politics before and after Independence. His scholarship and charisma were unparalleled. During my youth I was more impressed by Nehru's modern outlook than by Mahatma Gandhi's homespun philosophy. But I did not have an opportunity to interact with him as he was too senior a leader.

Of all Nehru's successors I would rate his daughter Indira Gandhi very high essentially because she was a staunch nationalist and had the courage to take on the world when it came to safeguarding Indian interests. Unfortunately, she had strong autocratic traits. Whoever did not toe her line was treated with suspicion. Since I was close to Yashwantrao Chavan, I was always seen as belonging to the 'other camp'. Not that I cared.

I vibed well with her son Rajiv as we were of the same age (he was younger to me by about three-and-a-half years) and also because he was keen to take the nation on the path of science and technology. He started on a promising note, ushering in the 'computer age' in India despite resistance from trade unions and political opponents. It then seemed that Rajiv was all set to play a long innings in politics. Unfortunately, the terrible incident in Sriperumbudur during the 1991 Lok Sabha election campaign cut his life short.

Rajiv made up for his lack of political experience with a readiness to reach out to people from different walks of life. My equation with Rajiv had its highs and lows, which reinforced the fact that, after all, he was a scion of the Gandhi family!

My longest political overlap has been with Sonia Gandhi. Unlike her husband Rajiv she is not very communicative. In the first few years after she entered politics, we shared a rather uneasy equation. But we both achieved a certain comfort level after I launched the NCP which joined the Congress-led UPA government in 2004.

For ten years Sonia Gandhi and I were together in the Lok Sabha. Since our seats were next to each other, we talked casually from time to time though we avoided discussing serious politics, especially anything relating to the Congress or the NCP. Official deliberations were restricted to the UPA of which she was the chairperson. Barring this, there was no social interaction between us. I must, however, admit that she did not in any way interfere in my ministerial work, not even an oblique query about a particular appointment or transfer in the departments under me.

Rahul, who is widely, and, unsurprisingly, expected to be the next head of the Congress party, is still young and should be given more time to prove his credentials. Although he was elected to the Lok Sabha in 2004 he has started to take an active interest in party affairs only since early 2014 or so. It is good to see him visiting different parts of the country to meet people from various segments of society. However, the Congress party is in a very bad shape at present and a lot more needs to be done to set things right.

BALASAHEB THACKERAY

Balasaheb Thackeray. A good friend and an equally good opponent of mine. Though older than me by about 14 years, his political career started with the inception of the Shiv Sena in 1966, only a year before I got elected to the Maharashtra legislative assembly in the 1967 elections. Since then we crossed swords in the political field right till his death in November 2012.

A cartoonist par excellence, he was a fierce orator, a skill which he used to great effect in building his party. He was good at coining funny phrases and nicknames for his political opponents. I was one of his favourite targets. He would often call me 'maidyaacha pota' (a sack of flour), to make fun of my heavy girth!

In private meetings, however, Balasaheb was a warm person who stood by his friends through thick and thin. He had a treasure of anecdotes, and he was an excellent raconteur.

Few people know that he had good knowledge of medicinal herbs which he grew in the rear portion of Matoshree, his home in Bandra. I used to visit him there and often saw him recommending herbs from his own garden for someone's ailment or injury. When I was undergoing treatment for cancer in 2004, Balasaheb sent me a very touching letter. Addressing me as 'Dear Sharadbabu', as he always did in private, he went on to list several commandments relating to my dietary and working habits. 'I hereby direct you to take good care of your health,' he said.

I and my wife Pratibha would often visit Matoshree for gup-shup and dinner. Meenatai, Balasaheb's wife, was a great cook and a gracious host. She would serve us delicacies of Kayastha cuisine (the Kayastha community, to which the Thackerays belong, is well known for its passion for food). Balasaheb and Meenatai would also visit our home at Maheshwari Sadan. On a few occasions they were our guests at Varsha, the chief minister's official residence, when I was the chief minister.

Like the Thackerays, Sadanand Sule, my son-in-law, too is a Kayastha. He and Supriya, my daughter, went to Matoshree to seek Balasaheb's blessings a few days before their marriage. Balasaheb was happy to see both of them. He told Supriya that Sadanand was like his grandson. Balasaheb had a good equation with Sadanand's father who was then a very senior executive in Mahindra and Mahindra where the Sena has a union. Once a friend, always a friend was Balasaheb's credo. Although we often had to cross swords as our political views clashed, it didn't affect our friendship.

Drawing cartoons was Balasaheb's first love as was evident from the way he ran his weekly *Marmik*, where he lampooned all and sundry to make a point. After Balasaheb left his job at the *Free Press Journal* in Mumbai in the 1960s, he, B.K. Desai and I thought of launching a Marathi news weekly which would compare with the best in the world. We held several meetings at his residence to finalise the content, design and marketing plans. After everything was put in place, the issue of the launch date came up. It was said at the time that one of Balasaheb's sisters had 'divine' powers and that she could predict the future. Balasaheb called her over for consultation. We put her a question about our soon-to-be-launched magazine. The sister went into a trance and giving us an auspicious date for the launch, she said, 'The magazine has a bright future. Keep the first copy in the sanctum sanctorum of Siddhivinayak temple at Prabhadevi. You will see that all your copies are sold out in no time. Not a single copy will be in the market.' She was right. There was no trace of the magazine in the market as there were no takers. Soon, we had to wind up the joint venture.

In September 2006, Supriya was elected for the first time to the Rajya Sabha from Maharashtra. Soon after her candidature was announced by the NCP, Balasaheb called me up to offer his party's support. 'Sharadbabu, I have seen her since she was a knee-high girl. This is a big step in her career. My party will make sure that she goes to the Rajya Sabha unopposed.' I was deeply touched by the gesture. However, the Sena was in alliance with the BJP in Maharashtra. 'But what about the BJP?' I asked. Balasaheb's reply was instant and true to his character. 'Oh, don't worry about Kamalabai ('Kamal', lotus, being the BJP's poll symbol). She will do what I say.'

FAROOQ ABDULLAH

Large hearted and open-minded, Farooq has never been a 24-hour politician. He ran his government in all seriousness but also loved the good things in life and made no bones about it. Even people in the BJP admit to me in private that Farooq Abdullah's was one of the better governments that the state of Jammu and Kashmir has seen so far. I personally believe that Farooq, his father Sheikh Abdullah and son Omar deserve credit for their persistent efforts to keep Kashmir aligned with India through the decades.

Farooq has been a very close friend of mine for more than three decades. When militancy in Jammu and Kashmir was at one of its peaks, Farooq was worried about the well-being of his son. Omar and my daughter Supriya are more or less of the same age. So I had Omar staying at my home in Mumbai for four years to complete his college education. The family bond thus continues to run through the next generation as well.

SARAT CHANDRA SINHA

They don't make people like him anymore. An epitome of honesty and simplicity, Sarat Chandra Sinha belonged to a rare breed of politicians who practised what he preached. I consider myself fortunate for having worked with him in the Indian National Congress, the Congress (S) and also the NCP at successive stages in my political life.

I still remember the morning when I was hanging around with party colleagues at Azad Maidan in Mumbai where an All India Congress Committee (AICC) session was scheduled to start in the afternoon. I saw a tall, lean man walking towards us from the Victoria Terminus railway station with a suitcase in his hand and neatly tied bedding on his head. As he stopped in front of us, I was shocked to notice it was Sarat Chandra Sinha, the then chief minister of Assam! He had travelled for more than two days all the way from Guwahati to Mumbai in a third-class railway compartment because that was what he could afford. The AICC session was not a government engagement, it was a party affair, and therefore he had spent from his own pocket for the travel.

Sinha was the chief minister of Assam from 1972 to 1978 and also served the party in different capacities such as general secretary, vice-president and president for many years. Though a Congressman all his life, he left the parent party and joined us when we formed the NCP in 1999. His financial discipline was a lesson to all. Whether it was the maintenance of the party's Guwahati office or the election campaigns, Saratbabu would keep a detailed account right down to the last rupee. A man of the masses, he was also a good writer. Leading a principled life, he lived in a two-room apartment till he passed away in December 2005.

VASANTDADA PATIL

Maharashtra holds Vasantdada Patil in high esteem for his unflinching commitment to the rights and well-being of farmers. He was rooted in the soil of Maharashtra and was exceptionally sensitive to agrarian issues, be it the recurring drought, the cooperative movement or making sure that farmers got remunerative prices for their produce.

Dada was a simple man. He had scant regard for the trappings of power. His strength was his organisational ability. It would be no exaggeration to say that he knew almost every Congress worker by name. He was steeped in the Nehruvian culture of consensual politics and pluralism. Lack of formal education hardly deterred Dada from mastering the nuances of the state administration. In fact, his native wisdom would help resolve many a knotty issue which baffled the elite class of bureaucrats in Mantralaya.

I would like to share with my readers a story about the great leader. Dada was the chief minister of Maharashtra and I held the home portfolio in his cabinet. This was in the 1970s. Once, Dada had convened an urgent meeting of key IPS officers at Varsha, the chief minister's official residence. As home minister, I thought it my duty to arrive at about 9:45 a.m. for the meeting scheduled to begin at ten.

However, ten came and went and there was no trace of Dada. As time ticked by, I went to his room to remind him of the meeting. He had a visitor, a simple villager. Dada introduced him to me, saying, 'He is my friend. We were together in jail during the freedom struggle. His son is in the armed constabulary. But he wants a transfer to the Yellow Gate Police Station.'

The visitor's audacity irked me. First, he had detained the chief minister for a full 15 minutes for his personal problem. Second, his request that his son should be transferred to the Yellow Gate police station in Colaba was not a simple demand. The armed constabulary stood guard over ministers and VIPs.

There was not much chance of making any money on the side. The Yellow Gate police station, however, was close to the docks and was considered a lucrative posting, one that every cop secretly coveted.

'Dada, all those who want to make money ask for a transfer to the Yellow Gate police station,' I told the chief minister.

'Is that so?' he asked.

'Yes,' I said.

'In that case, let the boy spend two years in Yellow Gate. He has two daughters to marry off,' Dada said nonchalantly, leaving me dumbfounded!

BARRISTER SHESHRAO WANKHEDE

When I entered the Maharashtra legislature, Seshrao Wankhede was already a veteran in the state government as well as the Congress organisation. But he never allowed his seniority and experience to stand in the way. We struck a close rapport and the bond continues to be as thick as ever between our families even though he is no more.

Wankhede came from a wealthy, land-holding family in the Vidarbha region of Maharashtra and after becoming a barrister in England, he conducted a flourishing legal practice. Early in his political career, he became the first mayor of Nagpur. Years later, his daughter Kunda too was elected to that position and thus became the first woman mayor of Nagpur.

A man of extraordinary intelligence, Wankhede also had a great sense of humour which he used effectively to restore calm when temperatures rose in the legislature. He was the minister of industries and finance for some time, but according to me he truly excelled as speaker of the assembly. His sense of fairness and wit earned him tremendous respect from the treasury benches as well as the opposition in the House.

Wankhede was a terrific host. He owned a big farm at Katol,

near Nagpur. It was his regular practice to invite legislators from all political parties to his farmhouse during the winter sessions of the Maharashtra legislature in Nagpur. The informal atmosphere and camaraderie witnessed in those gatherings was infectious!

Wankhede was president of the Mumbai Cricket Association (MCA) for many years and could not get along much with Cricket Club of India chief Vijay Merchant. When Wankhede decided to construct a separate stadium (later named after him) in Mumbai, I could support his efforts because I was in charge of the sports ministry. That brought us closer.

He had two unfulfilled dreams. One was to smoothen the strained relations between the MCA and the Garware Club; he wanted me to look into the issue, which I did. The second was to host the cricket world cup final match in Mumbai. I am glad that I could fulfil that wish as well, and that too on a winning note!

S.M. JOSHI

One of Maharashtra's illustrious sons, S.M. Joshi became a household name during the historic Quit India movement, India's final struggle against the British Raj in 1942, because of his heroic deeds. He later played a key role in the Samyukta Maharashtra movement in the 1950s which led to the creation of a separate linguistic state for Marathis.

Steeped in Gandhian values and socialistic principles, Joshi was a man of unimpeachable integrity. A people's leader in the true sense of the term, he was Maharashtra's conscience-keeper. In 1978, I led Maharashtra's first non-Congress government. Joshi was a great help to me in keeping the coalition going. I considered him to be my 'high command'. He would iron out the differences, if any, in the alliance with wisdom and dexterity.

Joshi loved cricket and music. In the middle of a crucial

meeting, he would seek details of the test match being played that day. Age and eminence sat lightly on his shoulders. He kept himself away from the razmatazz of power. They don't make leaders like him anymore.

ABASAHEB KULKARNI

Abasaheb came from Sangli district, the place in south Maharashtra that was also home to another Congress stalwart, Vasantdada Patil. The two were quite close but Abasaheb had a mind of his own and pursued politics in accordance with his own convictions. He did not spare even his own acquaintances if he thought their actions were unfair or against the larger common good.

Abasaheb was wedded to Congress ideology. When Indira Gandhi set up V.V. Giri against the official Congress candidate in the 1969 presidential election, he did not dither for a moment and threw his lot with the party nominee. That move distanced him from Indiraji but he never regretted it.

In 1978, I walked out of the Vasantdada Patil-led ministry to lead the PDF government. Notwithstanding his earlier closeness to Vasantdada, Abasaheb stood by me at the time. He was also close to Chavansaheb. Yet, when Chavansaheb wanted us to keep the rebellion against Vasantdada on hold at the last moment, Abasaheb along with Kisan Veer told him firmly that it was too late to do so.

For me, Abasaheb was a role model when it came to setting up or running cooperative societies. He was studious by nature and meticulous in implementation. As a result, a large number of cooperative societies and spinning mills took roots in Ichalkaranji under his watchful eye.

Abasaheb made his mark as a Rajya Sabha member too. He spent hours in the parliamentary library, made copious notes and presented his case effectively during discussions in the House.

Everyone, including ministers as well as other members, would sit up and listen in rapt attention when he rose to speak.

LATA MANGESHKAR

I can recall my first meeting with Latadidi. She had come to Pune during the India-China war of 1962 to participate in a function hosted to gear up the nation for the war. The function was held under the aegis of the Rashtriya Nagarik Sabha with which I was connected as a youth worker.

Latadidi's soulful songs transcend barriers of caste, creed and community. She is a symbol of national integration. I love many of her songs, especially those composed by greats such as C. Ramchandra, Madan Mohan, S.D. Burman, Roshan and Salil Chowdhury, among many others.

I was the chief minister when she began to work on the nitty gritty of her pet project, a hospital to commemorate the memory of her father, Master Dinanath Mangeshkar. I cleared the files for the land in Pune on which the hospital came up.

I hosted a concert in her honour at my New Delhi residence when she was decorated with the Bharat Ratna, the country's highest civilian honour, in 2002. Noted classical vocalist Malinitai Rajurkar sang at the Delhi concert and Latadidi heard the singer in rapt attention for nearly two hours. A special function to felicitate Didi was held in Mumbai as well, under the aegis of the Y.B. Chavan Centre.

Didi and I once shared the dais at a function in Pune. I requested her to hum a few lines of her favourite composition. 'I don't believe in humming. I like to sing,' she said and asked me for my favourite number of hers. I requested her to sing 'Jayostute Shri Mahanmangale', the famous poem penned by Veer Vinayak Damodar Savarkar. She sang the song, to the sheer delight of the gathering. And mine, of course!

DILIP KUMAR

To tell you the truth I have no fascination for Hindi films, and have hardly any friends in the cinema world. However, Dilip Kumar has been an exception. Like scores of his fans, I admired him immensely as a thespian though I do not quite remember when we met for the first time. It was probably several years ago, through Bombay Pradesh Congress Committee (BPCC) president barrister Rajani Patel. The three of us grew quite close. Since our families also got acquainted, all of us went on long vacations in India and abroad whenever time permitted.

Dilip Kumar is a terrific orator who can keep the audience spellbound for long. As a personal friend, he volunteered to address many of my election rallies in Baramati. He would call up my Pune-based childhood friend Vitthal Maniyar and ask, 'Suna hai elections aayee hain. Bataaiye kab jaanaa hai?' (I hear elections have been announced. Tell me when I should go.) Keeping aside his other engagements, he stole time between his shooting schedules and travelled all the way from Mumbai to Baramati to address my poll rallies. The turnout was always huge and the crowd lapped up every word he said.

A year ago, Dilip Kumar published his autobiography wherein he mentioned my name as a mediator who, along with Rajani Patel, helped sort out a complication in his personal life, which had to do with his second marriage, to Asma Rehman. What he has written is a fact. It was solely on the request of his wife Saira Banu and Dilip Kumar himself that we intervened and I am happy that things worked out well.

There was some discomfort between us when he came to meet me following Sanjay Dutt's arrest by my government in the Mumbai bomb blast case in 1993. He was saddened by the discomfiture of his friend Sunil Dutt (Sanjay Dutt's father) and wanted me to be a little lenient. Citing the strong evidence against the young actor, I turned down his request. Though a certain chill crept into our ties after that, relations between Saira Banu and my family continue to be as warm as ever. He is now 93 and ailing. I went to meet him some time ago, but unfortunately he could not recognise me.

PU LA DESHPANDE

P.L. Deshpande, or Pu La as he was fondly called by his friends and admirers, was Maharashtra's cultural ambassador. He earned nationwide fame because of his Marathi plays and books such as *Vyakti Aani Valli* and *Apporvaiee*, to name a few.

As a student of the BMMS college in Pune, I acted in Pu La's *Tuze Aahe Tujpaashi*, a breezy comedy which Marathis immensely loved. Both Pu La and Sunitabai, his fabulously talented wife, reigned over Maharashtra's cultural scene for nearly five decades. I have seen all of Pu La's plays. Not once or twice, but many times. I was not a film buff; I loved Marathi plays, and I particularly liked Pu La's plays as he would make you laugh and think as well, about life's foibles and follies.

Pu La, noted scholars Tarkateertha Lakshman Shastri Joshi, Govardhan Parikh and A.B. Shah cast a magical spell on four generations of Maharashtrians. They were the Renaissance people who celebrated Maharashtra's pluralistic and inclusive culture.

RAMNATH GOENKA

The first time I met Ramnath Goenka, or RNG, as he was fondly known among friends, was in the mid-1970s. He fought with all his might against the Indira Gandhi government during Emergency and did not hesitate to stake the future of his newspaper group for the cause. Since some of us from the Congress were also unhappy with the Emergency, we were drawn to RNG. After Emergency was lifted in 1977, he stood firmly in support of the Janata Party.

RNG's equation with the Janata Party president, Chandrashekhar, was excellent and since I too was close to Chandrashekhar, I started interacting regularly with the old man in his Express Tower penthouse at Nariman Point in Mumbai. After I formed a coalition government with the Janata Party in 1978, we grew closer.

Chatting with RNG was a lively experience. He had very strong views on most issues and individuals. He had a running feud with industrialist Dhirubhai Ambani, but he shared a close bond with Nusli Wadia. The RNG-Ambani fight and the Ambani-Wadia business rivalry are well documented and have become part of the country's folklore. I had personal differences with Dhirubhai but I must admit that he had a vision and the necessary drive to translate his vision into reality.

NUSLI WADIA

My friendship with Nusli has stood the test of time for close to four decades now. One of my early interactions with him came during my first tenure as the Maharashtra chief minister. There is a place called Toshakhana (treasure-house) near the city collector's office in Mumbai. During British rule, gifts and expensive mementos received by government officials were stored in the Toshakhana. The treasure remained intact even after the British left. In it was found a big bag of silver coins. The tag on it said it was left by Sir Dinshaw Petit, great-grandfather of Nusli Wadia, who had gifted it to the government for undertaking afforestation and water conservation projects in the then Bombay province. I called Nusli over to discuss what he wanted to do with the treasure bequeathed by his ancestor. He immediately cashed the silver coins, added his own contribution and set up a trust for supporting projects as desired by Sir Petit. This marked the beginning of our friendship.

Whenever time permits, which is very rare, I visit Nusli

either at his Mumbai residence or at his beautiful nineteenth-century house on a sprawling 22-acre plot near Lonavala. What both of us still remember fondly are our chat sessions at Ramnath Goenka's Mumbai penthouse where Atal Bihari Vajpayee was also an occasional visitor. Nusli and Atalji shared a great equation and they would often shout and scream at each other as all close friends do. The tone and tenor of their friendship did not change even after Atalji became the prime minister.

RAHUL BAJAJ

My first contact with the Bajaj family was not with Rahul but with his uncle Ramkrishna who had supported our Youth Front which had campaigned against V.K. Krishna Menon in an election in Mumbai. Even after the election, I continued visiting his house but did not interact with Rahul much because he generally kept a low profile at the time. However, with the passage of time we came closer and the bond became thicker after Rahul shifted his base to Pune to lead his automobile empire, Bajaj Auto. The Akurdi-based plant happens to fall in my Lok Sabha constituency of Baramati.

Over the years, Rahul has grown in stature to become a prominent spokesman of Indian industry and as everyone knows by now, he does not mince words. A stickler for clean, above-board transactions, he has carried forward the family tradition of supporting a number of social causes by making handsome donations.

The Bajaj family runs about 30-35 trusts at present. Rahul, my childhood friend Vitthal Maniyar and I form a close group. If Vitthal fails to send him a list of some genuine voluntary organisations by the middle of March every year, Rahul gives him a reminder call. As soon as the recommended names reach him, donation cheques go out, without a question asked.

CYRUS POONAWALLA

Maverick is the word that best describes Cyrus, my friend since our college days. His family was in the furniture business, but Cyrus was fond of cars, with a special liking for the Rolls Royce which he couldn't afford when we were in college. He had a car, but of some other make. He modified the exterior to give it a Rolls Royce look and one day drove into the Brihan Maharashtra Commerce College (BMCC) campus in style. Everyone stood around the car and gaped. His antics spared no one, not even the faculty.

Though a commerce student, Cyrus got down to developing vaccines because that was the dire need in an agrarian country such as India. He studied immuno-biology and went on to earn a doctorate in the subject. Subsequently, he developed a polio vaccine, and a range of other pharmaceutical products which are sold today across the globe.

As chairman of the Poonawalla Group, which includes the Serum Institute of India, he is the ninth richest person in India as per the *Forbes* March 2015 rankings. He was awarded the Padma Shri in 2005 for his contribution in the field of medicine, but Cyrus, true to his type, makes light of all his achievements.

Cyrus sells his vaccines on a 'no loss, no profit' basis in India. 'Why?' I once asked him. 'I don't need to make a profit in India. Let our countrymen get vaccines at a low price. I make enough money in the overseas markets,' he replied matter-of-factly.

GAMA

This is one well-known name among all my relatives, friends and acquaintances from different fields. Yet, you will never find him bragging about his closeness to me or his interactions with any of the national or international luminaries over all these years. His name is Gama. Strictly speaking, he is my driver. Frankly, he is much more than that.

It was about 40 years ago that Gama was 'gifted' to me by Dr M.R. Shah who used to practise in Baramati at the time. The doctor was one of my staunchest supporters and canvassed for me in elections. I heard stories of how passionately he went about the task. Some of them were really hilarious and obviously exaggerated. For instance, it was said that when a local patient went to him to take an injection, the doctor would insert the needle into the patient's arm and ask, 'Who are you going to vote for?' Only after the patient took my name would the doctor withdraw the needle.

The Congress gave me a jeep for party work but I did not have a driver. When I approached Dr Shah to ask if he could help me find one, he readily passed on his own driver to me. Since then Gama has been with me as one of my most dedicated, trusted assistants. I love travelling by road and must have crisscrossed the state of Maharashtra times beyond count so far. Gama has carried out the duty without a frown on his face. There has not been a single accident in the last 40 years, which speaks volumes not only for his driving skill but also how well he maintains my car. He is very cryptic in communication and will just say, 'Let us not use this car,' if he finds a technical fault in the vehicle. Since I have full faith in his capability, I abide by his veto without question.

By now, he has come to know the exact locations of people I have met in practically every city or village in Maharashtra. Since he is so familiar with the routes, travelling becomes hassle-free. Whether my trips are long or short, I generally take someone with me to discuss issues on the way, including, high-profile politicians, public servants, celebrities, industrialists and my party's office-bearer. This saves a lot of time which is otherwise taken up by long-drawn meetings. The discussions are often done in strict confidence. Most people avoid discussing sensitive topics in the presence of their drivers. I have no such problem because I know from experience that Gama does not utter a single word about what he hears when driving.

Public figures do not have fixed work hours. Taking meals and medicines on time thus becomes the first casualty. Gama serves as my unofficial custodian in such matters. Before setting out, he ensures that my travel kit is complete with clothes, cash, medicines and relevant papers. If meetings stretch over several hours, he pesters my staff with questions about whether I have taken my meals and medicines at the prescribed time. If he is not satisfied with the response, he just barges in to remind me about it.

Sometimes, however, he tends to cross the line. I remember an incident when the Inspector General of Police (IGP) of Maharashtra was scheduled to meet me at a particular time. I am a stickler for keeping my appointments and therefore freed myself of all other engagements to meet the IGP on time. For some reason, the police officer reached late and unfortunately for him, met Gama at the door.

When he asked Gama whether I had arrived, Gama coldly told him, 'Look at your watch. Saheb has been waiting for you for a long time.' Hearing this, I pulled him up. 'Gama, he is the IGP of the state,' I said. 'That is fine,' he replied, 'but he must come on time.' Everyone, including myself, has now learnt to accept Gama as he is. In fact, qualities like these have endeared him to all and one.

✤ TWENY-SIX ✤

Epilogue

EQUANIMITY IS A DESIRABLE virtue at 75. Memories make you tender, happy, sad, remorseful, proud, angry, frustrated, dejected and determined—all at once. As you grapple with nostalgia the future invites you into the realm of the unknown and you are filled with anticipation and uncertainty.

What matters in the present, therefore, is that small pause when you take stock of what you have gained and lost, weigh what you have against what you had desired and what has eluded you all your life—the task undone.

Hence, I decided to pause and ponder.

It has so far been a fascinating journey. As a primary school student in Katewadi village, I had never thought that I would step into a high school in the tehsil town of Baramati. But I did. Pune, the hallowed education hub, was then a distant dream. But I met my dream in a Pune college. 'Someday I will surely go to Mumbai,' I thought then. And I did make it to the great city.

Delhi, the next logical destination, greeted me in the 1990s. Camping now at 6 Janpath, I not only frequent Mumbai, Pune, Baramati and Katewadi through the year, but also keep visiting places overseas in my quest to learn and share what I learn. The biggest inspiration that has kept me going through the twists and turns of life is my mother Sharadabai, or just Bai, about whom I have written in detail in the chapter 'An Early Start'. Bai continues to inspire and guide me even today though she passed away in 1975. She exposed me to the magical world of books—books which helped me understand life. Books opened up new horizons before me.

I often felt deprived as I did not know many languages; I still do. But the feeling of deprivation is somewhat mitigated because of the worldwide translation movement which blends continents and languages.

I was lucky to have a mentor like Yashwantrao Chavan in the early part of my political life. I have written separately in this book about his cultured, reassuring personality. He could read people well and went out of his way to groom those he found promising. I have sought to follow the tradition, not just in politics but also in several other fields. Besides Chavansaheb and Vasantdada Patil, many stalwarts have blessed me with their affection and support. I can say with a tinge of legitimate pride that leaders like S.M. Joshi, Chandrashekhar, Karpoori Thakur, Biju Patnaik, Sarat Chandra Sinha have walked with me in various phases of my life and career. I thank them all.

As things stand today, I believe that there is a lot that the younger generation can contribute towards the progress of the nation. Our youth have already made a mark in numerous fields, both in India and abroad. Many are doing commendable work in the social sector. I would urge them to also look at active politics as an important means to nation-building. This was the mantra Chavansaheb gave me in the 1960s and it stays valid to this date. Politics is a force multiplier where policy decisions are taken, impacting multitudes of people in the country.

I do not, however, approve of the practice of 'full-time politics' which is in vogue at present. Social initiatives across different fields—education, research, industry, trade, literature, culture, sport, empowerment of the disadvantaged, among others—play a vital role which no politician should ignore. Active involvement in apolitical fields and interactions with those engaged in social institutions add value to politics. It enables one to actively support social causes and also understand issues at the grassroot level. If you are part of the government, the feedback helps you to see how well policy decisions are getting translated into reality. And if you are in the opposition, you can take the rulers to task for any wrongdoing you notice. Politics bereft of a burning urge to contribute to society's all-round progress is worthless. Moreover, to be able to lend a strong development angle to the politics you practice, you must engage regularly with those involved in development work. There is also a collateral benefit in reaching out as much as possible. The wider the network you have, the better it is for your politics. I can vouch for this from my personal experience.

Though ideologically aligned with the Congress, I did not hesitate to walk out of the mother party when I saw it digressing from its core democratic values or when I found the intra-party atmosphere stifling. I never shied away from maintaining cordial relations with members of other parties because I believe that political differences do not mean personal enmity. It is another matter that people who frown upon my cross-party relations do not mind approaching me for hammering out a broad political understanding in times of crisis. And believe me, such situations occur quite frequently in these days of coalition politics. If someone says it raises a question about my individual credibility, I simply do not bother because my conscience is clear.

Did cross-party networking cost me politically? I don't think so. Even if it did, I would be the last person to resort to the politics of exclusion.

Let me touch upon another widely circulated myth that sometimes creeps into gossip columns, too. Am I the richest politician in the country? Or one of the richest? I have learned to take such loose talk in my stride. While I find the accusation laughable, I also understand where the perception comes from. Whether in power or in the opposition, I never refuse help to anyone if the cause is just. Since the support offered is unconditional, it generates tremendous goodwill. It is difficult to quantify the number of people I must have helped this way in the last 50-odd years of my public life. Many look for an opportunity to reciprocate in whatever way they can. While some offer their time for my party's work, the affluent ones come forward with logistical support or actual monetary help. This probably creates an impression of my being a very wealthy person. Let me say one thing. No amount of money can make a person or a party thrive in present-day politics. The growth comes only through mass support and mass support comes only if one empathises with people.

Another salacious topic which regularly provides grist to the gossip mills is 'Sharad Pawar's love for land'. Despite numerous clarifications in the past, such accusations are routinely hurled at me because they are either politically motivated or they emanate from empty minds. Unlike most politicians I love travelling by road because it enables me to meet people and observe different terrain along the route. I have been doing it for the last 60 years. This apparently makes it easy for idle minds to link any upcoming big projects at any location with my name. All I can say is: God bless them!

The constraints of running a small party like the NCP are severe. Other parties with pockets of influence in certain areas across the country face similar limitations. Though all of them are mass-based, they are sometimes required to take to 'guerrilla tactics' when faced with the giant armies of the big two—the Congress and the BJP. I know that political pundits credit me with having mastered this art. The 2014 assembly elections in Maharashtra threw up a hung House with the BJP falling a little short of a clear majority. The BJP could have easily formed the government in collaboration with its traditional ally, the Shiv Sena (which it eventually did). However, the Sena was making things difficult for the BJP. Sensing an opportunity to drive a wedge between the saffron partners, I unilaterally announced unconditional support to the BJP from outside if it wanted to form the government on its own. That created quite a flutter in the saffron camp. Following a lot of hard bargaining, the BJP-Sena finally formed a joint government. However, the psychological rift still persists between the two allies and this is what I was aiming at.

The rule is simple: when in a position of relative weakness, make a move that will keep your opponents guessing. By the time they gather their wits and arrive at a conclusion, you move a few steps forward. A mind-game? Or a game of chess? Call it what you like.

Whatever I have said about grooming the youth is being attempted in the NCP at present. We hold regular workshops for party workers at different levels and encourage them to launch initiatives on a range of social issues. They perform exceedingly well when they are entrusted with responsibilities and offered support. Citing examples from my own 'internship period' in the 1960s, I tell them calamities like droughts or floods offer an excellent opportunity for a young political worker to be truly useful, to connect with the masses and hone his or her leadership skills.

Sixteen years have passed since the inception of the NCP. It is gratifying to note that we have been able to develop an impressive multiple-layered leadership during the period. Most of the NCP councillors and legislators are young and have risen through the ranks. I take personal interest in the grooming of second-rung leaders by encouraging them to read, speak, travel and interact as much as they can. For instance, I took five or six young leaders from my party to Brazil so that they would understand how well that country was doing in the field of agriculture. We also went to the US where they were exposed to the functioning of the United Nations and the World Bank. It gladdens me to know that Jayant Patil, one of the most promising second-rung leaders of the NCP, still keeps in touch with those institutions with a view to keeping himself abreast of the latest developments. If he retains the zest, he will go far in public life.

It is not just the NCP that I have confined myself to. Wherever I go, I make it a point to interact with young people and impress upon them the need to join or create institutions engaged in enhancing the quality of people's lives. No matter whether I am in New Delhi, Mumbai, Pune, Baramati or on tours, the flow of visitors from different parties, fields and institutions wanting to share notes or seeking advice continues unabated. That keeps me going. I am aware that a lot needs to be done, but at this age I am compelled to utilise my energy very judiciously.

I make it a point to steal time from my busy schedule for leisure and relaxation. After a long, hard day, it is sheer delight to listen to Indian classical music before retiring to bed. The old habit of reading books and periodicals continues. Going back in time to catch up with childhood acquaintances in Baramati is always a pleasure. Of late, however, the 'old boys' meetings are tinged with sadness as I mostly get to hear about the demise of one or the other of my old friends. That, I suppose, is the bane of growing old.

For decades I have managed to take time out to go on long vacations every year. Kashmir was a favourite destination till some years ago. England continues to be on the list. Coorg in Karnataka, Alibaug on the Maharashtra coast and many other places are new additions. Most of the holidays are in the company of close friends and their families. Otherwise it is just my wife Pratibha and me.

And once the much-needed breaks are over, I look forward to returning to where I belong—with the Common Man of India.

Acknowledgements

I WOULD LIKE TO thank all the people and organisations who helped me put together my memoir: Akash Sakharia, Ambarish Mishra, Anand Paranjpe, Anant Bagaitkar, Aurobind Patel, Chandra Aaiyyanger, Datta Balsaraf, F.M. Shinde, Hemant Takle, Jabbar Patel, Jaya Shetty, Jerry Pinto, Neelesh Raut, Nilu Damle, Pratab Aasbe, Sada Dumbre, Satish Raut, Sharad Kale, Siddheshwar Shimpi, Suresh Bhatewar, Uday Jadhav, Uma Shankar, Vidya Pratishthan Baramati, Vijay Naik, Vitthal Maniyaar and the Yashwantrao Chavan Pratishthan.

Appendix I

My letter of 1969 to Y.B. Chavan on the state of the Congress party at the time. This is a translation of the Marathi original.

March 31, 1969

Shri Yashwantrao Chavan
1 Race Course Road
New Delhi

Respected Saheb,

I have been contemplating to write to you for the past few days. When I met you briefly some time ago, I vented my sentiments but could not share my observations and thoughts on several key issues due to lack of time. Please pardon me if you found my outburst disturbing.

A newcomer to politics like me finds the prevailing political situation in the country quite distressing. Though the Congress is in a bad shape, the party High Command appears least concerned about it. As things stand, there is little that can attract the young generation or the educated class to the Congress. In fact, the Congress worker often becomes a target of the youth's ire. I would not blame the young generation for this sorry state.

Mired in self-centred power games, we have moved far away from our prime responsibility of being the voice of the people. Our bond with the masses has diluted; we have also abandoned the process of sharing the party's stand and policies on various issues with our constituents. In the absence of any guidance from the Congress leadership, the party workers find it near impossible to reconnect with the youth, especially because the latter have noticed how far we have digressed from our long-cherished ideals. Probity in public life has become a thing of the past. Since the leadership has failed to stop the rot, the common is completely fed up with the overall climate.

The nation is grappling with many serious challenges, such as the Mysore-Maharashtra border issue or the dispute over river water sharing between Andhra Pradesh and Maharashtra. The late Pandit Jawaharlal Nehru had the capacity to resolve these issues; his stature was such that no one could have opposed any decision he took. But, despite his huge mass appeal, he did not do this, making it even more difficult for the present leadership to make a breakthrough. The young generation and probably even the historians will hold Nehru responsible for this.

The situation is not much different as far as the state of the party in Maharashtra is concerned. People have conferred upon you the moral right and the stature to pull up erring and irresponsible party members in the state. Failure on your part to act against unsavoury elements in the party at this juncture would weaken the Congress organization. If that happens, the people of Maharashtra would probably blame you as they would blame Nehru for reasons explained earlier. This is what I honestly feel about the issue. So please pardon me for my candour.

No matter how daunting the situation is, scores of party workers like me are determined to work dedicatedly at our locations. We are fully aware that you have been instrumental in giving us an opportunity to serve actively in politics and we intend to carry on the good work.

In my humble opinion, the Congress in Maharashtra is faced with several political challenges at the moment and they are not going to go away anytime soon. One of the biggest challenges is the weakening of emotional integrity across the Vidarbha, Marathwada and Western Maharashtra regions of the state. The demand for smaller states is gaining momentum in the country. Since supporting parochial sentiments translates into impressive electoral gains, such demands will acquire prominence in future.

Some of the signs are already visible in the Vidarbha region. The Congress leadership there is cut off from the masses and the youth. It is obvious that the latter would never be able to connect with rich peasants and members of the business community who dominate the party top brass in Vidarbha. As the leadership is clueless about the youth's aspirations, the latter are feeling dejected. Despite being ideologically close to our party, they have started moving away. We need to act quickly to set things right in that region.

People in Marathwada generally feel they have got a raw deal from the state leadership of our party. Several local political leaders and newspapers actively fan the sentiment of injustice. This is detrimental to the integrity of the state and the interests of our party.

The situation in Western Maharashtra is somewhat different. The masses and the youth from this region are simmering with anger against those Congress leaders who wield immense financial and political clout by virtue of their positions of power in zilla parishads and the cooperative sector. There is a feeling that these positions are being grossly misused to suppress or terrorise people who don't fall in line. This is reflecting very badly on the Congress image and needs to be corrected quickly.

There are several other issues but I have chosen to touch upon only a select few which I consider of paramount importance. Many of those who would be voting for the first time in the 1972 general elections were born in post-independence India and are not much conversant with the Congress party's role in the freedom struggle. The Congress party needs to understand that leaders of impeccable character, and fired with a nationalist spirit, would hold appeal for the youth.

Political parties with extreme Left ideology will pose a stiff challenge to the Congress in the elections. Our party will do well to choose clearly between the socialist model of economic development and the mixed economy model because that will help us identify our constituents without any ambiguity.

I have penned my thoughts in this letter openly because I feel you alone possess the openness and the maturity to empathize with party workers like me on these issues.

I look forward to your response, and if possible, a meeting with you to discuss this further.

Yours sincerely,
Sharad Pawar

Appendix II

This is the letter P.A. Sangma, Tariq Anwar and I wrote to Sonia Gandhi after the CWC meeting where the 'foreigner' issue came up.

May 15, 1999

Smt Sonia Gandhi
President, All India Congress Committee
24 Akbar Road
New Delhi–110001

Respected Congress President,

It is with a deep sense of responsibility and an overwhelming sense of concern that we write to you. The founders and leaders of the Congress party like your eminent grandfather-in-law had always encouraged a tradition of free and uninhibited exchange of views amongst Congressmen. They have built the foundation of Indian democracy on the four pillars of liberty of opinion, freedom of expression, responsibility of action and above all nation before self. We believe we are being true to these ideas in placing our views before you.

Madam President, we belong to a generation which had the good fortune to have, as role models, people like Mahatma Gandhi, Pt. Nehru, Maulana Azad, Subhash Chandra Bose, Sardar Patel, Lal Bahadur Shastri and Indira Gandhi. It is under their tutelage that we learnt about the value of sacrifice, and the intensity of national pride. They taught us to be Indians first and Congressmen next. Your family has, more than once, made the supreme sacrifice to uphold these ideals.

After the demise of Rajivji the party felt orphaned. Like most orphans, its condition deteriorated. With the slow decline of the Congress party, the forces of communalism, violence and fundamentalism, which would divide and break the country, grew from strength to strength. As a result the country plunged from crises to crises. The last three years have seen more political, social and economic turbulence in this country than the previous 45.

Right thinking people were leaving the Congress. The poor, the underprivileged, the minorities and the youth were disillusioned with the party.

It was at such a bleak time, Madam, that some of us came to you. We had all watched with respect and admiration the great dignity with which you and your children bore the series of blows that life dealt you.

We also sensed the genuine affection and care that you had for Congressmen and the Congress party. At this critical juncture in the party's life we came to you and requested you to take over the reins of the party. We felt that the real respect the Congress party had for your family would rejuvenate the organisation And we are not wrong. Your presence in the party gave it a new life. The disintegration stopped. Congressmen started returning to the fold.

For the past months, we have observed the maturity and dignity you have brought to the high office of the Congress president. You have kept the fold together, consulted with senior colleagues and motivated the youth. Through all this ran a clear purpose that the party so cherished by your family did not perish. Such selflessness is not new to India, and this ability to put the party's interest above yourself gave us hope and strength.

With clarity of purpose you concentrated on the party without getting involved in the political battles fought on the ground and on the floor of Parliament. Despite tremendous pressure, you resisted the temptation to fight elections. Both at the AICC session in Delhi and at Panchmarhi, you very rightly reminded us that keeping the party strong and vibrant was as important as running a government. When the fractured outcome of the general elections [was] out, you and the party accepted the verdict of the people of India that the Congress party had not fully lived up to their expectations. Other political parties were given a chance to take this great county forward. At all times you intuitively understood and respected the often unstated wishes of the Indian people.

However, of late we have noticed what we hope is only a temporary aberration. We believe that this is the work of a few self-seeking individuals, we pray that you are able to discharge yourself from such minds.

Soniaji, you have lived as daughter-in-law to India for the past 30 years. You have in your own way absorbed much of this great country's spirit. You are in the line of many non-Indians who have loved and adopted this country and worked for its benefit. The Congress party which you now lead was the brainchild of a Scotsman, Sir A.O. Hume. The seat you occupy has once adorned Annie Besant. It is in this selfless tradition that we see your services to the party and the nation.

Madam President, India is a country with a history and tradition going back for [thousands] of years. It is a confident culture and a proud nation. Above all it is a country which is self-sufficient in every sense of the word. India has always lived in the spirit of the Mahatma's words: "Let the winds from all over sweep into my room", but again he said "I will not be swept off my feet". We accept with interest and humility the best which we can gather from the North, South, East or West and we absorb them into our soil.

But our inspiration, our soul, our honour, our pride, our dignity, is rooted in our soil. It has to be of this earth.

Soniaji, you have become a part of us because you have all along respected this. We therefore find it strange that you should allow yourself to forget it at this crucial juncture.

It is not possible that a country of 980 million, with a wealth of education, competence and ability, can have anyone other than an Indian, born of Indian soil, to head its government.

Some of us have tried to initiate and open broader discussions on this issue within the party. It is an issue which affects not just the security, the economic interest and the international image of India, but hits at the core pride of every Indian. Unfortunately this initiative has been thwarted at every stage.

At the risk of repetition we would like to emphasise that, as Congressmen, we look up to you as a leader who kept the party together and is a source of strength to all of us. We hope that you will continue in this role for many years. But, as a responsible political party, we also have to understand the genuine concern of the average Indian who may or may not be a Congressman. That Indian is concerned about the person who will guide the course of his destiny for at least five years.

India's prime ministership is probably the single most difficult job in the world today. A country the size of a subcontinent, with a population of 980 million. A vibrant, vocal democracy, a struggling economy, fissiparous forces tearing the social fabric, insurgency and terrorism which cuts at national unity. No government anywhere in the world faces the type of complex problems and multidimensional issues that need attention in India. A person who is to take the reins of this country needs a large measure of experience and understanding of public life. That is why the founders of the party insisted that people who aspired for higher positions should first spend time working their way up. This way the party worker got acquainted with the complexity of issues in the country.

The average Indian is not unreasonable in demanding that his Prime Minister have some track record in public life. The Congress party needs to respect this very justifiable expectation. We need to understand that during an election campaign every Congress worker has to be able to be aggressive about his party's line. Our workers cannot afford to be either defensive or apologetic. This will negatively affect the party's performance.

We believe, Madam President, that even now it is not too late. Let this great party once again move forward in the direction of Rajivji's dream—a strong resurgent India leading the world into the 21st century. Rajivji's dream was shared by all of us. We look to you to lead the party to fulfil this dream.

We have discussed this matter today in the CWC at great length. We stand by the views we have expressed there. There can be no two opinions that this personalized campaign started by the BJP against you is reprehensible and needs to be opposed strongly. At the same time we would again state that the issue raised by us in today's meeting is real as far as this country is concerned and cannot be wished away.

We believe that it is our responsibility as Congressmen and political leaders to formally place on record our view and request the CWC and you to consider the following suggestion which we feel would set at rest the controversy currently being debated across the country.

(1) The Congress Manifesto should suggest an amendment to

> the Constitution of India, to the effect that the offices of the President, Vice President and Prime Minister can only be held by natural born Indian citizens.

We would also request that you, as Congress president, propose this amendment. This will be in line with your own consistent stand that your sole concern in entering public life was to revive and rejuvenate the party for which Panditji, Indraji and Rajivji gave their all. Such a stand will not only further enhance your status but also give strength to the Congress party as it goes to the polls.

We urge you to consider the issues that we have raised in the same spirit and seriousness with which we have raised them. We believe that in the larger interests of the party and the country you would accept the suggestion we have made.

With regards

Yours sincerely,

[P.A. Sangma] [Tariq Anwar] [Sharad Pawar]